Writer
**DON LAWRENCE
MIGUEL QUESADA
PHILIP CORKE**
Artists

JOHN BURNS
Exclusive Webshop Hardcover Art

Pages 5-112 **THE DON LAWRENCE COLLECTION STUDIO**
Pages 114-240 **SIMON BOWLAND**
Letters

PYE PARR
Design

Thanks to:
Rob van Bavel and **Steve Holland**

ReBELLiON

Creative Director and CEO: **Jason Kingsley**
Chief Technical Officer: **Chris Kingsley**
Head of Publishing: **Ben Smith**
Publishing Manager: **Beth Lewis**
Production Manager: **Dagna Dlubak**
2000 AD Editor In Chief: **Matt Smith**
Senior Graphic Novel Editor: **Keith Richardson**
Graphic Novel Editors: **Oliver Pickles** & **Olivia Hicks**
Graphic Design: **Sam Gretton, Oz Osborne, & Gemma Sheldrake**
Reprographics: **Joseph Morgan, Emma Denton, & Rich Tustian**
2000 AD Brand Manager: **Michael Molcher**
Senior Digital Marketing Executive: **Casey Davoren**
Trade and Special Sales Manager: **Owen Johnson**
Archivist: **Charlene Taylor**
Rights Manager: **Reitha Pattison**

Paperback ISBN: 9-781-78618-564-8
Webshop Hardback ISBN: 9-781-78618-784-0

Published by Rebellion,
Riverside House, Osney Mead, Oxford, UK, OX2 0ES

treasuryofbritishcomics.com
www.rebellion.co.uk

Printed in Turkey by Imago.
First published: August 2022
10 9 8 7 6 5 4 3 2 1

Printed on FSC Accredited Paper.
A CIP catalogue record for this book
is available from the British Library.

For information on other Rebellion graphic novels visit 2000ad.com.

THE RISE
AND FALL OF

THE TRI

E

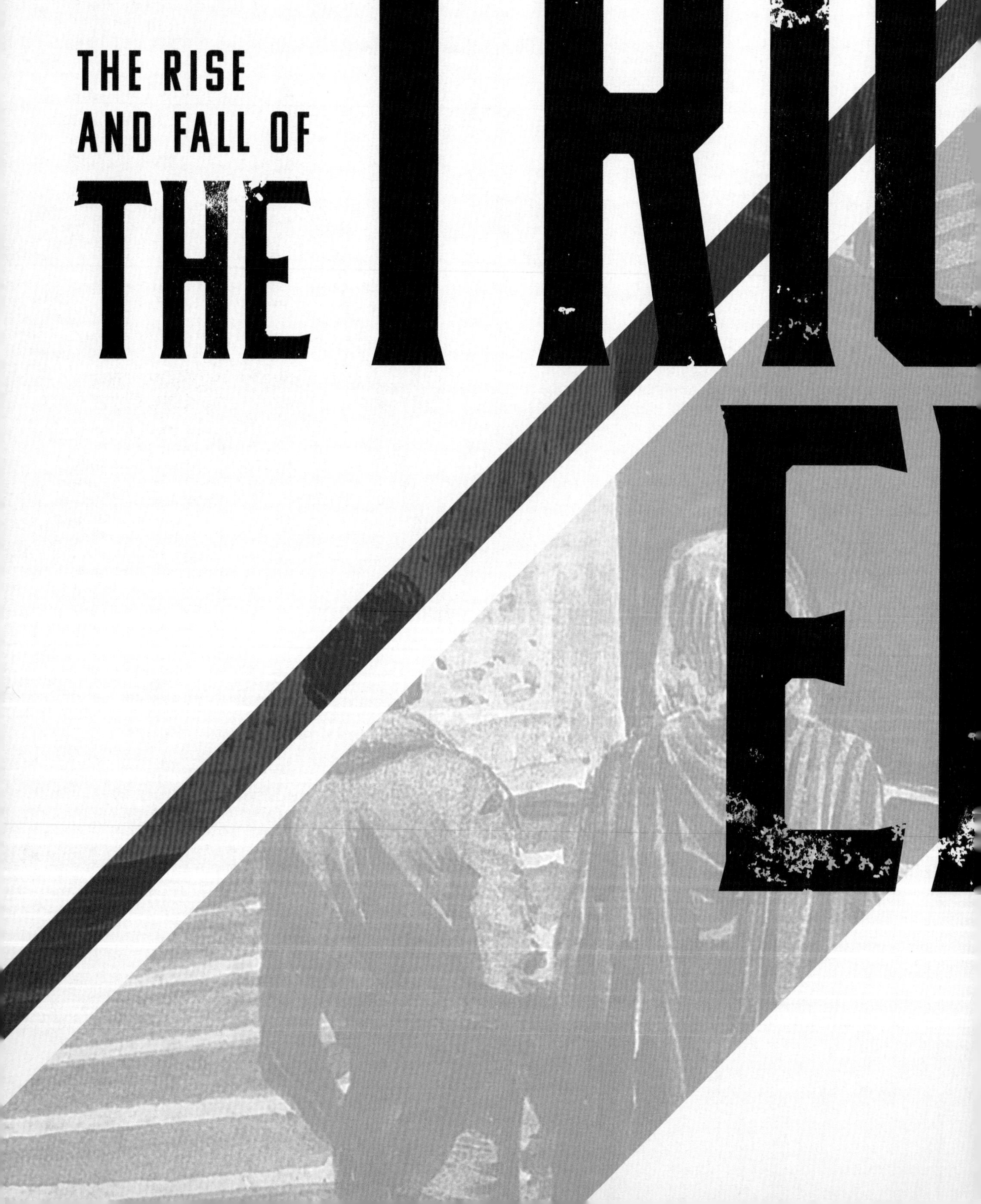

AN

MPIRE

WRITER
MIKE BUTTERWORTH
ARTISTS
DON LAWRENCE
MIGUEL QUESADA
PHILIP CORKE

VOLUME  IV

XXXVII

THE TRIGAN EMPIRE
JOURNEY TO ORCADIA

Originally published in *Look and Learn* 579 - 587
17th February 1973 – 14th April 1973
Story by Mike Butterworth
Art by Don Lawrence

THE END OF THE THIRD YEAR OF ZISS BROUGHT GREAT DISSENSION IN THE TRIGAN EMPIRE. IN THE LAND OF THARV, THERE WERE RIOTS AND STREET BATTLES.

DOWN WITH THE EMPIRE!

FREEDOM FOR THARV!

TRIGO HIMSELF PREPARED TO LEAVE FOR THE TROUBLE SPOT. AS HE BOARDED HIS AIRCRAFT AT TRIGAN CITY AIR TERMINAL...

GOOD LUCK IN YOUR GREAT MISSION, IMPERIAL MAJESTY!

...A TRANSPORTER CRAFT BEGAN A DISASTROUS TAKE-OFF!

THE EMPEROR HIMSELF WAS AMONG THE FIRST TO REACH THE SCENE OF THE CRASH.

TRIGO INSPIRED ALL BY HIS SELF-SACRIFICING GALLANTRY.

TAKE HIM CAREFULLY – THERE ARE MORE INJURED MEN INSIDE!

TRIGO LOWERED HIMSELF INTO THE BODY OF THE GIANT CRAFT.

COME BACK, MAJESTY! THE WHOLE THING COULD BLOW UP!

AND THEN...

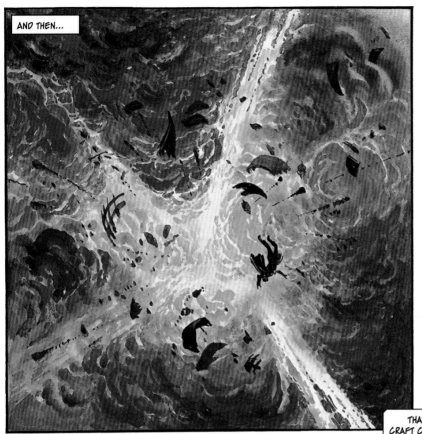

LATER – MUCH LATER – THEY FOUND THEIR EMPEROR AND TOOK HIM AWAY.

PERIC – ELEKTON'S GREATEST SCIENTIST – SPOKE THE GRAVE NEWS.

THAT TRANSPORTER CRAFT CONTAINED A CARGO OF ATOMIC WASTE. IN THE EXPLOSION, HIS IMPERIAL MAJESTY ABSORBED ENOUGH OF A SPECIAL KIND OF RADIATION TO UPSET THE BALANCE OF HIS BODY STRUCTURE – AS I WILL SHOW YOU...

IT WAS MANY DAYS BEFORE YOUNG JANNO WAS SUMMONED TO THE IMPERIAL PALACE BY HIS FATHER, THE EMPEROR'S BROTHER.

HOW... HOW IS HE?

LAD, WHAT PERIC HAS TO TELL US IS A NATIONAL SECRET. WHAT WE SHALL SEE AND HEAR TODAY CONCERNING THE EMPEROR MUST NEVER BE DIVULGED OUTSIDE THESE WALLS!

PERIC TOOK THEM TO HIS PRIVATE LABORATORY IN THE PALACE.

PREPARE YOURSELVES FOR A SHOCK!

THE EMPEROR OF THE TRIGANS LAY UNDER A SMALL, TRANSPARENT DOME.

IT'S UN-BELIEVABLE.

IT IS BAD – BUT WORSE IS TO FOLLOW!

OH, NO!

THE EMPEROR'S TISSUES ARE FURTHER REDUCING IN SIZE! IN A SHORT TIME, HE WILL BE SHRUNK TO MICROSCOPIC PROPORTIONS! LATER STILL, HE WILL BECOME A SINGLE ATOMIC PARTICLE, WHICH WILL SPLIT AND EXPLODE TO NOTHING!

JANNO, BRAG AND THE GREAT SCIENTIST PERIC STARED DOWN AT THE DIMINUTIVE FIGURE UNDER THE TRANSPARENT DOME.

HIS IMPERIAL MAJESTY IS RECOVERING CONSCIOUSNESS!

TRIGO'S EYES OPENED – TO SEE THE THREE GIANT HEADS LOOMING ABOVE HIM!

AAAAGH!

WHAT– WHAT HAS HAPPENED TO ME?

THEY TOLD HIM... EVERYTHING!

YOU MEAN... I MUST PERISH?

IT IS BY NO MEANS CERTAIN, IMPERIAL MAJESTY. I HAVE EVERY HOPE OF DEVISING A MEANS OF REVERSING THE PROCESS IN YOUR TISSUES BEFORE... BEFORE YOU DISINTEGRATE INTO NOTHING!

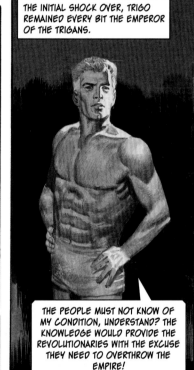

THE INITIAL SHOCK OVER, TRIGO REMAINED EVERY BIT THE EMPEROR OF THE TRIGANS.

THE PEOPLE MUST NOT KNOW OF MY CONDITION, UNDERSTAND? THE KNOWLEDGE WOULD PROVIDE THE REVOLUTIONARIES WITH THE EXCUSE THEY NEED TO OVERTHROW THE EMPIRE!

BUT REVOLUTIONARY ELEMENTS IN THE CAPITAL HAD ALREADY TAKEN TO THE STREETS. WITHIN DAYS, THEY WERE MASSING AT THE IMPERIAL PALACE.

WE WANT TRIGO!

COME OUT AND TALK TO US, TRIGO!

ARE YOU SCARED?

FURIOUS THAT THE EMPEROR WOULD NOT COME FORTH AND HEAR THEIR GRIEVANCES, THEY RESORTED TO VIOLENCE!

DOWN WITH THE EMPIRE!

BURN THE PALACE!

TRIGO, WHO IN THE COURSE OF THE FEW DAYS HAD SHRUNK TO A THIRD OF HIS SIZE ON RECOVERING CONSCIOUSNESS, HEARD THE APPROACHING MOB.

IF THEY FIND ME, THEY'LL TRAMPLE ME UNDERFOOT LIKE AN INSECT!

THE MOB BURST INTO THE LABORATORY.

THIS IS WHERE THAT OLD FOOL PERIC DABBLES WITH HIS SPELLS! SMASH IT UP! SMASH EVERYTHING!

THE TRIGAN EMPEROR WAS FORCED TO COWER FROM HIS OWN PEOPLE AMONGST THE WRECKAGE OF PERIC'S LABORATORY.

I AM HELPLESS... HELPLESS!

NO SOONER HAD THE MOB GONE ON THEIR WAY WHEN HE SAW... IT!

A WEAPON – I MUST HAVE A WEAPON!

HA!

WITH A SHARP WEAPON IN HIS HAND, THE EMPEROR FELT GOOD FOR THE FIRST TIME SINCE HIS DISASTER!

NOT SO HELPLESS AFTER ALL!

HAH!

HE HAD JUST DISPATCHED HIS FIERCE OPPONENT, WHEN HE HEARD THE VOICE OF PERIC, THE SCIENTIST.

DESTROYED! RUINED! A LIFETIME'S WORK! AND WHAT OF THE EMPEROR?

I'M HERE, PERIC!

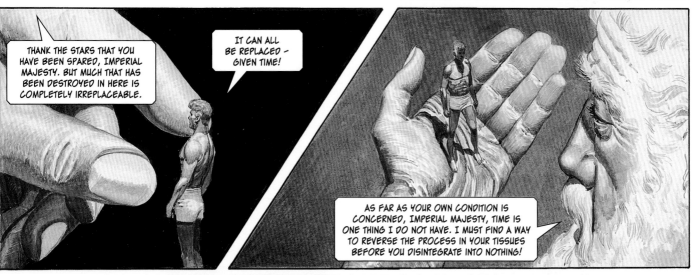

THANK THE STARS THAT YOU HAVE BEEN SPARED, IMPERIAL MAJESTY. BUT MUCH THAT HAS BEEN DESTROYED IN HERE IS COMPLETELY IRREPLACEABLE.

IT CAN ALL BE REPLACED – GIVEN TIME!

AS FAR AS YOUR OWN CONDITION IS CONCERNED, IMPERIAL MAJESTY, TIME IS ONE THING I DO NOT HAVE. I MUST FIND A WAY TO REVERSE THE PROCESS IN YOUR TISSUES BEFORE YOU DISINTEGRATE INTO NOTHING!

BY NIGHTFALL, THE REVOLUTIONARIES' FURY HAD SPENT ITSELF. BUT THE IMPERIAL PALACE LAY IN RUINS.

A TRUCE WAS DECLARED. THE EMPEROR'S BROTHER, BRAG, MET LEADERS OF THE REVOLT AND THE MORE MODERATE POLITICAL GROUPS.

WHERE IS THE EMPEROR? IT'S USELESS TO TALK OF REFORMS, WHEN THE ONLY MAN WHO CAN MAKE THEM REFUSES TO SHOW HIMSELF!

THE EMPEROR WILL APPEAR... IN... IN GOOD TIME!

THE LEADER OF THE MODERATES SPOKE UP...

LORD BRAG — YOU MUST PRODUCE THE EMPEROR BY THE END OF THE LUNAR MONTH OR WE SHALL HAVE NO ALTERNATIVE BUT TO AGREE TO THE DECLARATION OF A REPUBLIC!

BRAG KNEW THAT TRIGO WAS AS GOOD AS DOOMED ALREADY.

IF — IF MY BROTHER DOES NOT APPEAR WITHIN THE TIME YOU HAVE GIVEN, WOULD I BE ACCEPTABLE IN HIS PLACE?

NO, MY LORD, YOU WOULD NOT! IT'S TRIGO — OR NOTHING!

AND SO...

IT'S ALL UP TO YOU, PERIC. YOU'VE GOT TO RESTORE THE EMPEROR TO HIS PROPER SIZE BY THE END OF THE LUNAR MONTH OR THE TRIGAN EMPIRE IS FINISHED!

I AM NOWHERE NEAR THE ANSWER TO THE PROBLEM, LORD BRAG. MEANWHILE, THE EMPEROR IS SHRINKING FAST! LOOK!

BRAG LOOKED. HIS BROTHER WAS LIVING IN THE NIGHTMARE WORLD OF THE MICROSCOPIC!

EVEN AT THAT MOMENT, TRIGO WAS IN DEADLY PERIL!

I AM DONE FOR!

BY ALL THE STARS! THIS IS HORRIBLE!

MY GREATEST PROBLEM IS TO PROTECT HIM FROM PREDATORY BACTERIA. UNFORTUNATELY, IN KEEPING HIM ALIVE AND NOURISHED, I AM ALSO KEEPING ALIVE THE CREATURES THAT COULD DESTROY HIM!

TRIGO SEIZED A PIECE OF MICROSCOPIC DEBRIS AND PREPARED TO SELL HIS LIFE DEARLY TO THE PREDATORY BACTERIA.

THE EMPEROR OF THE TRIGANS WAS SNATCHED UP IN A DEADLY GRIP.

AAAAAGH!

BUT IN THE PROCESS OF BEING TRANSFERRED TO A GAPING MOUTH, TRIGO SUDDENLY FELT THE CLAW RELEASE HIM.

HE FELL HEAVILY AND FELT THE BONE OF HIS RIGHT ARM BREAK ASUNDER. AND THERE HE LAY – HELPLESS – WHILE THE MONSTERS BATTLED.

SOME TIME LATER, IN THE NORMAL WORLD OF TRIGAN, JANNO LANDED HIS AIRCRAFT...

MESSAGE FROM PERIC, LIEUTENANT.

IT MUST BE NEWS OF MY UNCLE TRIGO!

IT WAS A SUMMONS. AND IT TOOK JANNO RUSHING WITH ALL HASTE TO THE MAKESHIFT LABORATORY THAT ELEKTON'S TOP SCIENTIST HAD CONSTRUCTED IN THE RUINS OF THE IMPERIAL PALACE.

WHAT IS IT, PERIC? IS MY UNCLE...?

HE IS INJURED. HIS ARM WAS BROKEN IN A FIGHT WITH PREDATORY BACTERIA!

HIS CHANCE OF SURVIVAL IN THE VIOLENT WORLD OF THE MICROSCOPIC IS NOW ALMOST NIL – UNLESS SOMEONE GOES TO HIS ASSISTANCE!

YOU MEAN...?

I AM AS YET UNABLE TO REVERSE THE PROCESS AND RESTORE THE EMPEROR TO THE NORMAL WORLD – BUT I CAN REDUCE YOU TO MICROSCOPIC SIZE AND SEND YOU TO HELP HIM!

JANNO TOOK A DEEP BREATH... AND...

ALL RIGHT, PERIC. I'LL GO. I'LL TAKE MY CHANCE IN THAT NIGHTMARE WORLD WITH MY UNCLE!

MEANWHILE, IN THE HEADQUARTERS OF THE TRIGAN CITY REVOLUTIONARY PARTY...

WHAT'S GOING ON? WHERE IS TRIGO?

THEY'VE HIDDEN HIM. IT'S SOME KIND OF TRICK, I TELL YOU! IF HE'S ALIVE, WHY DOESN'T HE COME FORWARD?

THAT NIGHT, ONE OF THE REVOLUTIONARIES CREPT TORWARDS THE RUINS OF THE IMPERIAL PALACE.

THEY SAY THAT'S WHERE PERIC DABBLES WITH HIS ACCURSED SPELLS. IF ANYONE KNOWS WHERE TRIGO IS, IT'S PERIC!

WHAT DEVILRY'S GOING ON HERE?

JANNO AND PERIC WERE IN THE LABORATORY.

ARE YOU READY TO DESCEND INTO THE NIGHTMARE WORLD OF THE MICROSCOPIC?

YES, I AM! GET IT OVER WITH!

KRA-A-A-KKK! JANNO SLUMPED, UNCONSCIOUS, AS A MASSIVE SHOCK WAVE PASSED THROUGH HIS BODY.

UUUUGGHHH!

INSTANTLY, HIS BODY STRUCTURE HAD COMPLETELY CHANGED!

I HAVE ACCELERATED THE EFFECT — IN NO TIME HE WILL BE REDUCED TO MICROSCOPIC SIZE, LIKE THE EMPEROR!

CAREFULLY, THE GREAT SCIENTIST PERIC CARRIED THE TINY, UNCONSCIOUS FIGURE TO THE LABORATORY BENCH.

WHEN HE RECOVERS CONSCIOUSNESS, HE WILL BE UNDER MY MICROSCOPE — IN THE TEEMING, PERIL-RIDDEN WORLD THAT THE EMPEROR NOW INHABITS!

OUTSIDE THE WINDOW OF THE MAKESHIFT LABORATORY, THE EAVESDROPPER WAS RUDELY CHALLENGED!

WHO'S THAT?

HUH?

HE REACTED SWIFTLY — AND WITH VIOLENCE!

HAH!

...BUT THE IMPERIAL GUARDSMAN WAS QUICKER AND MORE DEADLY!

YUUUGGH!

THE GUARDSMAN DRAGGED HIS PRISONER IN TO PERIC.

CAUGHT HIM SNOOPING OUTSIDE YOUR WINDOW, EXCELLENCEY.

BY ALL THE STARS! HE'S ONE OF THE REVOLUTIONARY LEADERS! I KNOW HIS FACE WELL.

WHAT DO I DO WITH HIM, EXCELLENCY?

LOCK HIM UP. IF HE WERE TO REPEAT WHAT HE SAW OR HEARD IN THIS LABORATORY TONIGHT, IT COULD MEAN THE END OF THE TRIGAN EMPIRE!

SOME TIME LATER, JANNO RECOVERED CONSCIOUSNESS – AND LOOKED INTO THE FACE OF THE EMPEROR.

UNCLE!

JANNO! WHAT ON ELEKTON ARE YOU DOING IN THIS INFERNAL PLACE?

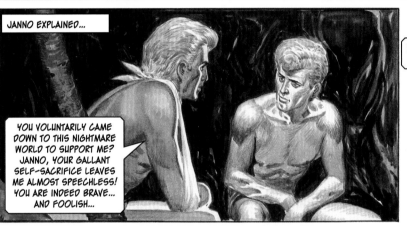

JANNO EXPLAINED...

YOU VOLUNTARILY CAME DOWN TO THIS NIGHTMARE WORLD TO SUPPORT ME? JANNO, YOUR GALLANT SELF-SACRIFICE LEAVES ME ALMOST SPEECHLESS! YOU ARE INDEED BRAVE... AND FOOLISH...

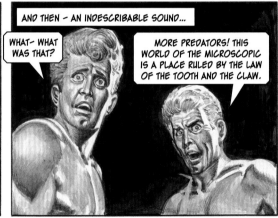

AND THEN – AN INDESCRIBABLE SOUND...

WHAT– WHAT WAS THAT?

MORE PREDATORS! THIS WORLD OF THE MICROSCOPIC IS A PLACE RULED BY THE LAW OF THE TOOTH AND THE CLAW.

THE GROUND SHOOK BENEATH THEM AS A MOUNTAINOUS FORM MOVED PAST.

THE SIZE OF THE THING!

BY ALL THE DEMONS! WE HAVE MADE A SUDDEN AND FANTASTIC REDUCTION IN SIZE!

THEN IT SEEMED TO TRIGO AND JANNO THAT THEY WERE CAUGHT UP LIKE LEAVES IN A STORM AND BORNE AWAY THROUGH A NEVER-ENDING VOID!

TRIGO AND HIS NEPHEW JANNO WERE WHIRLED THROUGH UNCHARTED SPACE, PAST UNKNOWN WORLDS.

AFTER WHAT SEEMED A LIFETIME, THEY RECOVERED CONSCIOUSNESS IN BRIGHT SUNLIGHT.

WHERE— WHERE ARE WE?

NOT ON ELEKTON, THAT'S FOR SURE! I'VE CIRCUMNAVIGATED OUR PLANET MANY TIMES BUT I'VE NEVER SEEN THIS TYPE OF COUNTRY!

PRESENTLY, THEY HEARD VOICES AND A CRAFT GLIDED INTO SIGHT.

THEY WERE ADDRESSED – IN THE COMMON LANGUAGE OF THEIR OWN PLANET.

WELCOME TO ORCADIA. WE HAVE BEEN EXPECTING YOU.

THE TRIGANS WERE TOO ASTOUNDED TO SPEAK. THEIR WONDER INCREASED WHEN THEY CAME TO A FABULOUS CITY.

THEIR GUIDE LED THEM INTO A GREAT HALL.

THE PERSONS FROM THE UPPER WORLD, GREAT ONE!

IT IS GOOD. PLEASE APPROACH, MY FRIENDS.

THEN BEGAN THE ANSWERS TO THE QUESTIONS THAT TEEMED IN THE TRIGANS' MINDS.

WE DETECTED YOUR APPROACH. IN THE DISTANT PAST, OUR PEOPLE INHABITED THE PERILOUS WORLD THAT YOU CALL THE MICROSCOPIC. INDEED, WE ARE EVEN FAMILIAR WITH YOUR NATIVE PLANET - WHICH IS WHY WE SPEAK YOUR LANGUAGE.

BUT... WHAT IS THIS PLANET? WHERE IS ORCADIA?

TAKING THE SCALE OF YOUR NATIVE PLANET, ORCADIA MOVES IN SPACE ABOUT THE NUCLEUS OF A SINGLE ATOM!

JANNO STARED AT HIS UNCLE IN AWE.

I... I DON'T UNDERSTAND.

THINK OF IT THIS WAY, LAD... UNDER PERIC'S MICROSCOPE IN THE PALACE LABORATORY IN TRIGAN CITY IS A MICROSCOPIC WORLD MADE UP OF A TEEMING MASS OF ATOMIC PARTICLES - WORLDS WITHIN WORLDS. WE ARE NOW ON ONE OF THOSE SUB-MICROSCOPIC WORLDS!

MEANWHILE, IN TRIGAN CITY, THE REVOLUTIONARY WHO HAD BEEN CAUGHT OUTSIDE PERIC'S LABORATORY WAS RECOVERING HIS SENSES.

GIVE ME A HAND TO CARRY THIS ANIMAL TO THE LOCK-UP!

HE SEIZED HIS CHANCE!

UUUUGH!

AAAAGH!

PRESENTLY, HE WAS BACK AT HIS PARTY'S SECRET HEADQUARTERS.

OH, IT'S YOU. WHAT DID YOU FIND OUT?

PLENTY!

HE TOLD HIS FANTASTIC STORY OF WHAT HE HAD SEEN AND HEARD THAT NIGHT IN THE LABORATORY AT THE PALACE.

I TELL YOU IT'S TRUE! TRIGO AND THAT NEPHEW OF HIS ARE UNDER PERIC'S MICROSCOPE! WE CAN DESTROY THEM AS EASILY AS SNAPPING A FINGER - SO!

THE REVOLUTIONARIES TOOK NEW HEART AT THE NEWS OF THE EMPEROR'S TRUE FATE. THEY SWARMED INTO THE STREETS.

TRIGO IS NO MORE!

DOWN WITH THE EMPIRE!

THERE IS NO EMPEROR!

FOR THE SECOND TIME, THEY BROKE INTO PERIC'S LABORATORY.

LET'S SEE WHAT YOU'VE GOT UNDER YOUR MICROSCOPE, PERIC!

AAAAH!

THE GREAT SCIENTIST TRIED TO SHIELD HIS PRECIOUS APPARATUS FROM THEM... IN VAIN.

NO! NO!

OH, YES!

THE SLIDE WAS RIPPED FROM UNDER THE MICROSCOPE AND HELD ALOFT.

BEHOLD! INSIDE THIS THING LIES TRIGO, FORMER EMPEROR OF ALL THE TRIGANS, AND HIS NEPHEW, THE HIGH AND MIGHTY LORD JANNO...

THE SLIDE WAS DASHED TO THE FLOOR AND GROUND UNDER A HEAVY HEEL!

FAREWELL, EMPEROR! FARE-WELL, JANNO!

WHEN THE MOB HAD DEPARTED, THE EMPEROR'S BROTHER, BRAG, FOUND THE GREAT SCIENTIST ON HIS KNEES.

HAVE THEY...?

THEY KNEW WHAT THEY WERE COMING FOR – AND THEY HAVE SMASHED THE PRECIOUS SLIDE TO PIECES AND ALL THAT IT CONTAINED!

THEY HAVE SLAIN MY BROTHER AND MY SON AS SURELY AS IF THEY HAD STRUCK OFF THEIR HEADS!

NOT QUITE! ATOMS CANNOT BE DESTROYED BY SUCH SIMPLE MEANS.

BUT THERE IS NOW NOTHING I CAN DO TO RETURN THEM TO THE WORLD OF THE NORMAL – NOTHING! THE ATOMIC PARTICLE IN WHICH THEY ARE CONTAINED CAN NEVER BE FOUND AGAIN – NEVER!

MEANWHILE, IN THE SUB-MICROSCOPIC WORLD OF ORCADIA, TRIGO AND JANNO WERE LEARNING MUCH FROM THE SPLENDID OLD MAN WHO RULED THAT PLANET.

THIS IS THE NERVE CENTRE OF OUR SCIENCE AND TECHNOLOGY, BY MEANS OF WHICH WE ARE ABLE TO PROBE INTO UNIVERSES BEYOND OUR OWN.

YOU SAID, GREAT ONE, THAT YOU ARE FAMILIAR WITH OUR NATIVE PLANET - ELEKTON?

NOT ONLY YOUR PLANET BUT WITH THE VERY STREETS OF YOUR CAPITAL CITY, TRIGO. BEHOLD...

THEY SAW THE FAMILIAR BROAD STREETS... AND HEARD AN UNFAMILIAR CRY!

TRIGO IS DEAD!

LONG LIVE THE REPUBLIC!

THE OLD MAN GAZED AT TRIGO WITH COMPASSION.

DO NOT GRIEVE FOR YOUR LOST EMPIRE, TRIGO. I KNOW YOUR GREAT WORTH AND I WILL APPOINT YOU AS MY SUCCESSOR. WHEN I AM GONE, YOU SHALL REIGN ON ORCADIA. WHAT DO YOU SAY?

JANNO STARED AT HIS UNCLE...

WILL MY UNCLE ACCEPT? ARE WE NEVER TO SEE ELEKTON AGAIN?

TRIGO POINTED TO THE FLICKERING SCREEN AND ANSWERED IN RINGING TONES...

I THANK YOU FOR THE HONOUR YOU OFFER ME, GREAT ONE - BUT MY COUNTRY NEEDS ME AND I AWAIT PERIC'S SCIENCE TO RETURN US BOTH TO OUR NORMAL STATE!

ORCADIA'S ANCIENT RULER SHOOK HIS HEAD SADLY.

TRIGO, I AM FAMILIAR WITH THE WORK OF ELEKTON'S GREATEST SCIENTIST BUT I REGRET TO TELL YOU THAT THERE ARE NOT ENOUGH RESOURCES ON ALL YOUR PLANET TO BRING ABOUT YOUR RETURN!

YOU MEAN... WE CAN NEVER RETURN?

HOWEVER... IT IS WITHIN THE POWER OF THE SCIENCE AND TECHNOLOGY OF ORCADIA TO RETURN YOU TO ELEKTON!

MEANWHILE, IN TRIGAN CITY, THE REBELS WERE TRAMPLING UNDERFOOT THE LAST VESTIGES OF THE ONCE MIGHTY TRIGAN EMPIRE.

LONG LIVE THE REPUBLIC! LONG LIVE FREEDOM!

THE REVOLUTIONARY COMMITTEE ORDERED MASS ARRESTS...

I DEMAND TO KNOW WHAT YOU WANT WITH ME!

YOUR DAYS OF DEMANDING ARE OVER, BRAG! YOU'RE COMING WITH US!

THE INNOCENT AND THE GUILTY ALIKE... RICH AND POOR...

MY HUSBAND HAS DONE NOTHING! YOU CAN'T TAKE HIM!

HE WAS ONCE HEARD TO SHOUT "LONG LIVE THE EMPEROR" - THE PENALTY FOR THAT IS NOW DEATH!

EVEN PERIC'S GREAT AGE AND WISDOM DID NOT SAVE HIM...

GIVE ME ANOTHER TWO DAYS, I BEG YOU - IN TWO DAYS, THIS VITAL EXPERIMENT WILL BE FINISHED!

IN ONE DAY, OLD MAN, YOU WILL BE FINISHED!

A SPECIAL TRIBUNAL DISPENSED MASS "JUSTICE" TO THE PRISONERS.

GUILTY — ALL GUILTY!

THE VERDICT IS GUILTY — THE SENTENCE IS DEATH WITHIN A LUNAR DAY!

PERIC AND BRAG SPENT THE LONG NIGHT TOGETHER.

IF ONLY THEY HAD LET ME FINISH — I MAY HAVE FOUND A WAY OF BRINGING THE EMPEROR BACK!

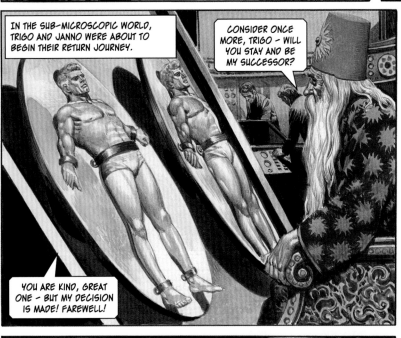

IN THE SUB-MICROSCOPIC WORLD, TRIGO AND JANNO WERE ABOUT TO BEGIN THEIR RETURN JOURNEY.

CONSIDER ONCE MORE, TRIGO — WILL YOU STAY AND BE MY SUCCESSOR?

YOU ARE KIND, GREAT ONE — BUT MY DECISION IS MADE! FAREWELL!

THE OLD MAN MADE A SIGN — AND...

THE TWO TRIGANS WERE WHIRLED THROUGH TRACKLESS SPACE...!

THEN CAME... TERROR!

UNCLE! WHERE ARE WE NOW?

IN THE WORLD OF THE MICROSCOPIC — ONLY IT'S A THOUSAND TIMES WORSE THAN I REMEMBER IT!

AT DAWN, THE CONDEMNED WERE TAKEN THROUGH THE SILENT STREETS OF THE CAPITAL TO THE PLACE OF EXECUTION.

BRAG AND PERIC MADE THE GRIM JOURNEY TOGETHER.

I HEAR NO CHEERS FROM THE CROWD.

THE REVOLUTION ISN'T POPULAR. IF MY BROTHER WERE TO REAPPEAR, THE WHOLE THING WOULD INSTANTLY COLLAPSE!

AT THAT SAME INSTANT, TRIGO AND JANNO WERE WADING FOR THEIR LIVES THROUGH MICROSCOPIC DUST..

I... I CAN'T GO ON MUCH FURTHER, UNCLE!

KEEP GOING, JANNO! WE'RE GROWING ALL THE TIME! SOON WE'LL BE ABLE TO OVERPOWER THOSE BEASTS!

TRIGO WAS RIGHT. THEIR INCREASE IN SIZE WAS SO RAPID THAT THEY WERE SOON MASTERS OF THE PREDATORY MICROBES.

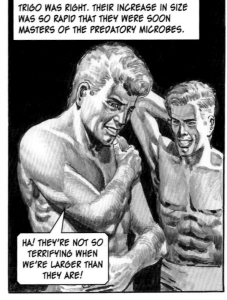

HA! THEY'RE NOT SO TERRIFYING WHEN WE'RE LARGER THAN THEY ARE!

AT A CERTAIN STAGE IN THEIR RE-GROWTH, THEY CAME OUT OF THE MICROSCOPIC AND INTO THE WORLD THEY KNEW.

WE'RE NO LONGER UNDER PERIC'S MICROSCOPE. THAT ACCOUNTS FOR THE GREAT NUMBER OF MICROBES WE ENCOUNTERED.

UNCLE - LOOK!

ANOTHER PREDATOR!

GNA-AGGHH!

FORTUNATELY, THEIR RE-GROWTH RATE WAS TOO SWIFT FOR THEIR WOULD-BE KILLER - A HOUSEHOLD PET!

SORRY TO DISAPPOINT YOU OVER A MEAL, OLD FELLOW!

GOOD. NOW WE'LL GO AND FIND PERIC.

WHEN THEY GOT OUTSIDE THE LABORATORY, THEY MET ONE OF THE OLD SCIENTIST'S ASSISTANTS.

IMPERIAL MAJESTY! THANK THE STARS - YOU LIVE!

WHERE'S YOU MASTER - WHERE'S PERIC!

THE REVOLUTIONARIES HAVE DECLARED A REPUBLIC! EVEN AT THIS MOMENT, PERIC AND YOUR BROTHER, LORD BRAG, ARE BEING LED TO EXECUTION!

EXECUTION!

IN THE GREAT SQUARE OF THE CITY, BRAG AND PERIC SHOOK HANDS AT THE FOOT OF THE DREAD SCAFFOLD.

FAREWELL, OLD FRIEND!

YOU FIRST!

FAREWELL, MY LORD.

AND THEN – IT HAPPENED!

STOP!

TRIGO!

WITH THE SUDDEN AND DRAMATIC APPEARANCE OF THE EMPEROR, THE REVOLUTION – AS BRAG HAD PREDICTED – INSTANTLY COLLAPSED!

MERCY, IMPERIAL MAJESTY!

LONG LIVE THE EMPEROR!

GRANTED!

TRIGO HAD JOURNEYED FROM THE WORLD OF THE SUB-MICROSCOPIC – AND SAVED HIS EMPIRE!

MY PEOPLE! TOGETHER WE WILL STAMP OUT ALL INJUSTICES AND INEQUALITIES IN OUR MIDST! WE WILL BUILD A NEW WORLD ON THE PLANET ELEKTON!

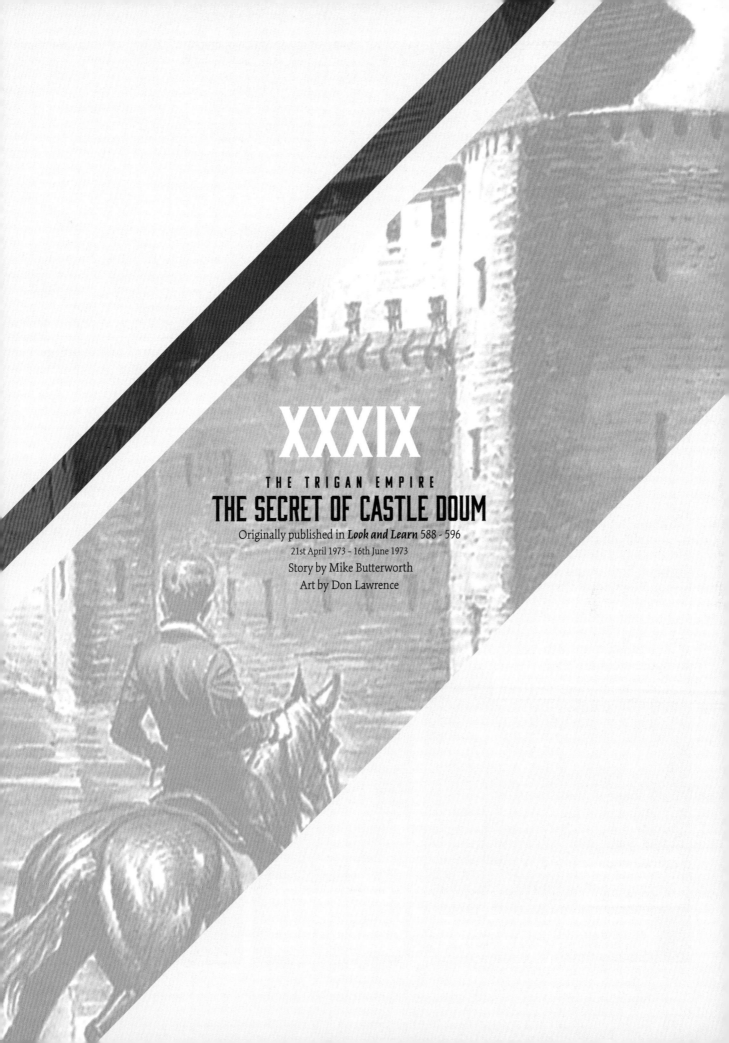

XXXIX

THE TRIGAN EMPIRE
THE SECRET OF CASTLE DOUM
Originally published in *Look and Learn* 588 - 596
21st April 1973 – 16th June 1973
Story by Mike Butterworth
Art by Don Lawrence

BY GENERAL CONSENT, THE FOUR TOP ACES OF THE TRIGAN AIR FLEET...

WERE JANNO, THE EMPEROR'S NEPHEW, ROFFA, KEREN - AND DUBAL.

DUBAL WAS THE YOUNGEST AND A NEWCOMER TO THE AIR FLEET. THIS DASHING, FEARLESS PILOT WON EARLY RENOWN BY SUCCESSFULLY LANDING A BLAZING AIRCRAFT.

LIEUTENANT DUBAL. YOU WILL USE YOUR EJECTION MECHANISM AND THAT'S AN ORDER.

NONSENSE. THESE THINGS COST TWENTY THOUSAND ZERSTS APIECE. HURRY UP WITH THOSE FIRE TRUCKS.

AFTER AN ARDUOUS SPELL OF DUTY, THE COMRADES' SQUADRON WAS DUE FOR LEAVE.

COME AND SPEND YOUR LEAVE WITH US. I CAN PROMISE SOME GOOD ZARGOT HUNTING.

THANKS. NOTHING WOULD PLEASE ME BETTER BUT IT'S MY COMING-OF-AGE, YOU KNOW, AND MY FATHER'S EXPECTING ME BACK AT CASTLE DOUM.

JANNO WAS SUDDENLY AWARE OF A BITTERNESS IN HIS FRIEND'S VOICE.

I DARE SAY MY FATHER AND I WILL SPEND MOST OF THE TIME QUARRELLING. HE DOESN'T LIKE ME - AND, IF THE TRUTH BE KNOWN, I DON'T LIKE HIM VERY MUCH EITHER.

WITH DUBAL'S STRANGE COMMENT IN HIS MIND, JANNO SPOKE TO HIS OWN FATHER THAT EVENING.

WHAT'S DUBAL'S FATHER LIKE? HE MAKES HIM SOUND A MONSTER.

I CAN TELL YOU THIS, LAD. WHEN HE WAS DUBAL'S AGE, DARRA WAS THE LIVELIEST, BRIGHTEST COMPANION YOU COULD WISH TO HAVE.

HE SEEMED TO CHANGE OVERNIGHT - IT WOULD HAVE BEEN AROUND THE TIME OF HIS COMING-OF-AGE- AND TURN FROM AN AMUSING, FUN-LOVING LAD, TO A SAVAGE AND MOROSE MAN. VERY STRANGE.

DUBAL'S FAMILY WERE OF THE ANCIENT VORG NOBILITY. FROM TIME IMMEMORIAL, THEY HAD LIVED AT THE GRIM ISLAND-FORTRESS OF CASTLE DOUM. IT WAS TO THE CASTLE THAT DUBAL WENT ON HIS LEAVE.

I HATE THIS PLACE. WHEN IT BECOMES MINE, I SHALL HAVE IT PULLED DOWN... EVERY STONE!

HIS FATHER, THE LORD DARRA, GREETED HIM WITH HIS ACCUSTOMED LACK OF WARMTH.

HELLO, FATHER. I HOPE I FIND YOU IN GOOD HEALTH.

YOU HOPE IN VAIN. I AM NOT LONG FOR THIS WORLD.

THEY SUPPED ALONE AND IN SILENCE WITH THE SOLITARY SERVANT, A GIANT VORG PEASANT, TO SERVE THEM.

AFTERWARDS, THE LORD DARRA SPOKE...

MY SON. TONIGHT YOU COME OF AGE AND IT IS MY UNFORTUNATE DUTY TO ADMIT YOU INTO THE TERRIBLE SECRET OF OUR FAMILY. I WOULD GIVE ANYTHING, MY BOY, TO SPARE YOU THE HORROR AND THE MISERY OF IT. BUT I AM FORCED TO TELL YOU.

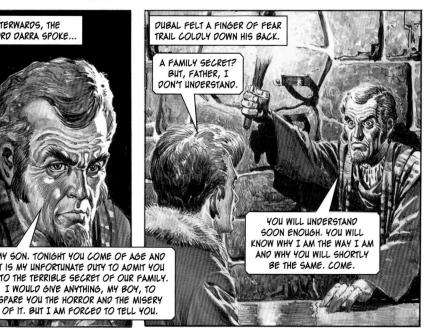

DUBAL FELT A FINGER OF FEAR TRAIL COLDLY DOWN HIS BACK.

A FAMILY SECRET? BUT, FATHER, I DON'T UNDERSTAND.

YOU WILL UNDERSTAND SOON ENOUGH. YOU WILL KNOW WHY I AM THE WAY I AM AND WHY YOU WILL SHORTLY BE THE SAME. COME.

THE LORD OF CASTLE DOUM LED HIS SON TO THE UPPERMOST PART OF THAT GRIM PILE, TO A LOCKED AND BARRED DOOR.

BEYOND THIS DOOR LIES THE SECRET OF CASTLE DOUM. PREPARE YOURSELF, MY POOR SON.

DAWN BROKE OVER THE GRIM PILE OF CASTLE DOUM...

THERE HAD BEEN NO SLEEP FOR DUBAL. ALL NIGHT, HE HAD GAZED WITH HAGGARD, TRAGIC EYES INTO THE DARKNESS.

IT CAN'T BE TRUE! THIS CAN'T BE HAPPENING TO ME!

HE LATER SOUGHT OUT THE LORD DARRA.

CAN NOTHING BE DONE, FATHER? DO WE HAVE TO LIVE UNDER THE SHADOW OF OUR DREADFUL SECRET?

YES, MY SON, WE DO!

I AM NOT LONG FOR THIS LIFE. WHEN I HAVE GONE, YOU WILL BEAR THE AWFUL BURDEN ALONE, TILL YOU TOO HAVE A SON WHO COMES OF AGE. THEN YOU WILL HAVE TO ADMIT HIM TO THE SECRET AT HIS COMING-OF-AGE.

AT THE END OF HIS LEAVE, DUBAL RETURNED TO DUTY WITH HIS COMRADES OF THE AIR FLEET.

HELLO, DUBAL! HOW WERE THINGS AT NIGHTMARE CASTLE?

HUH?

WHY DID YOU CALL IT THAT... WHY?

WELL, I MEAN, IT'S RATHER A GRIM-LOOKING PLACE YOU LIVE IN. HEY! I WAS ONLY JOKING!

NO ONE JESTS ABOUT CASTLE DOUM!

DUBAL! HAVE YOU TAKEN LEAVE OF YOUR SENSES?

UUUUGH!

THE PILOTS STARED IN SHOCKED HORROR AT THEIR COMRADE.

WHAT'S COME OVER YOU?

NO ONE JESTS ABOUT MY HOME, MY FAMILY, OR ME – DO YOU UNDERSTAND?

THEY WATCHED DUBAL STALK OUT – AND SOMETHING THAT HIS FATHER HAD TOLD HIM CAME BACK TO JANNO...

HE'S USUALLY SO CHEERFUL AND GOOD-NATURED.

IT WAS JUST THE SAME WITH DUBAL'S FATHER. HE CHANGED INTO A SAVAGE AND MOROSE MAN... AROUND THE TIME OF HIS COMING-OF-AGE.

FROM THAT DAY FORTH, DUBAL WAS NEVER THE SAME. HE TOOK TO SPENDING HIS NIGHTS IN LOW HAUNTS...

OH. IT'S YOU...

...WHERE HE PROCEEDED TO GAMBLE AWAY A FORTUNE AT AN ILLEGAL GAME OF CHANCE.

THE INEVITABLE HAPPENED. ONE MORNING, AFTER A NIGHT OF DISSIPATION, HE TOOK PART IN FORMATION FLYING...

DUBAL! YOU'RE OUT OF LINE! CORRECT YOUR POSITION!

DISASTER!

AAAGH!

27

TWO PILOTS EJECTED SAFELY FROM THEIR DOOMED CRAFT. THE THIRD – DUBAL – WAS UNCONSCIOUS.

HE WAS STILL IN HIS CRAFT WHEN IT PANCAKED INTO TRIGAN CITY HARBOUR!

LATER THAT DAY, UNDERWATER OPERATORS DIVED DOWN.

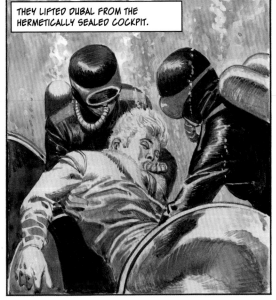

THEY LIFTED DUBAL FROM THE HERMETICALLY SEALED COCKPIT.

HE WAS TAKEN TO PERIC'S LABORATORY, WHERE THE GREAT SCIENTIST MADE HIS DIAGNOSIS.

HE IS HOVERING BETWEEN LIFE AND DEATH. AS YET, IT IS TOO EARLY TO DETERMINE WHICH STATE WILL CLAIM HIM.

IT WAS SOME DAYS BEFORE HIS COMRADE JANNO WAS ABLE TO VISIT HIM.

HAS HE RECOVERED CONSCIOUSNESS YET, PERIC?

BRIEFLY – AND ONLY PARTLY. THE BATTLE IS NOT YET OVER, JANNO. DEATH COULD STILL SNATCH HIM FROM MY GRASP!

WHEN JANNO WAS WITH HIM, DUBAL BEGAN TO BABBLE IN HIS DELIRIUM...

THE FAMILY SECRET... LOCKED ROOM... TOP OF THE CASTLE...

BY THE STARS! WHAT'S HE SAYING?

FAMILY SECRET? LOCKED ROOM? I WONDER! CAN THIS HAVE ANYTHING TO DO WITH THE STRANGE CHANGE WE'VE NOTICED IN HIM?

JANNO DECIDED TO VISIT DUBAL'S FATHER AT CASTLE DOUM.

SINCE IT'S A FAMILY SECRET, I'D BETTER BE DISCREET. LORD DARRA WON'T THANK ME FOR MEDDLING IN HIS AFFAIRS.

HE ARRIVED AT THE GRIM ISLAND-FORTRESS THAT HAD BEEN IN DUBAL'S FAMILY SINCE TIME IMMEMORIAL.

I'VE PURPOSELY LEFT IT TOO LATE TO SET OFF BACK TO TRIGAN CITY BEFORE DARK. THE OLD MAN WILL HAVE TO INVITE ME TO STAY OVERNIGHT, OUT OF COURTESY.

JANNO MET THE LORD DARRA FOR THE FIRST TIME.

I HAVE BROUGHT YOUR SON'S EFFECTS, MY LORD. HE IS NOT OUT OF DANGER, YET, BUT PERIC HAS GREAT HOPES.

YOU ARE KIND, LIEUTENANT JANNO. ALLOW ME TO OFFER YOU MY HUMBLE HOSPITALITY FOR THE NIGHT.

IN THE MIDDLE OF THE NIGHT, THE YOUNG PILOT LEFT HIS BEDCHAMBER...

NOW... TO UNCOVER THE SECRET OF THE LOCKED ROOM!

HE WAS OBSERVED!

29

IN THE UPPERMOST PART OF THE CASTLE, JANNO CAME UPON THE OBJECT OF HIS SEARCH.

THE LOCKED ROOM! BEHIND IT LIES THE FAMILY SECRET!

AND THEN...

WHAT'S THAT? AAAAAAAGH!

HE WAS FELLED BY A BLOW OF A MASSIVE HAND!

ACCURSED SPY!

UUUUUUH...

LORD DARRA'S HAGGARD EYES BLAZED WITH FURY...

HE RECOVERED CONSCIOUSNESS LATER — MUCH LATER — IN A DANK AND AIRLESS DUNGEON. THE OWNER OF CASTLE DOUM STOOD BEFORE HIM...

HOW DARE YOU BETRAY MY HOSPITALITY? WHAT DO YOU KNOW? ANSWER, OR I WILL DESTROY YOU WITH MY OWN HANDS!

I KNOW NOTHING — SAVE THAT YOU HAVE A FAMILY SECRET!

YOU KNOW THAT?... HOW?

YOUR SON SPOKE OF IT IN HIS DELIRIUM. HE BABBLED OF THE LOCKED ROOM. I TOLD NO-ONE, BUT DETERMINED TO COME HERE AND FIND FOR MYSELF WHAT CHANGED HIM FROM A FUN-LOVING COMRADE TO A MOROSE AND BITTER MAN!

LORD DARRA WAS SILENT FOR A LONG WHILE. AND THEN...

I HAVE NO ILL-FEELING TOWARDS YOU, YOUNG MAN, AND I WISH YOU NO HARM. FURTHERMORE, I HAVE TOO MUCH SORROW ON MY MIND TO ADD TO IT THE BURDEN OF YOUR DEATH. HOWEVER...

...THE SECRET MUST BE KEPT AT ANY PRICE. YOU MUST, THEREFORE, STAY HERE IN THIS DUNGEON TILL YOUR DYING DAY!

LATER, IN THE GREAT HALL OF HIS GLOOMY CASTLE, LORD DARRA SPOKE WITH HIS VORG MANSERVANT.

NOW, URGAL, WE MUST LAY A FALSE TRAIL. THE ENQUIRERS WILL SOON BE HERE...

YES, MY LORD.

TRUE ENOUGH, INVESTIGATORS OF THE TRIGAN POLICE SOON TRACED THE MISSING PILOT TO CASTLE DOUM.

THE LIEUTENANT VERY KINDLY BROUGHT MY WOUNDED SON'S PERSONAL EFFECTS. HE STAYED OVERNIGHT AND DEPARTED IN THE MORNING.

THANK YOU FOR YOUR HELP, MY LORD.

SOME DAYS LATER, THEY FOUND JANNO'S HOVER-AUTO AT THE FOOT OF THE SEA-LASHED CLIFFS BENEATH THE ROAD TO TRIGAN CITY.

THAT'S THE ANSWER! HE OVERSHOT THE BEND AND WENT OVER!

IT WAS ASSUMED THAT JANNO'S BODY HAD BEEN CARRIED AWAY BY THE STRONG TIDES. A DAY OF NATIONAL MOURNING WAS DECLARED FOR THE POPULAR MEMBER OF THE IMPERIAL FAMILY.

A FLIGHT OF HIS COMRADES DROPPED A TOKEN OF THE AIR FLEET'S SORROW AND RESPECT.

IT WAS SOME DAYS LATER THAT KEREN RECEIVED A STRANGE NOTE THAT CONTAINED STAGGERING NEWS AND A PROMISE OF FUTHER INFORMATION TO COME...

NO! IT CAN'T BE TRUE! IT CAN'T!

FEW PEDESTRIANS EVER TACKLED THE ENORMOUS LENGTH OF THE TRIGAN BAY BRIDGE. BUT THE FOLLOWING DAY, AT AN APPOINTED TIME, KEREN DID JUST THAT.

THAT MUST BE... HIM!

KEREN AND THE STRANGER MET IN THE MIDDLE OF THE BRIDGE.

YOU ARE THE WRITER OF THE NOTE?

I AM. AND YOU ARE LIEUTENANT KEREN OF THE AIR FLEET.

IN THE NOTE, YOU CLAIM TO HAVE PROOF THAT JANNO DIDN'T PERISH IN THAT CAR CRASH.

THAT IS TRUE. LET ME EXPLAIN...

"I AM A BOTANIST BY PROFESSION," WENT ON THE STRANGER. "SOME DAYS AGO, I WAS TAKING PICTURES OF WILD PLANT LIFE WHEN I SAW A STRANGE THING HAPPENING ON THE CLIFF ROAD BELOW..."

I'LL HAVE A PICTURE OF THIS!

HE PASSED A PRINT TO KEREN.

WHY! THAT FELLOW'S PUSHING JANNO'S HOVER-AUTO OVER THE CLIFF!

QUITE SO. AND NOTICE THAT JANNO IS NOT IN IT!

WHO IS THIS MAN IN THE PICTURE?

I HAVE FOUND THAT OUT – BUT IT WILL COST YOU A THOUSAND THULLARS FOR THE INFORMATION!

YOU MEAN...?

SAY NOTHING TO ANYONE, OR THE DEAL IS OFF. BRING ME A THOUSAND THULLARS TO THIS SPOT IN TWO DAYS FROM NOW AND I WILL LEAD YOU TO THE MAN WHO FAKED YOUR COMRADE'S DEATH!

KEREN HAD NO CHOICE BUT TO AGREE TO THE STRANGER'S PROPOSITION. THE STRANGER WATCHED HIM GO WITH A CUNNING GRIN.

POOR YOUNG FELLOW – LITTLE DOES HE KNOW WHAT I HAVE IN STORE FOR HIM!

THAT SAME EVENING, THE STRANGER JOURNEYED TO CASTLE DOUM.

AND NOW... THE SECOND PART OF MY FOOLPROOF LITTLE SCHEME TO MAKE A DOUBLE FORTUNE!

THE VORG SERVANT URGAL ANSWERED THE KNOCK.

JUST ASK YOUR MASTER IF HE WANTS TO BUY A PICTURE – THIS PICTURE!

AAAAAAH! WHERE DID YOU GET THAT?

IT WAS THEN THAT THE VORG SERVANT LEAPT ON THE SNEERING STRANGER WITH A HOWL OF BESTIAL FURY.

SOON, THE STRANGER WAS STANDING BEFORE LORD DARRA.

DOES... DOES ANYONE ELSE KNOW OF THIS?

YES, MY LORD. ONE PERSON – A COMRADE OF THE UNFORTUNATE YOUNG MAN WHO OWNED THE CAR.

GAAAAAH! PERISH, SPY!

HAVE A CARE! AT MY DEATH OR DISAPPEARANCE, ANOTHER PRINT OF THE PICTURE IS SENT TO THE EMPEROR HIMSELF!

URGAL! PUT HIM DOWN!

YOUR TERMS?

THE YOUNG OFFICER WHO HAS SEEN THE PRINT – GIVE ME A THOUSAND THULLARS AND I WILL DELIVER HIM INTO YOUR HANDS SO THAT YOU CAN DISPOSE OF HIM YOURSELF!

TWO DAYS LATER, KEREN MET THE MYSTERIOUS STRANGER AGAIN ON THE TRIGAN BAY BRIDGE.

YOU HAVE BROUGHT THE MONEY?

YES.

HERE... AND IN RETURN YOU WILL LEAD ME TO THE MAN WHO FAKED JANNO'S DEATH!

YES! HERE ARE YOUR INSTRUCTIONS. BUT YOU WILL SAY NOTHING OF THIS TO ANYONE, OR JANNO'S LIFE WILL BE IN DANGER. YOU WILL JOURNEY TO CASTLE DOUM...

CASTLE DOUM? THE HOME OF LORD DARRA, FATHER OF DUBAL?

THE VERY SAME! LORD DARRA WILL BE EXPECTING YOU. HE WILL HELP YOU FURTHER IN YOUR QUEST FOR YOUR COMRADE.

THAT SAME DAY, KEREN PREPARED TO SET OFF FOR CASTLE DOUM. BEFORE HE LEFT THE AIR FLEET BASE, HE WROTE A LETTER AND PLACED IT IN HIS DESK...

JUST IN CASE...

DURING THE JOURNEY, HIS MIND PUZZLED OVER THE MYSTERY OF HIS MISSING COMRADE.

WHAT CAN LORD DARRA KNOW OF JANNO'S DISAPPEARANCE? WHAT CAN BE THE CONNECTION?

ARRIVING AT THE GRIM ISLAND-FORTRESS, HE WAS ROWED ACROSS THE DARK LAKE.

KEREN ENTERED THE DARK PORTALS.

HO, THERE! ANYONE ABOUT?

AND THEN... *IT HAPPENED!*

AAAAAGH!

INSTANTS LATER, HE WAS LYING STRETCHED OUT AT THE FEET OF THE SINISTER OWNER OF CASTLE DOUM.

HE STILL LIVES, MY LORD!

GOOD! I DO NOT WANT HIS DEATH ON MY CONSCIENCE. TAKE HIM AND PUT HIM WITH THE OTHER!

LATER - MUCH LATER - KEREN RECOVERED CONSCIOUSNESS, TO FIND HIMSELF LOOKING UP INTO THE FACE OF HIS COMRADE, JANNO.

BY ALL THE STARS! JANNO!

I'M SORRY TO SEE YOU IN THIS HOLE, KEREN!

WHAT'S IT ALL ABOUT? WHO'S BEHIND IT ALL?

LORD DARRA! THERE'S A FAMILY SECRET - A LOCKED ROOM - I DON'T KNOW MUCH ABOUT IT. I ONLY KNOW THIS...

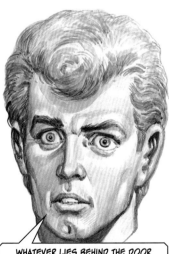

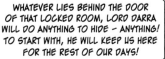

WHATEVER LIES BEHIND THE DOOR OF THAT LOCKED ROOM, LORD DARRA WILL DO ANYTHING TO HIDE - ANYTHING! TO START WITH, HE WILL KEEP US HERE FOR THE REST OF OUR DAYS!

IN DUE COURSE, WHEN IT WAS REALISED THAT KEREN WAS MISSING, HIS QUARTERS AT THE AIR FLEET BASE WERE SEARCHED. THE LETTER WAS FOUND IN HIS DRAWER.

ROFFA! THIS IS ADDRESSED TO YOU!

TO ME? WHAT CAN IT BE?

ROFFA OPENED THE LETTER AND READ IT.

WHAT DOES IT SAY, ROFFA?

ER... IT'S NOTHING. JUST A NOTE FROM KEREN THANKING ME FOR SOMETHING. HE... HMM... HE MUST HAVE FORGOTTEN TO HAVE IT DELIVERED.

AS HE STUMBLED OVER THE AWKWARD LIE, THE TRUE CONTENTS OF KEREN'S MESSAGE BURNT IN HIS MIND...

"JANNO STILL ALIVE – FOLLOW ME TO CASTLE DOUM – TRUST NO-ONE – TELL NO-ONE!"

THAT EVENING, ROFFA STOOD GAZING AT THE BLACK BULK OF CASTLE DOUM.

MY BEST PLAN IS TO ACT THE COMPLETE INNOCENT... KEEP MY MOUTH SHUT AND MY EYES AND EARS OPEN!

PRESENTLY, THE YOUNG AIR FLEET PILOT WAS INTRODUCING HIMSELF TO THE GRIM-FACED OWNER OF THE ISLAND-FORTRESS.

AND TO WHAT DO I OWE THE HONOUR OF THIS VISIT, LIEUTENANT ROFFA?

WELL, LORD DARRA, YOUR SON WAS A MEMBER OF MY SQUADRON AND I THOUGHT YOU'D LIKE TO HEAR THE LATEST NEWS OF HIM...

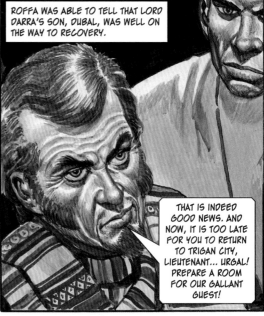

ROFFA WAS ABLE TO TELL THAT LORD DARRA'S SON, DUBAL, WAS WELL ON THE WAY TO RECOVERY.

THAT IS INDEED GOOD NEWS. AND NOW, IT IS TOO LATE FOR YOU TO RETURN TO TRIGAN CITY, LIEUTENANT... URGAL! PREPARE A ROOM FOR OUR GALLANT GUEST!

NIGHT FELL OVER CASTLE DOUM. AS ELEKTON'S TWIN MOONS ROSE, THREE DARK FIGURES SLIPPED INTO THE WATER.

AT ABOUT THE SAME TIME, ROFFA LEFT HIS BEDCHAMBER AND BEGAN HIS EXPLORATION OF THE CASTLE.

WHAT— WHAT WAS *THAT?*

WHERE'S *HE* OFF TO AT THIS TIME OF THE NIGHT?

LORD DARRA PAUSED BEFORE A DOOR. THERE WAS A CLATTER OF HEAVY LOCKS AND BOLTS. THE DOOR CREAKED OPEN...

WHAT – OR WHO – DOES HE KEEP LOCKED IN *THERE?*

SUDDENLY, SOME SIXTH SENSE MADE ROFFA LOOK ROUND – JUST IN TIME TO AVOID A PAIR OF MASSIVE, CLUTCHING HANDS!

GAAAAAAAGH!

HE RAN FOR HIS LIFE!

SEIZE HIM, URGAL!

ROFFA CLAMBERED THROUGH AN ARCHED WINDOW AND OUT INTO THE NIGHT.

IF ONLY I HAD A WEAPON. THAT BRUTE COULD REND ME LIMB FROM LIMB!

HE SET OFF ACROSS THE PERILOUS ROOFTOPS OF CASTLE DOUM!

HOW DID I LET MYSELF GET INTO THIS SITUATION!

ROFFA EDGED CAREFULLY AWAY FROM THE VORG UNTIL HE COULD GO NO FURTHER. THEN HE TURNED TO FACE HIS HUGE PURSUER.

ROFFA DUCKED TO AVOID THE CLUTCHING HANDS – SLIPPED – AND FELL!

GAAAAAAAGH!

AAAAAAAAGH!

AND SO, AT THE PERIL OF HIS OWN LIFE, THE BIG SERVANT RESCUED ROFFA.

BUT THE URGENT CRY OF LORD DARRA ECHOED ACROSS THE VOID...

HE SCRABBLED, CLUTCHED AT SOMETHING AND WAS LEFT HANGING BY HIS FINGERTIPS!

THE GIANT VORG BROKE OFF A PIECE OF MASONRY AND RAISED IT ALOFT.

I'M DONE FOR NOW!

PERISH, ACCURSED SPY!

NO! SPARE HIM, URGAL! I WILL NOT HAVE HIS DEATH ON MY CONSCIENCE.

SOON, ROFFA WAS CARRIED TO SAFETY.

AND NOW... PUT HIM WITH THE OTHERS. HE CAN REMAIN THERE TILL THE END OF HIS DAYS! THE SECRET MUST BE KEPT!

A VOICE ANSWERED LORD DARRA FROM THE GLOOM!

NO, MY LORD!

WHAT?!

THE MASTER OF CASTLE DOUM SAW THE FACE OF HIS EMPEROR – AND FELL TO HIS KNEES!

IMPERIAL MAJESTY! I– I DO NOT UNDERSTAND...

THERE IS MUCH *I* DO NOT UNDERSTAND, MY LORD! BUT FIRST, YOU WILL RELEASE YOUR PRISONERS.

SOON, THE DUNGEON DOOR WAS OPENING FOR JANNO AND KEREN.

UNCLE! I NEVER EXPECTED TO LOOK UPON YOUR FACE AGAIN.

NOR WOULD YOU HAVE DONE – IF KEREN HAD NOT THOUGHT TO LEAVE A NOTE BEHIND FOR ROFFA!

HAPPILY FOR THE THREE OF YOU, THE PEOPLE AT AIR FLEET HEADQUARTERS WERE ASTUTE ENOUGH TO GUESS THAT THERE WAS MORE TO KEREN'S LETTER THAN ROFFA WAS WILLING TO DIVULGE. AND SO... THREE OF US CAME AFTER YOU, ROFFA!

THE EMPEROR TURNED TO THE MASTER OF CASTLE DOUM.

AS FOR YOU, LORD DARRA, SINCE YOU HAVE DONE NO REAL HARM TO ANY OF THESE THREE, YOU WILL BE PARDONED. BUT ONLY ON ONE CONDITION...

WHAT CONDITION, MAJESTY?

THAT YOU OPEN THE LOCKED DOOR AND REVEAL YOUR FAMILY SECRET THAT HAS BEEN THE CAUSE OF ALL THIS TROUBLE! *NOW... IN MY PRESENCE!*

BOLTS AND LOCKS WERE OPENED AND THE INMATE OF THE LOCKED ROOM WAS REVEALED TO THE EMPEROR OF THE TRIGANS.

THERE, IMPERIAL MAJESTY, IS OUR DREADFUL FAMILY SECRET!

TRIGO'S REPLY WAS IMMEDIATE – AND TYPICALLY BLUNT!

THAT IS THE SON OF THE SEVENTH LORD DARRA! THE BLOOD OF MONSTERS RUNS IN OUR VEINS.

NONSENSE! I DON'T BELIEVE A WORD OF IT!

THE GREAT SCIENTIST PERIC EXAMINED THE CREATURE FROM CASTLE DOUM... AND CONFIRMED THE EMPEROR'S OPINION!

QUITE OUT OF THE QUESTION! THIS CREATURE'S CELL STRUCTURE IS ENTIRELY ANIMAL. IT IS A SPECIES THAT WAS BELIEVED TO BE EXTINCT, BUT SOMETIMES OCCURS IN THE REMOTE ATTAT MOUNTAINS.

A LONG TIME PASSED BEFORE TRIGO'S QUESTION WAS ANSWERED. ONE DAY, A SERVANT DROPPED A VASE IN CASTLE DOUM – AND SOMETHING WAS INSIDE.

I WOULD SAY THAT, FOR THREE GENERATIONS, THE LORDS OF CASTLE DOUM HAVE BEEN THE VICTIM OF A CRUEL HOAX!

BUT WHO IS – OR WAS – BEHIND THE HOAX?

WHY... THERE'S A LETTER HIDDEN IN IT!

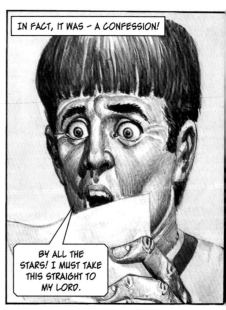

IN FACT, IT WAS – A CONFESSION!

BY ALL THE STARS! I MUST TAKE THIS STRAIGHT TO MY LORD.

IT HAD BEEN WRITTEN BY A CERTAIN ZUMATT.

"...INVESTIGATIONS INTO MY FAMILY HISTORY HAVE CONVINCED ME THAT I — ZUMATT — AM THE RIGHTFUL LORD DARRA. IF I CANNOT HAVE WHAT IS MINE, I WILL HAVE MY REVENGE..."

"MY GREAT OPPORTUNITY CAME," CONTINUED ZUMATT, "WHEN I WAS APPOINTED TUTOR AND GUARDIAN TO THE INFANT EIGHTH LORD..."

I WILL BE LIKE A FATHER TO YOU, MY LORD.

"THE MEANS OF MY REVENGE CAME WHEN I SAW A TRAVELLING SIDESHOW..."

WALK UP, WALK UP! ONLY HALF A ZERST TO SEE THE MONSTER FROM THE ATTAT MOUNTAINS!

"AS SOON AS I GAZED UPON THE MONSTER, THE PLAN SPRANG TO LIFE IN MY MIND."

HAH! WITH THAT CREATURE I CAN DESTROY THE PEACE OF MIND AND HAPPINESS OF COUNTLESS GENERATIONS OF DARRAS!

THE STRANGE AND DREADFUL CONFESSION CONCLUDED... "THE MOMENT OF MY TRIUMPH CAME ON THE DAY THAT MY YOUNG CHARGE CAME OF AGE!"

MY LORD, YOU MUST PREPARE YOURSELF FOR A SHOCK...!

SO ENDED THE SAGA OF THE LOCKED ROOM. LORD DARRA'S SON, DUBAL, MADE A COMPLETE RECOVERY FROM HIS AIR CRASH AND REJOINED HIS COMRADES...

KEREN, WHAT HAPPENED TO THAT FELLOW WHO SQUEEZED A THOUSAND THULLARS OUT OF YOU?

HE WAS CAUGHT AND SENTENCED FOR EXTORTION. REGRETFULLY HE HAD BY THAT TIME SPENT ALL MY MONEY!

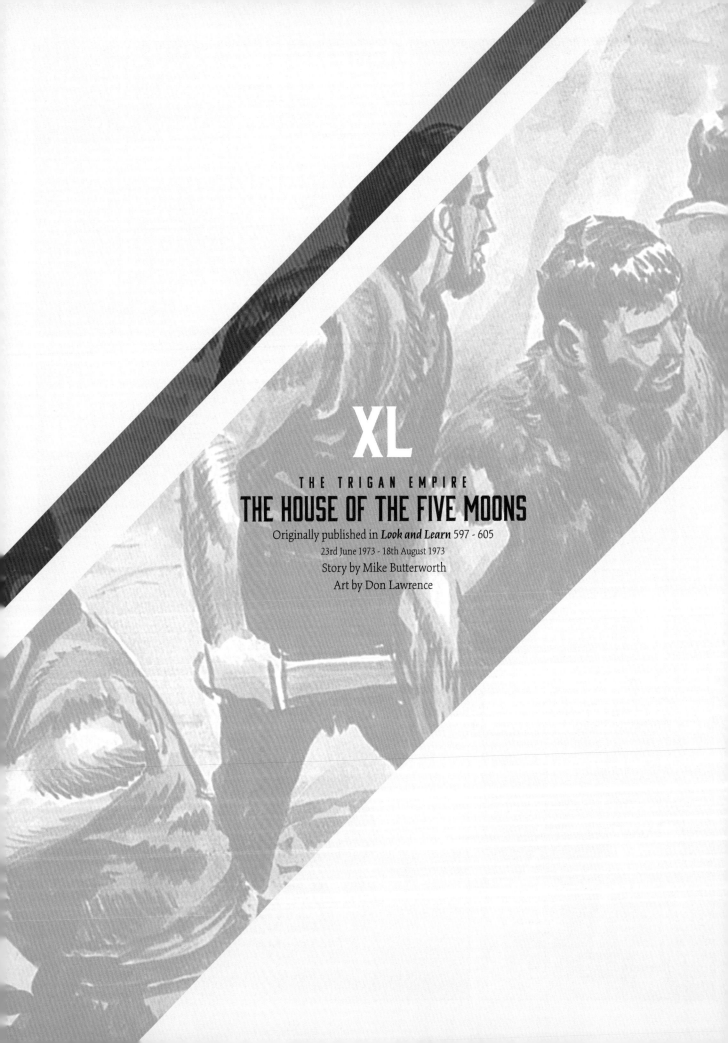

XL

THE TRIGAN EMPIRE

THE HOUSE OF THE FIVE MOONS

Originally published in *Look and Learn* 597 - 605

23rd June 1973 - 18th August 1973

Story by Mike Butterworth

Art by Don Lawrence

THE DAWN OF THE FOURTH YEAR OF ZISS WAS CELEBRATED WITH GREAT POMP AND SPLENDOUR AS THE ANNIVERSARY OF THE FOUNDING OF THE CITY AND EMPIRE. TRIGAN CITY WAS NOW THE WONDER OF THE PLANET ELEKTON.

THE AIR FLEET, AS EVER, PLAYED A PRINCIPAL PART IN THE CELEBRATIONS – FOR IT REPRESENTED THE MILITARY MIGHT OF THE TRIGANS.

HUMBLER TRIBUTES WERE PAID TO THE ANNIVERSARY. IN ONE OF THE POORER QUARTERS OF THE CITY, A GROUP OF STROLLING PLAYERS ACTED OUT THE EPISODE OF THE CITY'S FOUNDING.

THE ROLE OF TRIGO WAS PLAYED BY A FELLOW NAMED RUSS. A POOR ACTOR, HE WAS, NEVERTHELESS, DESTINED FOR A MEMORABLE FUTURE.

UPON THESE FIVE HILLS, I WILL BUILD A CITY AND NAME IT AFTER MYSELF! IT WILL BECOME THE GLORY OF OUR PLANET, ELEKTON!

AFTER THE SHOW, BACK IN HIS DRESSING ROOM...

BY ALL THE STARS! WHAT'S THIS? NOT A MESSAGE OF APPRECIATION FROM ONE OF MY MANY FANS?

IT WAS A MESSAGE THAT WAS TO BE IMPRINTED ON RUSS'S MIND TILL HIS DYING DAY!

"...BE PREPARED, AT A MOMENT'S NOTICE, TO PLAY THE GREATEST ROLE OF YOUR CAREER... IN REAL LIFE!"

43

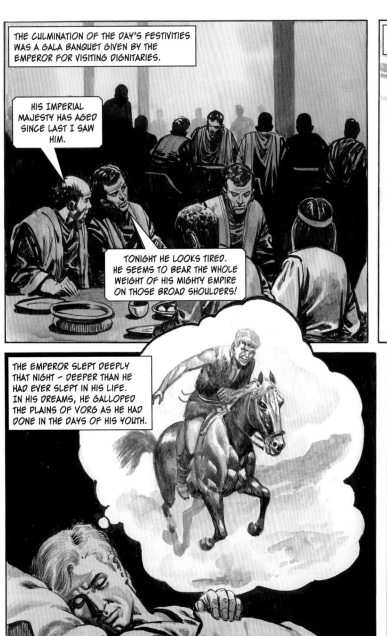

THE CULMINATION OF THE DAY'S FESTIVITIES WAS A GALA BANQUET GIVEN BY THE EMPEROR FOR VISITING DIGNITARIES.

HIS IMPERIAL MAJESTY HAS AGED SINCE LAST I SAW HIM.

TONIGHT HE LOOKS TIRED. HE SEEMS TO BEAR THE WHOLE WEIGHT OF HIS MIGHTY EMPIRE ON THOSE BROAD SHOULDERS!

THE EMPEROR SLEPT DEEPLY THAT NIGHT – DEEPER THAN HE HAD EVER SLEPT IN HIS LIFE. IN HIS DREAMS, HE GALLOPED THE PLAINS OF VORG AS HE HAD DONE IN THE DAYS OF HIS YOUTH.

TRIGO RETIRED EARLY TO HIS BEDCHAMBER.

GOOD NIGHT, SENTRY.

GOOD NIGHT TO YOU, IMPERIAL MAJESTY!

HE AWOKE EARLY AND WENT OUT TO HIS BATH.

I STILL FEEL HALF-ASLEEP...A COLD PLUNGE WILL LIVEN ME UP.

AND THEN...

HALT! WHAT ARE YOU DOING HERE IN THE EMPEROR'S QUARTERS?

FELLOW, HAVE YOU TAKEN LEAVE OF YOUR SENSES?

TRIGO WAS BUSTLED BACK, AT GUNPOINT, INTO HIS BEDCHAMBER.

THE EMPEROR'S GONE! WHERE IS HE? WHAT HAVE YOU DONE WITH HIS IMPERIAL MAJESTY, YOU ANIMAL?

BUT... I AM THE...

IT WAS IN THAT INSTANT THAT TRIGO CAUGHT SIGHT OF HIS FACE IN THE MIRROR... BUT IT WAS NOT HIS FACE!

IT CAN'T BE...! IT CAN'T!

THE GUARD'S SHOUTS BROUGHT OTHERS RUNNING.

OVERPOWER HIM! THAT ANIMAL HAS SPIRITED AWAY THE EMPEROR!

TRIGO PROTESTED... IN VAIN!

BUT...I AM THE...

WHAT WAS HE GOING TO SAY?

WE'LL FIND OUT SOON ENOUGH! INFORM THE LORD BRAG OF WHAT'S HAPPENED!

LATER THAT MORNING, JANNO LANDED HIS FIGHTING-CRAFT AND WAS IMMEDIATELY GIVEN A SUMMONS.

JANNO, YOUR FATHER WANTS YOU BACK AT THE PALACE... AND IT'S URGENT!

FOR THE REST OF THE DAY, THE HORRIFIED EMPEROR – STILL STUNNED FROM THE DREADFUL SHOCK OF SEEING ANOTHER MAN'S FACE REFLECTED BACK AT HIM – WAS CLOSELY QUESTIONED BY HIS OWN BROTHER AND NEPHEW.

JANNO ARRIVED AT THE IMPERIAL PALACE TO FIND BRAG AND THE IMPERIAL COUNCIL IN SESSION.

I CAME AS QUICKLY AS I COULD, FATHER. WHAT IS IT?

THE EMPEROR'S MISSING. A FELLOW WAS FOUND IN HIS APARTMENTS THIS MORNING... A COMPLETE STRANGER WHO CLAIMS TO BE THE EMPEROR!

IT'S ABSURD, OF COURSE – MERELY PART OF A DEEP-LAID CONSPIRACY – BUT I PROPOSE TO SUBJECT THIS IMPOSTOR TO CLOSE AND RIGOROUS QUESTIONING, JUST TO FIND OUT HOW WELL HE HAS BEEN BRIEFED ON THE DETAILS OF YOUR UNCLE TRIGO'S LIFE.

DESCRIBE THE CHARACTER OF YOUR FATHER! QUICKLY!

HE... HE WAS A KINDLY MAN...

THAT'S IN THE HISTORY BOOKS. BE MORE SPECIFIC!

AT THE END OF IT...

WELL, MY LORD? IS HE YOUR BROTHER?

OF COURSE NOT! MIND YOU, HE HAS BEEN BRIEFED IN DETAIL ON THE LIVES OF MEMBERS OF THE ROYAL FAMILY. THE PEOPLE BEHIND MY BROTHER'S DISAPPEARANCE HAVE BEEN VERY THOROUGH.

I CAN'T UNDERSTAND IT! WHY SHOULD THIS IMPOSTOR BE POSING AS MY BROTHER — AND WHERE IS TRIGO?

IN ANOTHER PART OF THE CITY, A THIRD-RATE THEATRICAL PERFORMANCE WAS JUST FINISHING. THE LEADING ACTOR — RUSS, WHO WAS PLAYING THE ROLE OF THE EMPEROR TRIGO — TOOK HIS BOW.

I THANK YOU, MY FRIENDS, FOR YOUR WILD APPLAUSE!

WHEN HE ENTERED HIS DRESSING TENT...

ANOTHER ONE OF THOSE STRANGE NOTES!

"THE TIME HAS COME FOR YOU TO STEP INTO THE GREATEST REAL-LIFE ROLE OF YOUR CAREER. BE AT THE HOUSE OF THE FIVE MOONS AT THE NINTH HOUR!"

"THE HOUSE OF THE FIVE MOONS" WAS A RAMSHACKLE TAVERN IN A SEEDY PART OF THE CITY DOCKLAND. ONE LIGHT BURNED IN AN UPPER WINDOW AS THE ACTOR APPROACHED IT THAT NIGHT.

AM I WISE... TO BE COMING TO THIS AWFUL PLACE?

IN ANSWER TO RUSS'S KNOCK, THE DOOR OF THE HOUSE OF THE FIVE MOONS CREAKED OPEN.

MY NAME IS RUSS AND I HAVE COME HERE BECAUSE...

WE KNOW WHO YOU ARE AND WHY YOU HAVE COME! ENTER!

THE TERRIFIED ACTOR WAS BROUGHT BEFORE A PERSONAGE IN A MASK.

YOUR NOTE PROMISED ME THE GREATEST ROLE OF MY CAREER!

THE NOTE DID NOT LIE!

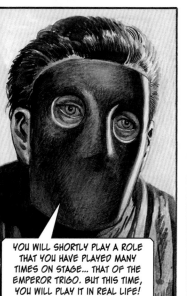

YOU WILL SHORTLY PLAY A ROLE THAT YOU HAVE PLAYED MANY TIMES ON STAGE... THAT OF THE EMPEROR TRIGO. BUT THIS TIME, YOU WILL PLAY IT IN REAL LIFE!

AT THE SAME MOMENT, TRIGO HIMSELF WAS LANGUISHING IN A CELL BELOW HIS OWN PALACE.

WHAT AM I GOING TO DO? THIS FACE, WHICH IS NOT MY OWN, HAS DEPRIVED ME OF MY EMPIRE, MY LIBERTY – AND WILL PERHAPS EVEN COST ME MY LIFE!

THIS IS AN ORDER TO TRANSFER THE UNKNOWN PRISONER TO THE TOP-SECURITY GAOL OF STARK ISLAND. IT IS SIGNED BY LORD BRAG AND THE COUNCIL.

TRIGO WAS TAKEN OUT, WHERE AN ARMED TRANSPORT AWAITED IN THE DAWN LIGHT.

GET ABOARD, PRISONER!

PRESENTLY, THEY WERE SPEEDING ACROSS TRIGAN CITY BAY – TOWARDS THE GLOOMY BULK OF STARK ISLAND GAOL.

47

AND THEN...

STRANGE CRAFT IN SIGHT, LIEUTENANT!

PREPARE TO OPEN FIRE AT MY ORDER!

A BIG CRAFT CAME AT THEM OUT OF THE MIST, GUNS BLAZING!

THE GUNNER ON THE ARMED TRANSPORT WAS IMMEDIATELY SILENCED. A BOARDING PARTY LEAPT FROM THE STRANGE CRAFT. IT WAS ALL OVER IN LESS TIME THAN IT TAKES TO TELL...

TRIGO HEARD HIS OWN NAME BEING SHOUTED...

THAT'S TRIGO. FELL HIM!

... THEN HIS WORLD DISSOLVED IN A SEA OF PAIN!

A VERY NEAT OPERATION!

ELEKTON'S SUNS HAD BARELY RISEN WHEN THEY CARRIED THE UNCONSCIOUS EMPEROR INTO THE HOUSE OF THE FIVE MOONS.

INFORM HIM THAT TRIGO IS OURS!

SOME TIME LATER, THE PERSONAGE IN THE MASK SHOWED HIS NEW PRISONER TO THE ACTOR RUSS.

BEHOLD – THE EMPEROR OF ALL THE TRIGANS.

BUT THAT ISN'T TRIGO! HIS FACE IS ON EVERY COIN. THAT FELLOW'S NOTHING LIKE TRIGO.

HE IS, NEVERTHELESS, TRIGO. WE HAVE THE MEANS TO CHANGE A MAN'S APPEARANCE WHILE HE IS UNCONSCIOUS. WITH THE CONNIVANCE OF THE GUARD OF THE IMPERIAL BEDCHAMBER, WE DID JUST THAT TO TRIGO THE OTHER NIGHT.

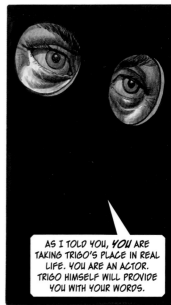

AS I TOLD YOU, *YOU* ARE TAKING TRIGO'S PLACE IN REAL LIFE. YOU ARE AN ACTOR. TRIGO HIMSELF WILL PROVIDE YOU WITH YOUR WORDS.

RUSS WAS FRIGHTENED. TORN BETWEEN AMBITION AND FEAR, HE CRACKED.

I'D NEVER GET AWAY WITH IT. I LOOK NOTHING LIKE TRIGO REALLY. I WON'T DO IT, YOU CAN'T MAKE ME.

WE WILL MAKE CERTAIN ADJUSTMENTS TO YOUR APPEARANCE THAT WILL FOOL EVEN HIS CLOSEST RELATIONS. *SEIZE HIM!*

RUSS WAS STRAPPED DOWN AND FORCIBLY ANAESTHETIZED.

YOU WILL SLEEP, AND WHILE YOU SLEEP YOU WILL RECEIVE THE FACE OF THE EMPEROR TRIGO, CORRECT DOWN TO THE VERY LAST WRINKLE.

AAAAAGH! DON'T HURT ME, I BEG YOU...

AS HE LAY THERE, UNCONSCIOUS, A MOULD WAS LOWERED OVER HIS FACE.

AND WHEN THE MOULD WAS REMOVED...

... THE TRANSFORMATION WAS COMPLETE!

LATER, RUSS STARED IN AWE AT HIS NEW FACE AND DYED HAIR.

BUT HOW... HOW DID YOU DO IT?

BEFORE WE GAVE TRIGO HIS NEW FACE, WE FIRST TOOK AWAY HIS OWN TO GIVE IT TO YOU, IN A MANNER OF SPEAKING.

THE MASKED MAN POINTED TO THE UNCONSCIOUS FIGURE OF THE TRIGAN EMPEROR.

THERE IS THE BRAIN, AND YOU ARE ITS MOUTHPIECE. WHAT WE HAVE NOW IS A SYNTHETIC EMPEROR, AN UNDETECTABLE FAKE!

AT DAWN THE FOLLOWING DAY, A MASSIVE FLEET OF FIGHTING SHIPS MOVED INTO POSITION OFF THE TRIGAN COAST.

THE INTRUDERS APPEARED ON THE DEFENCE SCREENS.

IT'S A MASSIVE ATTACK. THEY'RE WITHIN GUN RANGE OF TRIGAN CITY ITSELF!

SEND UP RECONNAISSANCE CRAFT!

AERIAL RECONNAISSANCE REVEALED THE DRAMATIC TRUTH.

IT'S THE ENTIRE CATON WAR-FLEET. THEIR GUNS ARE TRAINED ON THE CITY BUT THEY HAVE MADE NO HOSTILE MOVE TOWARDS ME.

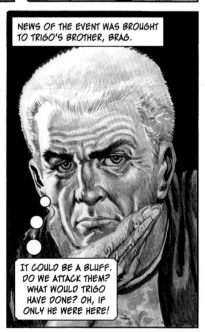

NEWS OF THE EVENT WAS BROUGHT TO TRIGO'S BROTHER, BRAG.

IT COULD BE A BLUFF. DO WE ATTACK THEM? WHAT WOULD TRIGO HAVE DONE? OH, IF ONLY HE WERE HERE!

ALL THAT MORNING, THE MIGHTY WAR-FLEET OF CATON LAY OFF THE TRIGAN COAST - GUNS AIMED.

IN THE IMPERIAL PALACE AT TRIGAN CITY, BRAG FINALLY CAME TO A DECISION...

WELL, LORD BRAG? DO WE WAIT FOR THEM TO BLOW THE CITY TO SMITHEREENS OR DO WE CALL THEIR BLUFF?

WE ATTACK FIRST! GIVE THE ORDER!

AND THEN, A WELL-KNOWN VOICE...

NO! CANCEL THAT ORDER!

THE EMPEROR HAD BEEN MISSING FOR DAYS. HE OFFERED NO WORD OF EXPLANATION BUT ISSUED ANOTHER ORDER.

HAVE MY PERSONAL AIRCRAFT MADE READY ON THE PALACE ROOF AND LET ME KNOW WHEN IT'S READY FOR TAKE-OFF!

YES, IMPERIAL MAJESTY!

BY ALL THE STARS! WHERE HAVE YOU BEEN, BROTHER?

I HAVE BEEN FOR A SHORT AND RESTFUL HOLIDAY - A BRIEF RESPITE FROM CARRYING AN EMPIRE ON MY SHOULDERS. AND WHAT DO I FIND WHEN I GET BACK...?

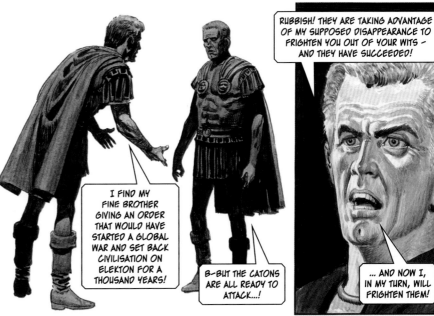

I FIND MY FINE BROTHER GIVING AN ORDER THAT WOULD HAVE STARTED A GLOBAL WAR AND SET BACK CIVILISATION ON ELEKTON FOR A THOUSAND YEARS!

B-BUT THE CATONS ARE ALL READY TO ATTACK...!

RUBBISH! THEY ARE TAKING ADVANTAGE OF MY SUPPOSED DISAPPEARANCE TO FRIGHTEN YOU OUT OF YOUR WITS - AND THEY HAVE SUCCEEDED!

... AND NOW I, IN MY TURN, WILL FRIGHTEN THEM!

AT NOON, A TRIGAN AIRCRAFT WAS SIGHTED APPROACHING THE CATON FLEET.

THEY'RE COMING STRAIGHT AT US! IF THEY TRY ANY TRICKS, BLOW THEM OUT OF THE SKY!

IT STREAKED TOWARDS THE FLAGSHIP...

STAND BY TO OPEN FIRE!

AND THEN... A FIGURE WAS EJECTED INTO THE AIR!

HOLD YOUR FIRE! HE'S COMING ABOARD!

THE NEWCOMER LANDED ON THE DECK OF THE FLAGSHIP AND WAS INSTANTLY SURROUNDED BY ARMED MEN. THEN... HE REVEALED HIS FACE!

BY ALL THE STARS! IT'S THE EMPEROR HIMSELF!

TAKE ME TO YOUR ADMIRAL!

BACK IN "THE HOUSE OF THE FIVE MOONS", THE PRISONER WAS IN THE BLACKEST DESPAIR.

THAT FELLOW CAN'T HANDLE A SITUATION LIKE THAT! HE'S ONLY A THIRD-RATE ACTOR, DRESSED UP TO RESEMBLE ME!

HE IS MORE THAN THAT! HE IS YOUR DUPLICATE! WITH YOUR FACE AND YOUR REACTIONS IMPLANTED IN HIS MIND!

AFTER THIS EPISODE, HE WILL BE ACCEPTED WITHOUT QUESTION AS YOU! FROM THEN ON, THE TRIGAN EMPIRE IS OURS, TO DO WITH AS WE PLEASE!

THERE WAS NO KEEPING THE PERIL FROM THE PEOPLE. WHEN NEWS OF THE WAR-FLEET BROKE, THEY TEEMED OUT OF TRIGAN CITY IN A PANIC-STRICKEN MASS.

THE ACCURSED CATONS ARE GOING TO BLOW THE CITY TO SMITHEREENS!

NO ONE CAN SAVE OUR CITY – NOT EVEN THE EMPEROR!

AT THAT MOMENT, THE FALSE TRIGO WAS FACE-TO-FACE WITH THE CATON COMMANDER ABOARD HIS FLAGSHIP.

THIS IS INDEED AN HONOUR, IMPERIAL MAJESTY. I WAS EXPECTING THE TRIGANS TO SEND SOMEONE TO SPEAK WITH ME. BUT... *YOU!*

ADMIRAL! I DEMAND TO KNOW WHAT YOU ARE DOING IN TRIGAN TERRITORIAL WATERS!

THE ANSWER CAME BACK, SMOOTHLY, COLDLY...

THE TRIGAN EMPIRE WILL SUBMIT TO THE RULE OF CATO, IMMEDIATELY, OR MY ORDERS ARE TO BOMBARD YOUR CAPITAL CITY UNTIL NOT ONE STONE STANDS UPON ANOTHER!

A THOUGHT-PATTERN CAME, ALL UNBIDDEN, TO THE MIND OF THE ACTOR IMPERSONATING TRIGO.

HE IS EITHER TELLING THE TRUTH OR HE IS BLUFFING. IN EITHER CASE, THE BOLD COURSE IS BEST!

THE SUPPOSED EMPEROR DEMANDED TO BE CONNECTED WITH HIS BROTHER ASHORE. THE CATONS WATCHED TENSELY AS THEY SPOKE.

BRAG! I APPOINT YOU THE EMPEROR OF THE TRIGANS IN MY PLACE. YOU WILL NOW CARRY OUT MY LAST ORDER...

YES, BROTHER, I AM LISTENING.

SEND THE AIR FLEET! HAVE THEM BLAST THE CATONS OUT OF THE WATER – AND ME WITH THEM!

NO! NO! NOT THAT!

IMPERIAL MAJESTY! THERE IS NO NEED TO CONDEMN THE PLANET TO A DESTRUCTIVE WAR THAT WOULD END CIVILISATION AS WE KNOW IT. I'M SURE WE CAN COME TO TERMS...

HE WAS BLUFFING!

BRAG! THE CATON WAR-FLEET IS SHORTLY ENTERING THE HARBOUR OF TRIGAN CITY ON A VISIT OF GOOD WILL! THEY WILL BE ESCORTED BY THE TRIGAN AIR FLEET!

SO IT WAS THAT THE MIGHT OF CATON SAILED MEEKLY INTO HARBOUR. THEY CAME AS VISITORS – BUT THEY LOOKED MORE LIKE A VANQUISHED FLEET!

JANNO WAS WITH THE ESCORTING AIR FLEET. HE LOOKED DOWN ON THE HUMILIATED CATONS AND REJOICED.

NO ONE ELSE ON ELEKTON COULD HAVE DONE IT BUT UNCLE TRIGO! HE'S GOT THE MAGIC TOUCH! HE'S A GENIUS!

THERE WAS A FEAST THAT NIGHT IN THE IMPERIAL PALACE, AT WHICH THE DOWNCAST CATON ADMIRAL WAS GUEST-OF-HONOUR.

ADMIRAL! LET US TOAST THE FUTURE FRIENDSHIP OF CATO AND THE TRIGAN EMPIRE!

JANNO NOTICED SOMETHING THAT SET HIM THINKING...

UNCLE TRIGO IS RIGHT-HANDED BUT THE MAN STANDING THERE IN HIS PLACE IS LEFT-HANDED!

THERE WAS A PRIVATE DOOR AT THE REAR OF THE IMPERIAL APARTMENTS, USED ONLY BY THE EMPEROR. LATE THAT NIGHT, A CLOAKED FIGURE EMERGED FROM IT. JANNO WAS LYING IN WAIT.

WHEREVER HE GOES... I'M GOING!

MYSTIFIED, JANNO FOLLOWED HIS QUARRY TO THE SEEDY PART OF THE CITY DOCKLAND.

WHAT WOULD THE EMPEROR OF THE TRIGANS BE DOING IN A PLACE LIKE THAT?

HE WENT CLOSER.

ONLY ONE LIGHT IN THE PLACE! IF I WANT TO KNOW THE ANSWER, I MUST FIRST RISK MY NECK...

THE THINGS I DO FOR THE TRIGAN EMPIRE!

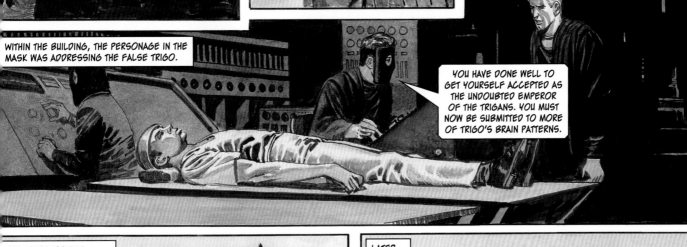

WITHIN THE BUILDING, THE PERSONAGE IN THE MASK WAS ADDRESSING THE FALSE TRIGO.

YOU HAVE DONE WELL TO GET YOURSELF ACCEPTED AS THE UNDOUBTED EMPEROR OF THE TRIGANS. YOU MUST NOW BE SUBMITTED TO MORE OF TRIGO'S BRAIN PATTERNS.

THE IMPOSTOR WAS CONNECTED TO THE MAN WHOSE FACE AND NAME HAD BEEN GIVEN TO HIM.

EVERY DAY, HIS THINKING GROWS MORE LIKE THAT OF TRIGO. IN THE END, HIS MIND WILL BE AN EXACT REPLICA OF TRIGO'S, SAVE IN ONE PARTICULAR... HE WILL OBEY *MY* WILL!

LATER...

AND NOW, MY FRIEND, YOU WILL RETURN TO THE PALACE. IN THE MORNING, YOU WILL HAVE BRAG AND JANNO ARRESTED AND EXECUTED FOR HIGH TREASON! WE WANT NO HEIRS TO THE IMPERIAL CROWN!

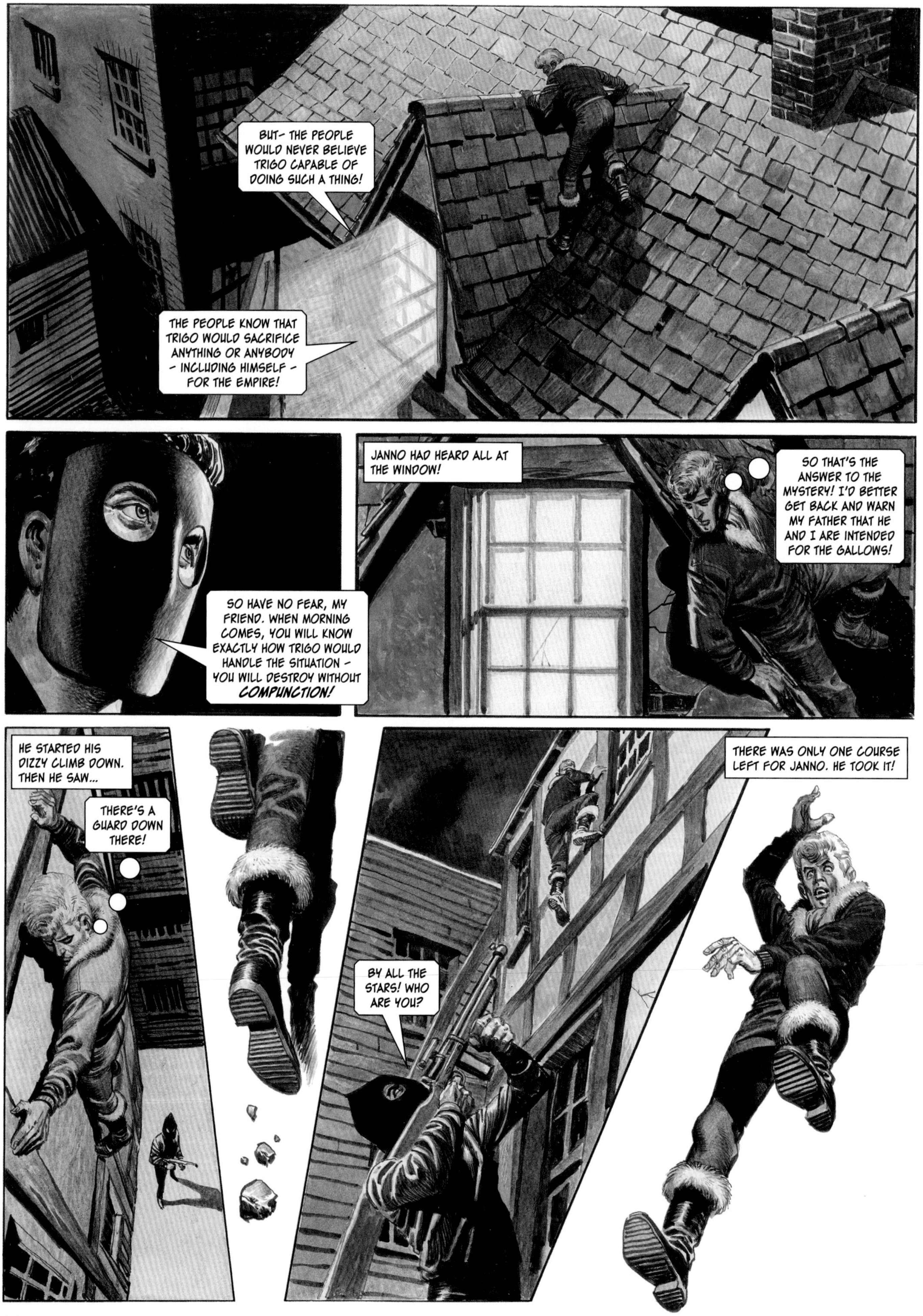
BUT- THE PEOPLE WOULD NEVER BELIEVE TRIGO CAPABLE OF DOING SUCH A THING!
THE PEOPLE KNOW THAT TRIGO WOULD SACRIFICE ANYTHING OR ANYBODY - INCLUDING HIMSELF - FOR THE EMPIRE!
SO HAVE NO FEAR, MY FRIEND. WHEN MORNING COMES, YOU WILL KNOW EXACTLY HOW TRIGO WOULD HANDLE THE SITUATION - YOU WILL DESTROY WITHOUT COMPUNCTION!
JANNO HAD HEARD ALL AT THE WINDOW!
SO THAT'S THE ANSWER TO THE MYSTERY! I'D BETTER GET BACK AND WARN MY FATHER THAT HE AND I ARE INTENDED FOR THE GALLOWS!
HE STARTED HIS DIZZY CLIMB DOWN. THEN HE SAW...
THERE'S A GUARD DOWN THERE!
BY ALL THE STARS! WHO ARE YOU?
THERE WAS ONLY ONE COURSE LEFT FOR JANNO. HE TOOK IT!

AAAAAH!

HE DRAGGED HIS VICTIM OUT OF SIGHT.

THIS FELLOW'S ABSENCE WON'T GO UNNOTICED FOR LONG. I DON'T HAVE MUCH TIME... SOMEONE'S COMING OUT!

JANNO SWIFTLY DUCKED INTO THE SHADOWS.

THERE GOES THE FAKE EMPEROR! PITY HE'S GOT AN ARMED ESCORT, OR I COULD HAVE DEALT WITH HIM MYSELF!

JANNO SPED BACK HOME AND ROUSED HIS FATHER FROM HIS SLEEP.

WAKE UP, FATHER! LISTEN TO WHAT I'VE GOT TO TELL YOU... AND LISTEN CAREFULLY.

WHAT? IS IT NEARLY DAWN ALREADY? I TOLD MY MAN ZITH TO WAKE ME IN GOOD TIME FOR THE ZARGOT HUNT.

BRAG LISTENED INCREDULOUSLY TO HIS SON'S TALE.

...IN OTHER WORDS, THE MAN WE THINK TO BE TRIGO ISN'T TRIGO AND HE'S BEEN ORDERED TO ARREST BOTH OF US FOR TREASON FIRST THING IN THE MORNING!

YOU MUST HAVE TAKEN LEAVE OF YOUR SENSES!

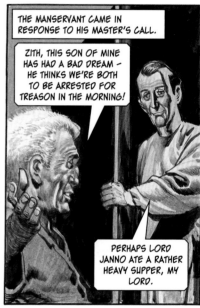

THE MANSERVANT CAME IN RESPONSE TO HIS MASTER'S CALL.

ZITH, THIS SON OF MINE HAS HAD A BAD DREAM – HE THINKS WE'RE BOTH TO BE ARRESTED FOR TREASON IN THE MORNING!

PERHAPS LORD JANNO ATE A RATHER HEAVY SUPPER, MY LORD.

FATHER! FOR THE LAST TIME – WILL YOU TAKE THIS MATTER SERIOUSLY?

NO, I WILL NOT! GRAB THIS ZARGOT SPEAR AND COME WITH ME!

NO SOONER HAD FATHER AND SON DEPARTED WHEN ZITH MADE A CALL...

"THEY KNOW! AT LEAST THE BRAT KNOWS! 'HOW DID HE FIND OUT?' WHAT'S THE USE OF ASKING ME?"

DAWN WAS BREAKING WHEN JANNO AND HIS FATHER REACHED THE VORG WILDERNESS, HUNTING GROUND OF THE SAVAGE ZARGOT.

THREE OF THEM!

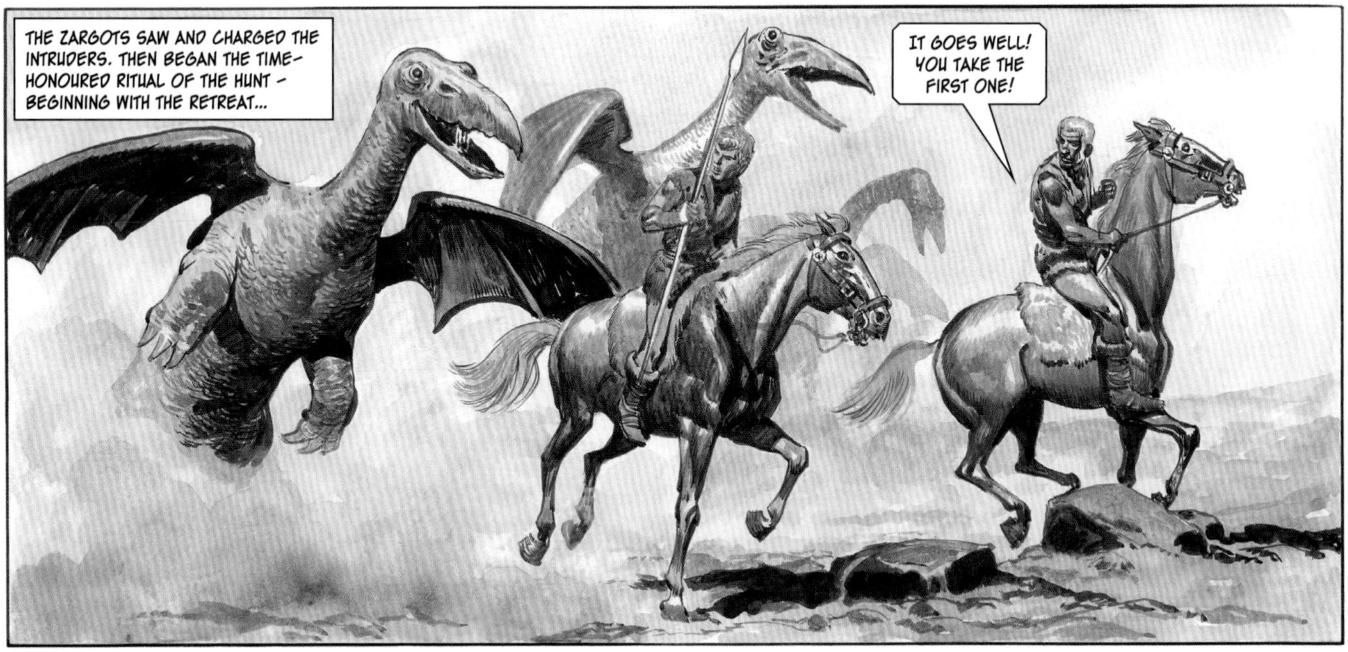
THE ZARGOTS SAW AND CHARGED THE INTRUDERS. THEN BEGAN THE TIME-HONOURED RITUAL OF THE HUNT - BEGINNING WITH THE RETREAT...
IT GOES WELL! YOU TAKE THE FIRST ONE!

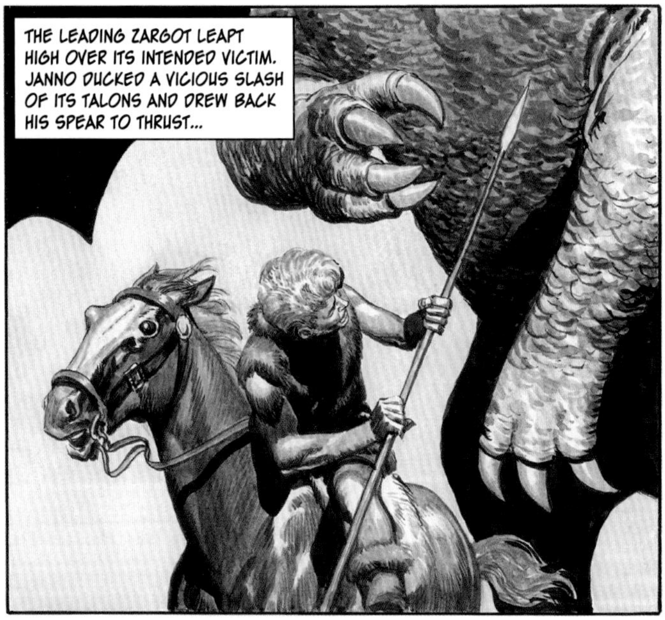
THE LEADING ZARGOT LEAPT HIGH OVER ITS INTENDED VICTIM. JANNO DUCKED A VICIOUS SLASH OF ITS TALONS AND DREW BACK HIS SPEAR TO THRUST...

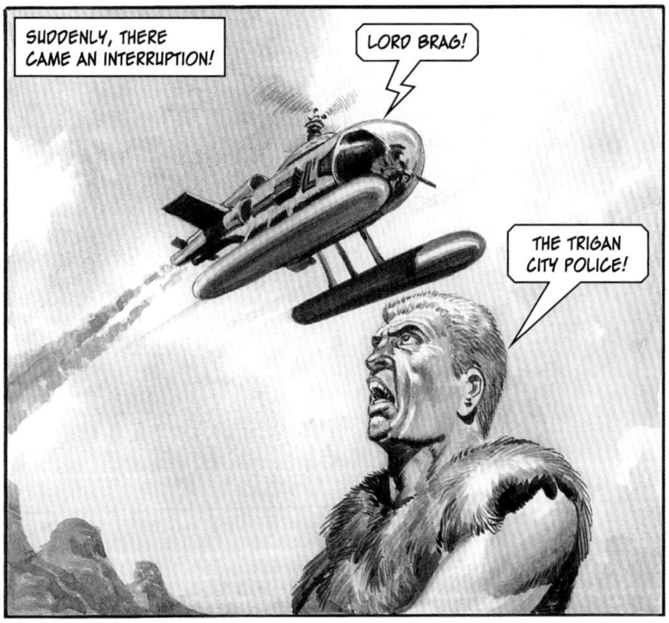
SUDDENLY, THERE CAME AN INTERRUPTION!
LORD BRAG!
THE TRIGAN CITY POLICE!

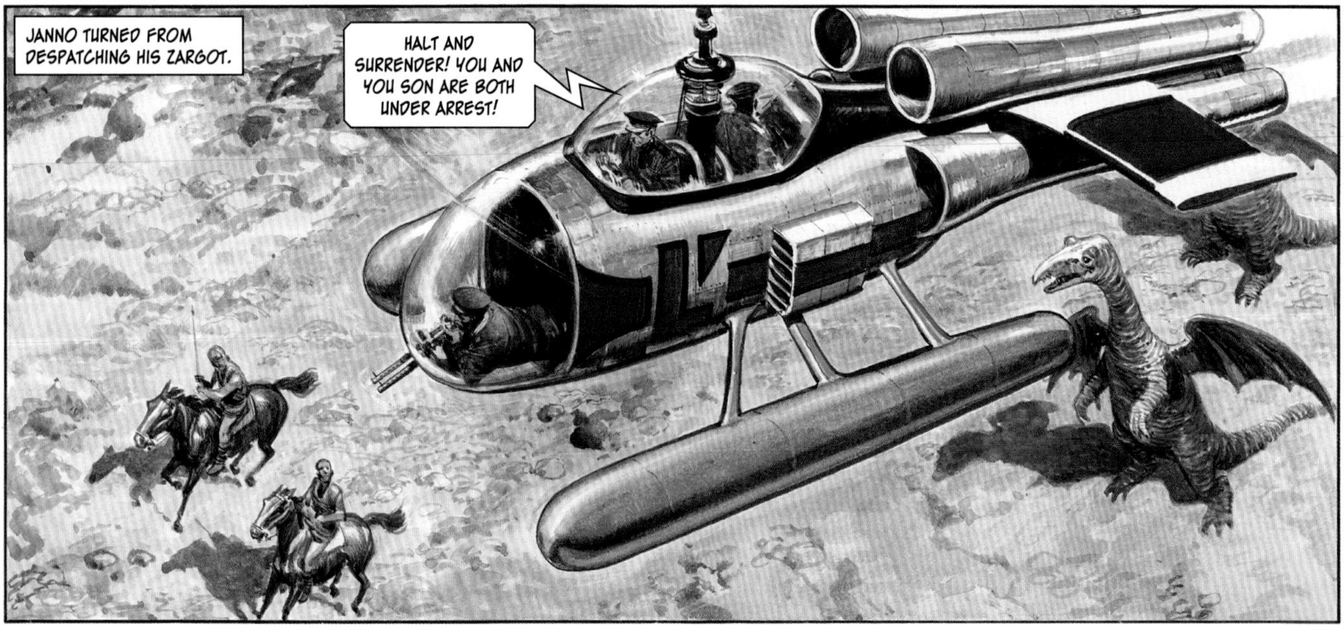
JANNO TURNED FROM DESPATCHING HIS ZARGOT.
HALT AND SURRENDER! YOU AND YOU SON ARE BOTH UNDER ARREST!

BRAG DELIBERATELY WHEELED HIS KREED INTO THE PATH OF AN ONCOMING ZARGOT!

FOR THE LAST TIME — HALT AND SURRENDER!

NO! BY ALL THE DEMONS IN DAVELI, I'LL DO NO SUCH THING!

THE ZARGOT LEAPT — BRAG DUCKED — AND THE SAVAGE BEAST CLUTCHED AT THE POLICE CRAFT WITH ITS VICIOUS TALONS!

RIGHT, JANNO — LET'S GET OUT OF HERE!

ONCE CONVINCED UPON A COURSE OF ACTION, THE STOLID BRAG ALWAYS MOVED WITH SPEED AND DECISION.

YOU BELIEVE ME NOW, FATHER?

I BELIEVE YOU, LAD! WE'LL GO AND RESCUE YOUR UNCLE — PICKING UP SOME HELP ALONG THE WAY!

FOR HELP, THEY CALLED UPON GROUPS OF WILD VORG HUNTERS — THOSE SPLENDID TRIBESMEN OF THE PLAINS WHO WERE FANATICALLY ATTACHED TO TRIGO.

THE EMPEROR IS IN PERIL! FOLLOW US!

IT WAS A LARGE BODY OF WELL-ARMED WARRIORS WHO BURST INTO THE SINISTER "HOUSE OF THE FIVE MOONS" AND SCATTERED THE MASKED GUARDS.

WHERE IS THE EMPEROR?

IN A TOP ROOM!

THE MASKED LEADER OF THE CONSPIRACY WAS ABOUT TO DISPATCH THE EMPEROR WITH A LETHAL DOSE OF POISON — WHEN THE DOOR WAS KICKED OPEN!

HOLD IT THERE!

THEY RIPPED OFF THE MASK, TO DISCOVER...

FATHER! IT'S YOUR MANSERVANT, ZITH!

WHO WOULD HAVE BELIEVED THAT HE...?

YES, MY LORDS! THE DESPISED MANSERVANT MADE HIMSELF EMPEROR IN ALL BUT NAME!

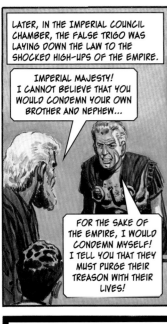

LATER, IN THE IMPERIAL COUNCIL CHAMBER, THE FALSE TRIGO WAS LAYING DOWN THE LAW TO THE SHOCKED HIGH-UPS OF THE EMPIRE.

IMPERIAL MAJESTY! I CANNOT BELIEVE THAT YOU WOULD CONDEMN YOUR OWN BROTHER AND NEPHEW...

FOR THE SAKE OF THE EMPIRE, I WOULD CONDEMN MYSELF! I TELL YOU THAT THEY MUST PURGE THEIR TREASON WITH THEIR LIVES!

BRAG ANSWERED FROM THE DOOR!

ONLY THE EMPEROR CAN CONDEMN US FOR TREASON — AND YOU, MY FINE FELLOW, ARE NOT THE EMPEROR!

HUH?

BRAG! WHAT ARE YOU SAYING?

GENTLEMEN — IN THE FACE OF ALL PROBABILITY, THIS MAN IS, AFTER ALL, WHOM HE CLAIMS TO BE — TRIGO, THE RIGHTFUL EMPEROR OF ALL THE TRIGANS!

LATER, PERIC HIMSELF SUPERVISED THE RESTORING OF TRIGO'S OWN FACE.

IN SIMPLE TERMS, WE ARE USING THE PROCESS THAT ZITH DISCOVERED. WE HAVE TAKEN A MOULD OF RUSS'S FACE — THE ONE THAT WAS TAKEN FROM TRIGO — AND WE ARE GIVING IT BACK TO THE EMPEROR.

TRIGO WAS WELL PLEASED WITH THE RESULT.

WHICH ONLY GOES TO PROVE THAT APPEARANCES ARE EVERYTHING!

WITH RESPECT, I DISAGREE, IMPERIAL MAJESTY. EVEN WITH YOUR FACE AND YOUR BRAIN-PATTERNS, THAT FELLOW RUSS WAS NEVER MORE THAN A THIRD-RATE ACTOR PLAYING A PART!

AS FOR RUSS — HE WAS PARDONED FOR BEING THE DUPE OF THE CONSPIRACY. HE WENT BACK TO THE STAGE, WHERE HE PLAYED TRIGO, AS BEFORE.

UPON THESE FIVE HILLS, I WILL BUILD A CITY AND NAME IT AFTER MYSELF!

XLI

THE TRIGAN EMPIRE
THE OUTLAW PLANET

Originally published in *Look and Learn* 606 - 610

25th August 1973 - 22nd September 1973

Story by Mike Butterworth

Art by Don Lawrence

THE EMPIRE GREW IN GREATNESS. EVERY DAY, BY LAND, SEA AND ATMOSPHERE, THE RICHES OF ELEKTON POURED INTO TRIGAN CITY.

PERIC, IN ADDITION TO BEING ELEKTON'S TOP SCIENTIST, WAS ALSO COMPTROLLER-GENERAL OF THE IMPERIAL TREASURY. EVERY LUNAR YEAR, THE TIME-LOCK OF THE TREASURY PERMITTED HIM TO ENTER.

ALONE IN THE MASSIVE, BOMB-PROOF BUILDING, PERIC HAD EXACTLY SIX LUNAR DAYS IN WHICH TO TAKE AN INVENTORY OF THE YEAR'S RICHES.

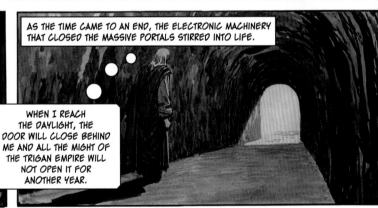

AS THE TIME CAME TO AN END, THE ELECTRONIC MACHINERY THAT CLOSED THE MASSIVE PORTALS STIRRED INTO LIFE.

WHEN I REACH THE DAYLIGHT, THE DOOR WILL CLOSE BEHIND ME AND ALL THE MIGHT OF THE TRIGAN EMPIRE WILL NOT OPEN IT FOR ANOTHER YEAR.

A FEW PACES FROM THE GREAT DOOR, THE OLD SCIENTIST WAS TAKEN BY A SUDDEN SEIZURE!

AAAH... AAAAAHHH!

THE EMPEROR WAS FENCING WITH HIS NEPHEW JANNO WHEN A FRANTIC MESSENGER SOUGHT HIM OUT.

WELL STRUCK, JANNO!

HA!

IMPERIAL MAJESTY!

PERIC WAS TRIGO'S OLDEST AND MOST VALUED FRIEND.

SIRE! PERIC IS LOCKED INSIDE THE IMPERIAL TREASURY!

WHA-A-A-AT?

BY ALL THE STARS! HE'S AS GOOD AS DEAD! THE TIME-LOCK CAN'T BE BROKEN!

BY EVENING, THEY MADE RADIO-VISUAL CONTACT WITH THE OLD SCIENTIST, WHO HAD BY THEN RECOVERED FROM HIS ATTACK.

HOW ARE THINGS WITH YOU, OLD COMRADE?

WELL, SIRE. I HAVE FOOD AND DRINK TO LAST ME PERHAPS THIRTY DAYS. BUT ATMOSPHERE ENOUGH TO LAST ME ONLY TWENTY-FIVE DAYS!

THE COUNCIL OF THE EMPIRE MET TO DISCUSS WHAT WAS INDEED A NATIONAL EMERGENCY.

NO POWER ON ELEKTON COULD BLAST OPEN - OR PIERCE THROUGH - THAT DOOR WITHIN TWENTY-FIVE DAYS!

PERIC IS ALREADY DOOMED! I MOVE THAT WE DECLARE A DAY OF NATIONAL MOURNING!

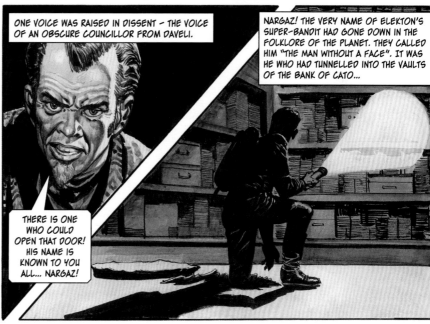

ONE VOICE WAS RAISED IN DISSENT - THE VOICE OF AN OBSCURE COUNCILLOR FROM DAVELI.

THERE IS ONE WHO COULD OPEN THAT DOOR! HIS NAME IS KNOWN TO YOU ALL... NARGAZ!

NARGAZ! THE VERY NAME OF ELEKTON'S SUPER-BANDIT HAD GONE DOWN IN THE FOLKLORE OF THE PLANET. THEY CALLED HIM "THE MAN WITHOUT A FACE". IT WAS HE WHO HAD TUNNELLED INTO THE VAULTS OF THE BANK OF CATO...

SINGLE-HANDED, HE HAD HI-JACKED AN AIR-TRANSPORT CARRYING THE CROWN JEWELS OF THARV!

NICE AND SLOWLY, PLEASE! LET US HAVE NO... UNPLEASANTNESS!

NARGAZ!

AND NOW HIS NAME WAS BEING RAISED IN THE SOLEMN COUNCIL OF THE EMPIRE.

BUT, SURELY, NARGAZ IS DEAD!

NOT DEAD! BUT HE HAS GONE TO A PLACE FROM WHICH THERE HAS NEVER BEEN, NOR EVER CAN BE, ANY RETURN!

THE TIME – THE FIRST HOUR OF THE NIGHT. THE PLACE – IMPERIAL AIR FLEET HEADQUARTERS. A MASKED INTRUDER REMOVED VITAL PLANS FROM A SAFE!

AT DAWN NEXT DAY, JANNO CLIMBED ABOARD HIS FIGHTING CRAFT.

SOMEWHERE NEAR THE CATON BORDER, HE WAS INTERCEPTED BY A TRIO OF HIS OWN SQUADRON-MATES! WARNING SHOTS WERE FIRED ACROSS HIS BOW!

WHAT IS THIS?

LAND IMMEDIATELY OR BE DESTROYED!

JANNO OBEYED... AND...

NOW, SEE HERE...!

STAND ASIDE! AND PUT YOUR HANDS ON YOUR HEAD! WE'RE GOING TO SEARCH YOUR CRAFT!

THE SEARCH WAS SWIFT – AND DECISIVE!

THE STOLEN PLANS!

TREACHEROUS ANIMAL! TAKE THAT!

AAAAH!

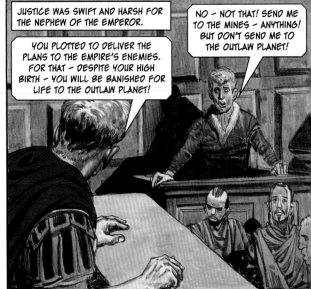

JUSTICE WAS SWIFT AND HARSH FOR THE NEPHEW OF THE EMPEROR.

YOU PLOTTED TO DELIVER THE PLANS TO THE EMPIRE'S ENEMIES. FOR THAT – DESPITE YOUR HIGH BIRTH – YOU WILL BE BANISHED FOR LIFE TO THE OUTLAW PLANET!

NO – NOT THAT! SEND ME TO THE MINES – ANYTHING! BUT DON'T SEND ME TO THE OUTLAW PLANET!

THE OUTLAW PLANET! THE VERY NAME STRUCK TERROR INTO THE HEARTS OF ALL ELEKTON. EVERY FIVE LUNAR YEARS, THIS ALIEN PLANET CAME WITHIN THE ORBIT OF ELEKTON.

THE USUAL FIVE-YEARLY BATCH OF ELEKTON'S WORST CRIMINALS WAS BEING LOADED ABOARD AN OUTER-ATMOSPHERE CRAFT... FOR TRANSPORT TO THE OUTLAW PLANET FOR THE REST OF THEIR DAYS!

ON THIS OCCASION, THE CONDEMNED TRAITOR JANNO WAS ONE OF THEIR NUMBER!

MOVE, ANIMALS! MOVE!

BLAST-OFF! AND THE PRISON-CRAFT ROSE SKYWARDS.

THE EMPEROR OF ALL THE TRIGANS WATCHED IT GO. WITH HIM WAS HIS BROTHER, BRAG – THE FATHER OF JANNO.

GOOD FORTUNE GO WITH YOU, LAD!

TRIGO! WE'RE SENDING HIM TO HIS DEATH!

WAS THERE NO OTHER WAY, TRIGO?

WHERE AN ARMY WOULD FAIL, ONE BRAVE YOUTH CAN SUCCEED! GIVEN LUCK, JANNO WILL BE BACK HERE IN TIME WITH NARGAZ!

YOU KNOW FULL WELL THAT IT WOULD TAKE AN ARMY TO GO UP TO THE OUTLAW PLANET, SECURE NARGAZ AND BRING HIM BACK TO BREAK INTO THE TREASURY AND RESCUE PERIC...

BUT NEITHER TRIGO, NOR HIS BROTHER, COULD GUESS ONE-HUNDREDTH PART OF THE PERILS LYING AHEAD OF JANNO!

TWO LUNAR DAYS LATER, THE PRISON-CRAFT ENTERED THE ORBIT OF THE OUTLAW PLANET AND BEGAN ITS DESCENT.

ONCE ON THE ALIEN GROUND, THE CRAFT'S DOORS OPENED AUTOMATICALLY TO RELEASE THE PANIC-STRICKEN CONVICTS.

GOT TO GET AWAY FROM HERE BEFORE IT GOES UP!

THEY SAID IT WOULD EXPLODE ALMOST AT ONCE!

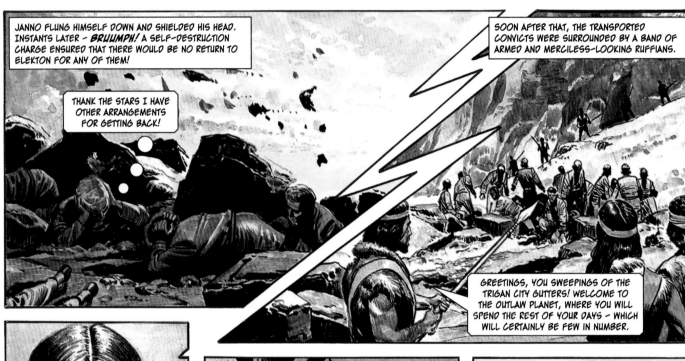

JANNO FLUNG HIMSELF DOWN AND SHIELDED HIS HEAD. INSTANTS LATER – *BRUUMPH!* A SELF-DESTRUCTION CHARGE ENSURED THAT THERE WOULD BE NO RETURN TO ELEKTON FOR ANY OF THEM!

THANK THE STARS I HAVE OTHER ARRANGEMENTS FOR GETTING BACK!

SOON AFTER THAT, THE TRANSPORTED CONVICTS WERE SURROUNDED BY A BAND OF ARMED AND MERCILESS-LOOKING RUFFIANS.

GREETINGS, YOU SWEEPINGS OF THE TRIGAN CITY GUTTERS! WELCOME TO THE OUTLAW PLANET, WHERE YOU WILL SPEND THE REST OF YOUR DAYS – WHICH WILL CERTAINLY BE FEW IN NUMBER.

SINCE IT'S WE WHO'VE FOUND YOU, YOU ARE ALL NOW MEMBERS OF THE GREEN FACTION. FROM NOW ON, YOUR LIVES WILL BE DEVOTED TO FIGHTING OUR ACCURSED ENEMIES THE BLUE FACTION! GOT THAT?

LATER, THE NEWCOMERS WERE INTERROGATED. JANNO KNEW THAT HIS LIFE WOULD BE WORTH NOTHING IF THE CONVICTS FOUND THAT HE HAD COME TO THEIR PLANET ON FALSE PRETENCES.

NEXT?

NAME – JANNO! BACKGROUND – PILOT IN THE TRIGAN AIR FLEET! CRIME – TREASON!

YOU LOOK LIKE PROMISING MATERIAL, JANNO. I ASSIGN YOU TO ONE OF OUR ACE KILLER-SQUADS! IT'S A GOOD LIFE IN THE KILLER-SQUADS – SHORT AND SWEET! HEH!

WHAT WILL BE MY DUTIES?

A THRILL RAN THROUGH JANNO'S VEINS AT THE MENTION OF THE NAME OF THE MAN FOR WHOM HE HAD COME TO THE OUTLAW PLANET.

THE LEADER OF THE ACCURSED BLUES IS THAT DOUBLE-DEALING SCOUNDREL, NARGAZ. DAY AND NIGHT, YOU WILL STRAIN EVERY NERVE AND SINEW TO ELIMINATE HIM!

HE WAS ISSUED WITH ROUGH CLOTHING OF SKINS AND GREEN HEADBAND AND SASH. HE THEN MET THE OTHER TWO MEMBERS OF HIS SQUAD.

AH, YOU'RE THE REPLACEMENT FOR OLD BRADDI. A GOOD KILLER WAS BRADDI!

WHAT HAPPENED TO HIM?

THE BLUES GOT HIM ON OUR LAST RAID! WE RAID AGAIN TOMORROW!

NEXT DAY, JANNO AND HIS NEW COMRADES STOOD AT THE FOOT OF A TOWERING MOUNTAIN RANGE.

THE BLUES' STRONGHOLD LIES BEYOND THE MOUNTAIN CREST. FIRST WE CLIMB THE MOUNTAIN!

ALL DAY, THEY TOILED UP THE VERTICAL ICE WALL.

SUDDENLY...

AAAAGGH!

... JANNO SAW THE REASON FOR HIS COMRADE'S FALL!

OH, NO!

67

THE AIR WAS FILLED WITH THE BEATING OF MIGHTY WINGS AND ANOTHER FEARSOME CREATURE CAME TO SAVE THE KILLER-SQUAD FROM THE MENACE OF THE FIRST!

A SLASH OF A KNIFE AND JANNO FELT HIMSELF RELIEVED OF THE BURDEN OF THE COMPANION WHO HAD BEEN ROPED TO HIM.

YOU CAN'T DO THAT!

I'VE DONE IT!

E-E-E-EHH!

JANNO LEARNED WHAT IT WAS TO BE A MEMBER OF A GREEN FACTION KILLER-SQUAD!

THAT WAS AN ACT OF COLD-BLOODED MURDER!

GET CLIMBING OR I'LL SERVE YOU THE SAME!

MUCH LATER THEY CAME TO A SNOW BRIDGE.

YOU CROSS FIRST AND TEST ITS STRENGTH! KEEP MOVING! YOU'RE NOT IN THIS GAME FOR YOUR HEALTH.

JANNO'S MERCILESS COMPANION FARED BADLY AT THE BRIDGE!

AAAAHHH!

THE YOUNG TRIGAN BATTLED HIS LONE WAY TO THE SUMMIT, WHERE HE SAW—

THE STRONGHOLD OF THE BLUE FACTION! LAIR OF NARGAZ THE FACELESS ONE!

CREEPING CLOSER, HE HEARD VOICES AND A NAME THAT SENT A SHOCK THROUGH HIM.

NARGAZ! THERE'S A GREEN KILLER-SQUAD SOMEWHERE ON THE MOUNTAIN!

WELL?

NARGAZ! IT'S HIM!

ONE OF OUR SENTRIES SIGHTED THEM BUT THEY MAY HAVE FALLEN PREY TO PREDATORS!

IF THE PREDATORS HAVE NOT GOT THEM... GET THEM!

THEN... JANNO ACTED!

HAH!

NARGAZ'S COMPANION WAS SENT SPINNING BY THE FLAT OF THE BLADE!

BY ALL THE STARS!

JANNO POINTED TO A SLEDGE, ROPED TO A STAKE.

GET IN THERE, NARGAZ!

WHO ARE YOU?

IF WE BOTH GET OFF THIS MOUNTAIN ALIVE, I'LL TELL YOU! GET IN!

JANNO'S BLADE SLASHED DOWN ON THE ROPE...

HERE WE GO!

...AND THEY BEGAN THE PLUMMETING DESCENT!

HALFWAY DOWN THE MOUNTAIN, THEY CAME TO A DIZZY BEND!

YOU'VE LOST CONTROL! WE'RE GOING OVER!

THERE WERE SOUNDS OF PURSUIT FROM HIGHER UP THE MOUNTAIN. JANNO KNEW HIS TIME WAS RUNNING SHORT.

KEEP YOUR LIFE, NARGAZ! I WANT YOU ALIVE OR NOT AT ALL. I'LL COME BACK AND GET YOU ANOTHER TIME. WE'LL MEET AGAIN! FAREWELL!

NO! WAIT!...

JANNO'S BREATH WAS DASHED FROM HIS BODY AS HE FELL INTO THE SOFT SNOW. MOMENTS LATER, HE SAT UP AND LOOKED ABOUT HIM.

AAAAAAGHHH!

EEEEEEGH!

MY SHOULDER'S SMASHED! WHAT IS IT TO BE, CURSE YOU – ARE YOU GOING TO KNIFE ME OR THROW ME INTO THE ABYSS?

WHO ARE YOU... AND WHAT DO YOU WANT OF ME?

JANNO TOLD THE SUPER-CRIMINAL EVERYTHING... AND WHEN HE WAS FINISHED...

LET'S GET THIS STRAIGHT – ON THE ORDERS OF THE TRIGAN EMPEROR YOU HAD YOURSELF FRAMED FOR TREASON AND SENT TO THIS CONFOUNDED PLANET IN ORDER TO BRING ME BACK, TO SMASH THE TIME-LOCK OF THE IMPERIAL TREASURY AND RESCUE SOME OLD FOOL WHO GOT HIMSELF TRAPPED IN THERE. HAVE I GOT IT RIGHT?

YES! HOW ABOUT IT, NARGAZ?

MY VANITY IS TOUCHED. I AM ALSO GRATEFUL TO YOU FOR SPARING MY LIFE. HOW DO WE GET BACK TO ELEKTON?

THAT NIGHT, JANNO FIRED A MINIATURE ROCKET THAT HE HAD SECRETED ON HIS PERSON. IT ROSE ABOVE NARGAZ'S MOUNTAINTOP LAIR AND SPED UP TO THE STRATOSPHERE.

THE SIGNAL BROUGHT DOWN AN ELEKTON OUTER-ATMOSPHERE CRAFT THAT HAD BEEN ORBITING THE OUTLAW PLANET...

BEFORE THE NEW MOONS, NARGAZ, YOU'LL BE BACK ON YOUR HOME PLANET!

THIS IS MY HOME PLANET, JANNO – AND DON'T YOU FORGET IT!

SO IT WAS THAT NARGAZ THE SUPER-CRIMINAL CAME BACK TO ELEKTON, FROM WHICH HE HAD BEEN BANISHED FOR LIFE. AND, BY A WRY TWIST OF FATE, HE WAS GREETED LIKE A RETURNING HERO.

THE HAND OF THE EMPEROR! I MUST BE DREAMING!

RESCUE MY OLD AND VALUED FRIEND FROM THAT LIVING DEATH, NARGAZ, AND YOU WILL EARN AN EMPEROR'S UNDYING GRATITUDE!

MANY PEOPLE ASSEMBLED TO WATCH THE LEGENDARY NARGAZ GET TO WORK ON THE TIME-LOCK OF THE TREASURY.

HMMM! THIS IS QUITE A LOCK YOU'VE GOT HERE. IF THEY'D BEEN AS GOOD AS THIS IN MY YOUNG DAYS, I'D HAVE HAD TO GIVE UP CRIME!

NEVERTHELESS, AFTER THREE DAYS' WORK, NARGAZ WAS ABLE TO DEFEAT THE LOCK – AND PERIC STUMBLED FORTH!

OLD FRIEND! I NEVER THOUGHT TO SEE YOU ALIVE AGAIN!

I CAN TELL YOU – CONFIDENTIALLY – IT WAS A CLOSE THING!

FOR HIS REWARD, NARGAZ ONLY ASKED ONE FAVOUR – TO BE TRANSPORTED BACK TO HIS INHOSPITABLE OUTLAW PLANET. AS HE EXPLAINED TO HIS NEW FRIEND JANNO...

HERE ON ELEKTON, I'D JUST BE A RETIRED THIEF. UP THERE, I'M BOSS OF HALF THE PLANET – A SOMEBODY!

XLII

THE TRIGAN EMPIRE
THE GLASS PALACE
Originally published in *Look and Learn* 611 - 612
29th September 1973 - 6th October 1973
Story by Mike Butterworth
Art by Don Lawrence

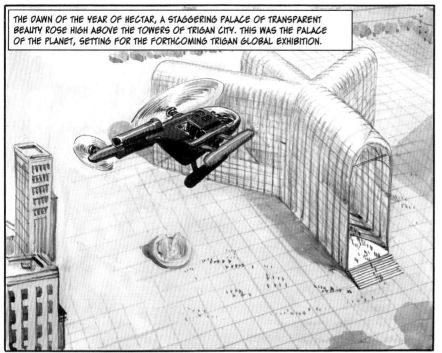

THE DAWN OF THE YEAR OF HECTAR, A STAGGERING PALACE OF TRANSPARENT BEAUTY ROSE HIGH ABOVE THE TOWERS OF TRIGAN CITY. THIS WAS THE PALACE OF THE PLANET, SETTING FOR THE FORTHCOMING TRIGAN GLOBAL EXHIBITION.

THE EMPEROR TRIGO INSPECTED THE VAST BUILDING.

IT IS MAGNIFICENT! MAGNIFICENT!

THE EXHIBITION WILL BRING TOGETHER THE PEOPLES OF THIS PLANET IN PEACEFUL ENDEAVOUR – AND THE PALACE WILL STAND FOREVER AS ONE OF THE WONDERS OF ELEKTON!

THAT NIGHT, IN A CELLAR SOMEWHERE IN TRIGAN CITY...

TRIGO MUST BE ELIMINATED!

THE MEN WERE EXTREMIST REVOLUTIONARIES, BENT ON SMASHING THE EMPIRE.

YOU WILL CARRY OUT THE ASSASSINATION!

THE KILLER-ELECT WAS A DOWNTRODDEN MAN NAMED YUPPA.

ME? BU-BUT I HAVE NO EXPERIENCE OF ASSASSINATION. ALL I HAVE EVER DONE IS WRITE REVOLUTIONARY LEAFLETS!

YOU WILL REQUIRE NO EXPERIENCE, MY FRIEND! YOU WILL DESTROY TRIGO WITH THE SIMPLEST, YET MOST DEVASTATING WEAPON IN THE UNIVERSE! LISTEN...

LATER, THE CONSPIRATORS' MEETING BROKE UP. THERE WAS A LAST WORD FROM THEIR LEADER.

RIGHT! IMMEDIATELY UPON RECEIPT OF THE NEWS THAT YUPPA HAS DONE HIS WORK, YOU WILL ALL MEET HERE TO DISCUSS THE NEXT MOVE!

ONE OF THE CONSPIRATORS WENT TO A NEARBY PUBLIC COMMUNICATOR.

GIVE ME THE IMPERIAL SECRET POLICE - SPECIAL SECTION...

BUT...

THEY ARE GOING TO ASSASSINATE THE EMPEROR! THE DAY OF THE OPENING OF THE PALACE! ONE MAN IS ASSIGNED FOR THE TASK! HIS WEAPON...

... THE POLICE SPY'S MESSAGE WAS NEVER FINISHED!

NO! NO! PLEASE... MERCY!

BACK AT THE HEADQUARTERS OF THE IMPERIAL SECRET POLICE...

THE RECEIVER'S GONE DEAD! I THINK AGENT SEVEN-FIVE-SIX HAS MET HIS END!

HIGH ABOVE THE EMPIRE'S FARTHEST-FLUNG FRONTIER, A PATROL OF FIGHTING CRAFT RECEIVED A MESSAGE.

CALLING LIEUTENANT JANNO... CALLING LIEUTENANT JANNO...

JANNO ANSWERING... GO AHEAD, PLEASE...

A DRAMATIC MESSAGE SOUNDED IN THE EAR OF THE EMPEROR'S NEPHEW.

THE EMPEROR IS THREATENED WITH ASSASSINATION! YOU WILL RETURN TO TRIGAN CITY AT ONCE AND MAKE YOURSELF AVAILABLE FOR SPECIAL PROTECTION OF THE IMPERIAL PERSON!

ON THE DAY OF THE OPENING OF THE PALACE, THE EMPEROR ENTERED THE VAST PORTALS OF THE TRANSPARENT BUILDING, FOLLOWED BY ALL THE RULERS OF ELEKTON.

THERE WERE OVER A MILLION PEOPLE INSIDE THE BUILDING. HIGH IN THE ROOF, JANNO AND HIS COMRADES KEREN AND ROFFA KEPT WATCH AS PART OF THE IMPERIAL BODYGUARD.

EVERYONE WHO CAME IN WAS SCREENED FOR WEAPONS. WHOEVER WANTS TO ASSASSINATE THE EMPEROR WILL HAVE TO DO IT WITH HIS BARE HANDS!

ONE OF THE VAST AUDIENCE SLIPPED AWAY AND TOOK A STAIRCASE THAT LED TO THE ROOF. IT WAS YUPPA, THE ASSASSIN!

HIGH ABOVE THE HEADS OF THE MULTITUDE, AMONG THE SKELETAL RIBS OF THE ROOF, YUPPA CROUCHED – AND WAITED.

IN A VERY SHORT WHILE, I SHALL GAIN ETERNAL GLORY AS THE MAN WHO DESTROYED A TYRANT!

AFTER A BRIEF BUT IMPRESSIVE OPENING CEREMONY, TRIGO LED HIS SOLEMN PROCESSION BACK THE WAY THEY HAD COME.

THEN IT HAPPENED – A TERRIBLE SHOUT!

FIRE!

THE WARNING ECHOED AND RE-ECHOED THROUGH THE VAST BUILDING. THERE WAS INSTANT, UNTHINKING PANIC IN THE MINDS OF THE MILLION PEOPLE PACKED WITHIN THE PALACE!

FIRE!

I'VE GOT TO GET OUT OF HERE! LET ME PASS!

WE'LL ALL BE ROASTED ALIVE!

MY BABY!

TRIGO FROZE IN HIS TRACKS AND HIS HEART MISSED A BEAT. FROM THREE DIRECTIONS, THE PANIC-STRICKEN MULTITUDE WAS CONVERGING UPON HIM!

GOT TO GET OUT OF THIS DEATH-TRAP!

EEEEH!

I'M DONE FOR! THEY'LL TRAMPLE ME TO PIECES!

SUDDENLY, THERE CAME ANOTHER SHOUT. ALL EYES LOOKED UP.

BY ALL THE STARS! LOOK AT THAT MADMAN!

HE'LL BE KILLED, SURE AS FATE!

THE SURGING MULTITUDE WAS STILL. EVERY LIVING PERSON IN THAT HUGE PALACE WATCHED, BREATHLESS, AS KEREN WALKED ACROSS THE DIZZY ABYSS!

KEREN HAD SPOTTED THE ASSASSIN. HE REACHED SAFETY AND SWIFTLY ARRESTED THE DEMORALISED YUPPA.

ARE YOU COMING QUIETLY – OR DO YOU WANT TO MAKE TROUBLE.

I... I DON'T W-WANT ANY TROUBLE, SIR!

SO ENDED AN ASSASSINATION ATTEMPT THAT – BUT FOR KEREN'S TIMELY INTERRUPTION – JUST COULD NOT HAVE FAILED. AS TRIGO COMMENTED AFTERWARDS...

IT WAS SIMPLE AND HIDEOUSLY CUNNING... THEY SOUGHT TO DESTROY ME WITH ONE OF THE MOST DESTRUCTIVE WEAPONS KNOWN – MOB PANIC!

THEY LOOKED TOWARDS THE BUILDING THAT WAS ONE OF THE WONDERS OF THE PLANET ELEKTON.

JUST IN CASE SUCH A THING HAPPENS AGAIN, I THINK WE'LL HAVE A FEW MORE DOORS PUT IN, EH?

IT WILL BE DONE IMMEDIATELY, IMPERIAL MAJESTY!

XLIII

THE TRIGAN EMPIRE
TERROR FROM TARRON

Originally published in *Look and Learn* 613 - 620

13th October 1973 - 1st December 1973

Story by Mike Butterworth

Art by Don Lawrence

ON THE MORNING OF THE FOURTH DAY OF THE SECOND MONTH OF THE YEAR HECTAR, ALL TRIGAN CITY FLOCKED TO SEE THE RETURN OF AN INTREPID VOYAGER OF OUTER SPACE.

THE RETURN CAPSULE HAS ENTERED ELEKTON'S ATMOSPHERE AND SHOULD BE IN SIGHT ANY MOMENT.

A GREAT CRY AROSE FROM THE WATCHING MULTITUDE, AS THE SILVER SPHERE DESCENDED OUT OF THE CLOUDS ON ITS PARACHUTE COMPLEX.

HERE HE COMES!

WELL DONE, ZACCO!

I KNEW HE'D MAKE IT!

ZACCO WAS THE SENIOR PILOT OF ELEKTON'S NEWLY FORMED OUTER-SPACE FLEET. BACK FROM THE FIRST LANDING ON ELEKTON'S LESSER MOON TARRON, HE EMERGED FROM HIS CRAFT – AND HIS COUNTENANCE CHILLED THE BLOOD OF ALL WHO LOOKED UPON HIM.

ZACCO WAS EXAMINED BY ELEKTON'S TOP SCIENTIST, PERIC, IN THE PRESENCE OF THE EMPEROR TRIGO HIMSELF.

THAT TERRIBLE PLACE... THE MOON TARRON! NO SOONER HAD I SET FOOT ON THAT ACCURSED MOON THAN I WAS AWARE OF THE PRESENCE OF UNSPEAKABLE EVIL.

WHAT IS IT THAT HAS DISTURBED YOU SO PROFOUNDLY, ZACCO?

HIS LISTENERS SAW IT ALL IN THEIR MINDS' EYES... "AFTER PERFORMING MY FIRST DAY'S TASK, I LAY DOWN TO SLEEP..."

"WHILE I SLEPT, I WAS MENACED!"

"MENACED – AND ATTACKED!"

E-E-EEEHH!

"IF I HAD NOT AWAKENED WHEN I DID, I SHOULD HAVE BEEN OVERPOWERED. AS IT WAS, I WAS JUST IN TIME TO CUT MYSELF FREE!"

WHEN HE HAD FINISHED HIS TERRIBLE TALE...

CALM YOURSELF, ZACCO. YOU ARE SAFE NOW!

AM I?... AM I?... I HAVE THE FEELING THAT SOME EVIL FORCE CAME BACK TO ELEKTON WITH ME... IN THE CAPSULE!

THE HISTORIC CAPSULE WAS LODGED IN THE OUTER-SPACE BASE UNDER GUARD. THAT NIGHT, A STRANGE THING HAPPENED.

LOOK! THE DOOR OF THE CAPSULE – IT'S OPENING!

COME OUT OF THERE – WHOEVER YOU ARE!

AAAAAGH! NO! NO!

KEEP AWAY! KEEP AWAY!

LATER, ZACCO RETURNED HOME TO HIS APARTMENT.

I SHALL NEVER FORGET THE AWFULNESS OF IT – NEVER! IT WILL HAUNT ME ALL MY LIFE!

HE SLEPT – AND WHILE HE SLEPT – THINGS HAPPENED!

AN IMPENETRABLE MASS OF FOLIAGE MOVED INEXORABLY TOWARDS THE SLEEPING OUTER-SPACE PILOT!

ZACCO WOKE WHEN TENDRILS OF THE PLANT TWINED ROUND HIS THROAT. INSTANTS LATER, HE WAS FIGHTING FOR HIS LIFE!

AAAAAGGH!

HE RETREATED BEFORE THE DESTRUCTIVE MASS TILL HE COULD GO NO FURTHER. THEN HE FELL... AND WAS SAVED!

EARLY NEXT MORNING, JANNO WAS BEING TESTED IN PERIC'S LABORATORY WEARING A NEWLY DESIGNED SPACE SUIT.

IT'S AN EMERGENCY, MASTER! ZACCO'S HAD AN ACCIDENT!

WELL, WHAT IS IT? CAN'T YOU SEE I'M BUSY?

THE ACE SPACE-VOYAGER WAS BROUGHT IN LATER. IT TOOK TWO BRAWNY IMPERIAL GUARDSMEN TO HOLD HIM DOWN!

BY ALL THE STARS! WHAT AILS HIM?

AAAAAAH! KEEP IT OFF ME! DON'T LET IT GET ME!

HE WAS FOUND AT DAWN, MASTER PERIC. UNCONSCIOUS HE WAS, LYING UNDER THE WINDOW OUTSIDE HIS APARTMENT. AND NO SOONER HAD HE RECOVERED CONSCIOUSNESS THAN HE STARTED TO RAVE ABOUT...

ZACCO'S CRIES AWAKENED ECHOES IN THE GREAT LABORATORY.

IT WAS JUST LIKE ON THE MOON TARRON! THE THING CAME AT ME! ENVELOPED ME - TRYING TO CHOKE THE LIFE OUT OF ME!

JANNO STARED AT THE SPACE-VOYAGER IN ALARM.

WHAT CAME AT HIM IN HIS OWN APARTMENT? THIS I HAVE TO SEE!

THOUGH ZACCO'S APARTMENT WAS CLOSED BY THE POLICE, THE EMPEROR'S NEPHEW HAD NO DIFFICULTY IN OBTAINING ADMISSION.

HE BABBLED OF A MONSTROUS THING THAT FILLED THE WHOLE ROOM AND TRIED TO CHOKE THE LIFE OUT OF HIM.

AS YOU SEE, LORD JANNO, THERE'S NOTHING HERE. IF YOU ASK ME, ZACCO'S GOING OUT OF HIS MIND.

ON THE WINDOW-SILL, UNNOTICED BY JANNO, WAS THE INNOCENT-LOOKING PLANT THAT WAS THE CAUSE OF IT ALL!

GOING OUT OF HIS MIND — OR BEING DRIVEN OUT OF HIS MIND? I WONDER?

MEANWHILE, BACK AT THE LABORATORY, PERIC HAD MANAGED TO SOOTHE THE SPACE-VOYAGER.

THERE'S NO ESCAPE FOR ME! I KNOW IT WILL COME AFTER ME AGAIN!

YOU'LL BE ALL RIGHT IN HERE, MY FRIEND. THIS ROOM IS HERMETICALLY SEALED, WITH ITS OWN AIR SUPPLY. NOTHING AND NO-ONE CAN ENTER WITHOUT YOUR KNOWLEDGE.

ZACCO RELAXED, ALONE IN HIS HERMETICALLY SEALED HAVEN.

NONE OF THEM BELIEVE ME. THEY THINK I'M GOING MAD — MAYBE I AM GOING MAD!

AND THEN... SUDDENLY...

AAAAAAAH!

...HE WAS SWIMMING FOR HIS LIFE!

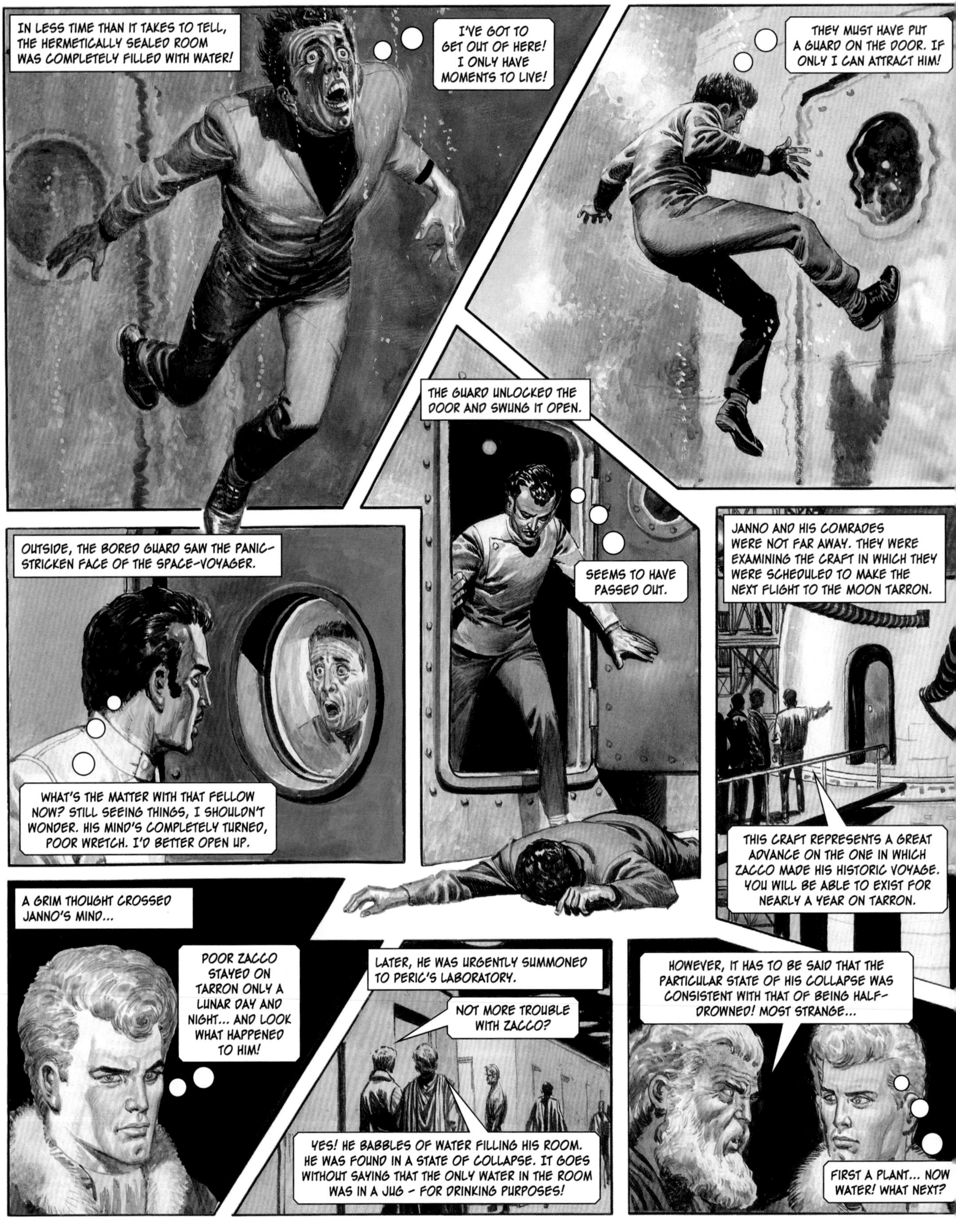

IN LESS TIME THAN IT TAKES TO TELL, THE HERMETICALLY SEALED ROOM WAS COMPLETELY FILLED WITH WATER!
I'VE GOT TO GET OUT OF HERE! I ONLY HAVE MOMENTS TO LIVE!
THEY MUST HAVE PUT A GUARD ON THE DOOR. IF ONLY I CAN ATTRACT HIM!
OUTSIDE, THE BORED GUARD SAW THE PANIC-STRICKEN FACE OF THE SPACE-VOYAGER.
WHAT'S THE MATTER WITH THAT FELLOW NOW? STILL SEEING THINGS, I SHOULDN'T WONDER. HIS MIND'S COMPLETELY TURNED, POOR WRETCH. I'D BETTER OPEN UP.
THE GUARD UNLOCKED THE DOOR AND SWUNG IT OPEN.
SEEMS TO HAVE PASSED OUT.
JANNO AND HIS COMRADES WERE NOT FAR AWAY. THEY WERE EXAMINING THE CRAFT IN WHICH THEY WERE SCHEDULED TO MAKE THE NEXT FLIGHT TO THE MOON TARRON.
THIS CRAFT REPRESENTS A GREAT ADVANCE ON THE ONE IN WHICH ZACCO MADE HIS HISTORIC VOYAGE. YOU WILL BE ABLE TO EXIST FOR NEARLY A YEAR ON TARRON.
A GRIM THOUGHT CROSSED JANNO'S MIND...
POOR ZACCO STAYED ON TARRON ONLY A LUNAR DAY AND NIGHT... AND LOOK WHAT HAPPENED TO HIM!
LATER, HE WAS URGENTLY SUMMONED TO PERIC'S LABORATORY.
NOT MORE TROUBLE WITH ZACCO?
YES! HE BABBLES OF WATER FILLING HIS ROOM. HE WAS FOUND IN A STATE OF COLLAPSE. IT GOES WITHOUT SAYING THAT THE ONLY WATER IN THE ROOM WAS IN A JUG - FOR DRINKING PURPOSES!
HOWEVER, IT HAS TO BE SAID THAT THE PARTICULAR STATE OF HIS COLLAPSE WAS CONSISTENT WITH THAT OF BEING HALF-DROWNED! MOST STRANGE...
FIRST A PLANT... NOW WATER! WHAT NEXT?

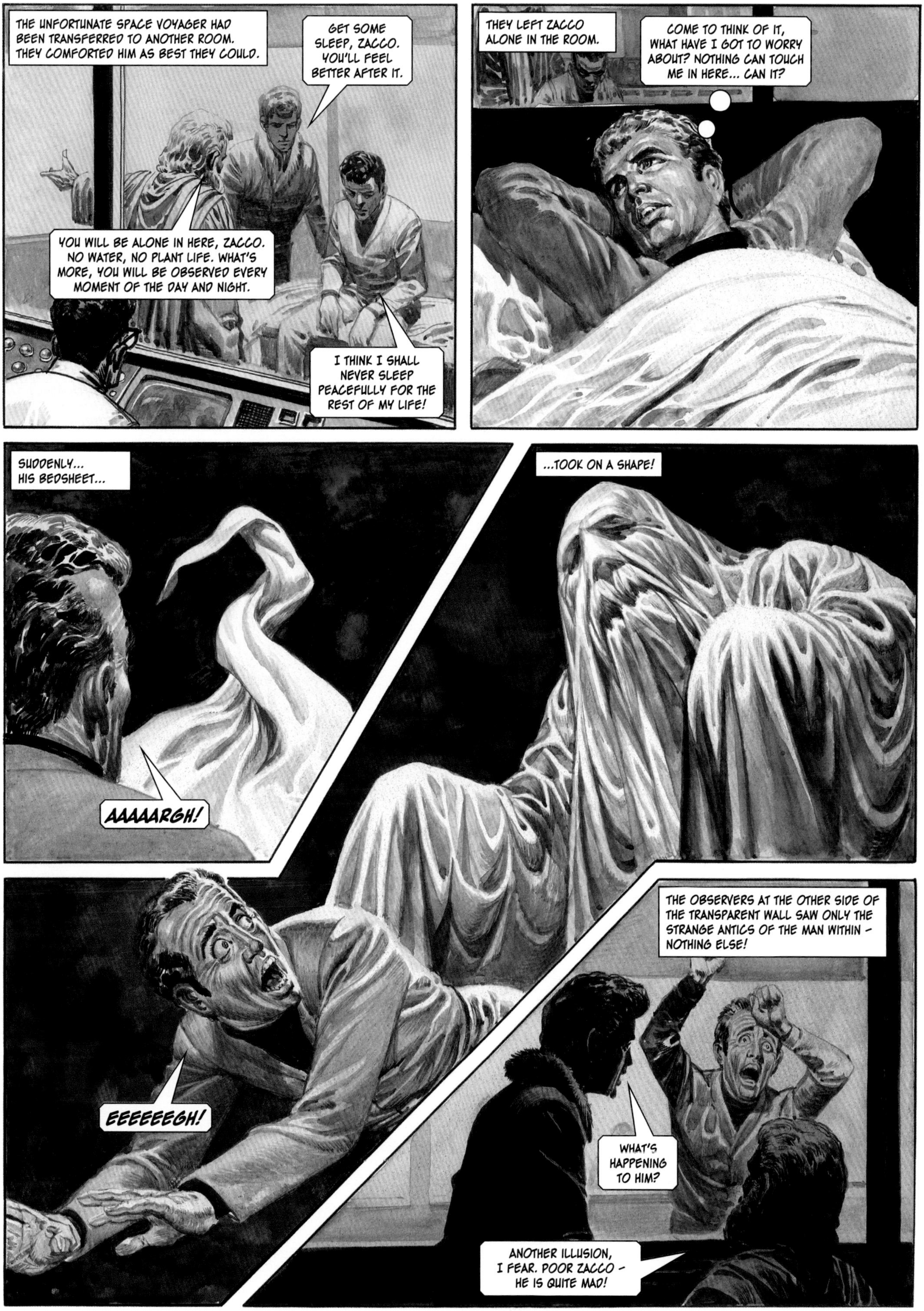
THE UNFORTUNATE SPACE VOYAGER HAD BEEN TRANSFERRED TO ANOTHER ROOM. THEY COMFORTED HIM AS BEST THEY COULD.
GET SOME SLEEP, ZACCO. YOU'LL FEEL BETTER AFTER IT.
YOU WILL BE ALONE IN HERE, ZACCO. NO WATER, NO PLANT LIFE. WHAT'S MORE, YOU WILL BE OBSERVED EVERY MOMENT OF THE DAY AND NIGHT.
I THINK I SHALL NEVER SLEEP PEACEFULLY FOR THE REST OF MY LIFE!
THEY LEFT ZACCO ALONE IN THE ROOM.
COME TO THINK OF IT, WHAT HAVE I GOT TO WORRY ABOUT? NOTHING CAN TOUCH ME IN HERE... CAN IT?
SUDDENLY... HIS BEDSHEET...
AAAAARGH!
...TOOK ON A SHAPE!
EEEEEEGH!
THE OBSERVERS AT THE OTHER SIDE OF THE TRANSPARENT WALL SAW ONLY THE STRANGE ANTICS OF THE MAN WITHIN - NOTHING ELSE!
WHAT'S HAPPENING TO HIM?
ANOTHER ILLUSION, I FEAR. POOR ZACCO - HE IS QUITE MAD!

ZACCO BEAT ON THE TRANSPARENT WALLS OF HIS CHAMBER – AS THE THING ENVELOPED HIM.

LET ME OUT! FOR PITY'S SAKE DON'T LET IT DESTROY ME!

THOSE OUTSIDE SAW ONLY THE FRIGHTENED MAN.

WHAT'S TO BE DONE WITH THE POOR, DELUDED FELLOW?

WELL – I'M GOING TO OPEN THE DOOR AND LET HIM OUT!

JANNO OPENED THE DOOR – AND THE SPACE-VOYAGER TOPPLED OUT INTO HIS ARMS.

WHAT AILS YOU, ZACCO? WHAT IS IT?

JANNO! AAAAH! THANK THE STARS! YOU'VE SAVED MY LIFE!

MY SHEET...! THE SHEET ON THE BED... IT ROSE UP AND ATTACKED ME!

HMMM!

FIRST A PLANT... THEN WATER... AND NOW THIS!

HE NEEDS REST AND A COMPLETE CHANGE. GET HIM AWAY FROM TRIGAN CITY INTO THE COUNTRYSIDE OR HE'LL HAVE A COMPLETE MENTAL BREAKDOWN.

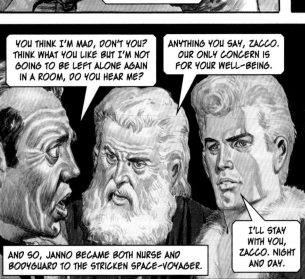

YOU THINK I'M MAD, DON'T YOU? THINK WHAT YOU LIKE BUT I'M NOT GOING TO BE LEFT ALONE AGAIN IN A ROOM, DO YOU HEAR ME?

ANYTHING YOU SAY, ZACCO. OUR ONLY CONCERN IS FOR YOUR WELL-BEING.

I'LL STAY WITH YOU, ZACCO. NIGHT AND DAY.

AND SO, JANNO BECAME BOTH NURSE AND BODYGUARD TO THE STRICKEN SPACE-VOYAGER.

HE HAS A BROTHER WHO LIVES ON THE COAST. I'LL TAKE HIM THERE.

IS IT HIS MIND – OR IS SOMETHING TRYING TO DESTROY HIM? SOMETHING HE BROUGHT BACK FROM THE MOON TARRON?

THE FOLLOWING DAY, JANNO PILOTED HIS CHARGE TO THE PLEASANT HOLIDAY COAST OF THE GREAT OCEAN.

THERE'S YOUR BROTHER'S VILLAGE. NO HARM COULD COME TO ANYONE IN A PLACE LIKE THAT.

ZACCO'S BROTHER AND HIS SMALL FAMILY LIVED IN A CHARMING VILLA OVERLOOKING THE SPARKLING BLUE SEA.

PLENTY OF FRESH AIR AND SUNSHINE, OLD FELLOW. WE'LL HAVE YOU FIT AGAIN IN NO TIME, YOU'LL SEE.

I FEEL BETTER ALREADY.

UNCLE ZACCO, THIS IS YAGGA. HE'S MY BEST FRIEND.

HE'S A VERY HANDSOME FELLOW. HELLO, YAGGA...

SUDDENLY, IT WAS AS IF A SHADOW HAD FALLEN ACROSS THAT IDYLLIC SCENE.

ZACCO! BY ALL THE STARS...

IT MOVED IN MY HAND! THE ACCURSED THING MOVED IN MY HAND!

AWWWW! HE'S DROPPED YAGGA AND HURT HIM!

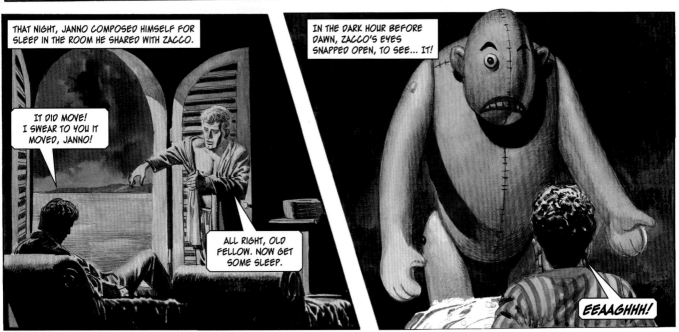

THAT NIGHT, JANNO COMPOSED HIMSELF FOR SLEEP IN THE ROOM HE SHARED WITH ZACCO.

IT DID MOVE! I SWEAR TO YOU IT MOVED, JANNO!

ALL RIGHT, OLD FELLOW. NOW GET SOME SLEEP.

IN THE DARK HOUR BEFORE DAWN, ZACCO'S EYES SNAPPED OPEN, TO SEE... IT!

EEAAGHHH!

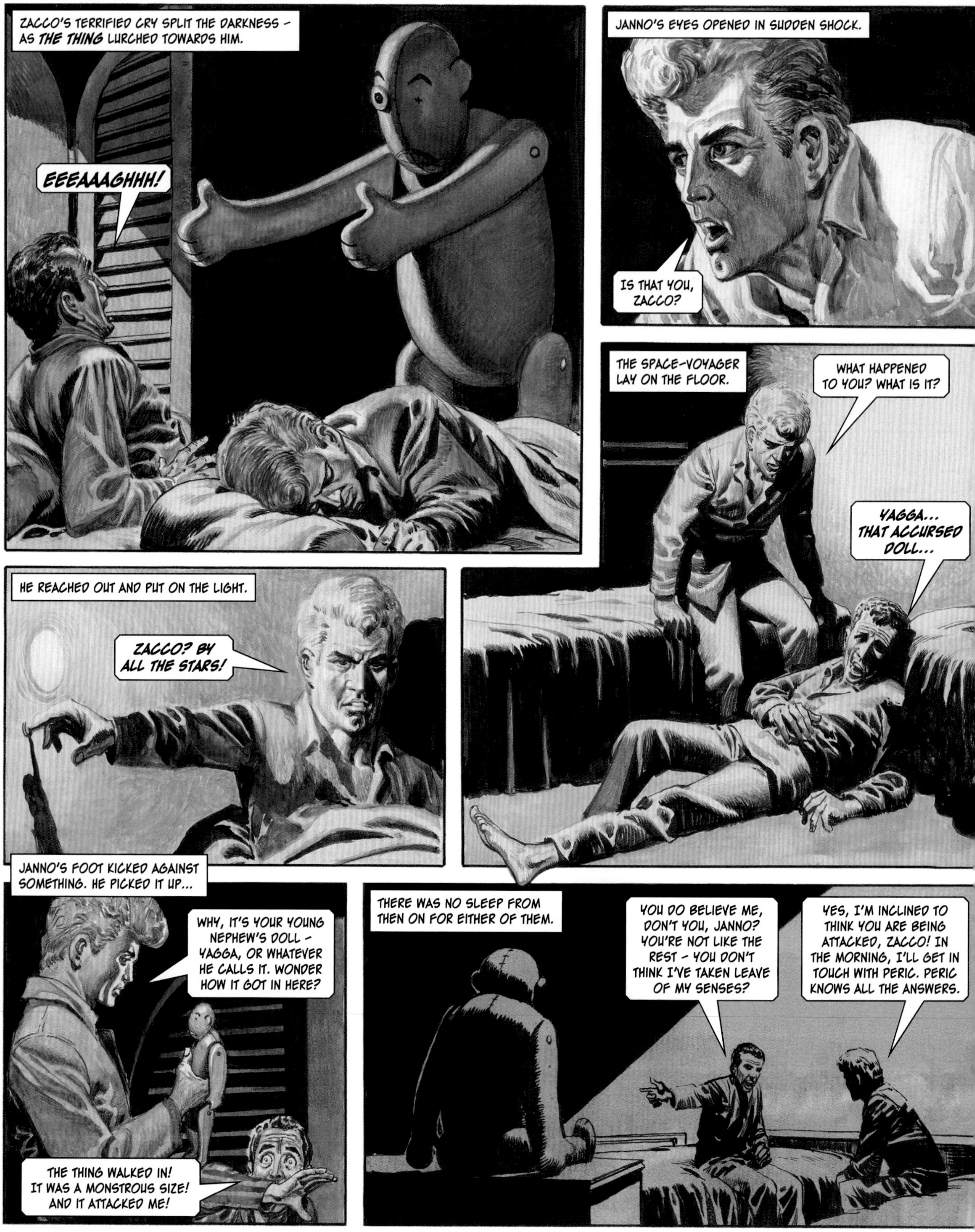

ZACCO'S TERRIFIED CRY SPLIT THE DARKNESS - AS THE THING LURCHED TOWARDS HIM.
EEEAAAGHHH!
JANNO'S EYES OPENED IN SUDDEN SHOCK.
IS THAT YOU, ZACCO?
THE SPACE-VOYAGER LAY ON THE FLOOR.
WHAT HAPPENED TO YOU? WHAT IS IT?
YAGGA... THAT ACCURSED DOLL...
HE REACHED OUT AND PUT ON THE LIGHT.
ZACCO? BY ALL THE STARS!
JANNO'S FOOT KICKED AGAINST SOMETHING. HE PICKED IT UP...
WHY, IT'S YOUR YOUNG NEPHEW'S DOLL - YAGGA, OR WHATEVER HE CALLS IT. WONDER HOW IT GOT IN HERE?
THE THING WALKED IN! IT WAS A MONSTROUS SIZE! AND IT ATTACKED ME!
THERE WAS NO SLEEP FROM THEN ON FOR EITHER OF THEM.
YOU DO BELIEVE ME, DON'T YOU, JANNO? YOU'RE NOT LIKE THE REST - YOU DON'T THINK I'VE TAKEN LEAVE OF MY SENSES?
YES, I'M INCLINED TO THINK YOU ARE BEING ATTACKED, ZACCO! IN THE MORNING, I'LL GET IN TOUCH WITH PERIC. PERIC KNOWS ALL THE ANSWERS.

IN THE SUNLIGHT OF EARLY MORNING, JANNO MADE HIS COMRADE COMFORTABLE ON THE PATIO.

YOU GET SOME SLEEP HERE IN THE FRESH AIR AND SUNSHINE. I'LL GET ON TO PERIC AND TELL HIM WHAT'S HAPPENED.

YES, JANNO. I REALLY THINK I COULD SLEEP NOW – FOR WHAT HARM COULD POSSIBLY COME TO ME IN THE BROAD LIGHT OF DAY?

THE SPACE-VOYAGER LAY HIMSELF DOWN AND ALMOST IMMEDIATELY WENT TO SLEEP.

AND THEN... A SHADOW FELL ACROSS HIM!

JANNO WAS SOON IN AUDIO-VISUAL CONTACT WITH ELEKTON'S TOP SCIENTIST.

DID YOU SEE THIS THING THAT ZACCO ALLEGES ATTACKED HIM?

I MIGHT HAVE, PERIC! I HAVE A FLEETING MEMORY ON THE POINT OF WAKING OF A HUGE FORM STOOPING OVER HIM!

PERIC HAD AN ITEM OF NEWS.

A STRANGE THING HAS HAPPENED. TWO GUARDS WHO WERE WATCHING ZACCO'S SPACE CAPSULE HAVE VANISHED. AT FIRST, IT WAS THOUGHT THAT THEY HAD DESERTED. NOW... I'M NOT SO SURE.

I THINK YOU HAD BETTER BRING ZACCO STRAIGHT BACK TO TRIGAN CITY, JANNO.

JANNO AGREED WITH THE SCIENTIST AND RETURNED TO HIS COMRADE.

SUPPOSING SOMETHING TRAVELLED BACK FROM THE MOON WITH ZACCO IN HIS CAPSULE! AND SUPPOSING THAT THE THING GOT OUT, DESTROYING THE GUARDS, THEN SEEKING OUT ZACCO TO DESTROY HIM!

THEN HE SAW...

ZACCO!

OH, NO! – NO!

ZACCO LAY IN A PATCH OF ALIEN SHADOW - GLISTENING WITH ICE CRYSTALS!

ZACCO! BY ALL THE STARS, YOU'RE FREEZING TO DEATH!

THE SPACE-VOYAGER'S PULSE WAS THE MEREST WHISPER AND HIS BREATHING HAD ALMOST CEASED!

HOW COULD ANYONE FREEZE IN THE HEAT OF THE MORNING SUN?

THERE WAS A SHADOW SURROUNDING THAT CHAIR... BUT NOW IT'S GONE! AND THE ICE WITH IT!

BUT... HOW?

JANNO DRAGGED HIS COMRADE INTO THE SUNLIGHT AND BEGAN TO CHAFE HIS ICE-COLD LIMBS.

ANOTHER FEW MOMENTS AND HE WOULD HAVE BEEN FROZEN!

WHAT'S HAPPENED TO HIM?

WHEN ZACCO RECOVERED HIS SENSES...

I- I CAN'T BEAR MUCH MORE OF IT, JANNO. IT'S DRIVING ME OUT OF MY MIND.

WE'RE GOING BACK TO TRIGAN CITY, OLD COMRADE. FROM NOW ON, YOU'RE GOING TO HAVE THE ENTIRE RESOURCES OF THE EMPIRE BEHIND YOU! YOU SEE, WE BELIEVE YOU NOW!

SOON AFTER, THEY TOOK OFF...

I'LL TELL YOU SOMETHING, ZACCO - THINGS HAVE CHANGED.

HOW'S THAT, JANNO?

WELL, UP TO THIS MORNING, WHATEVER IT IS THAT'S AFTER YOU HAS ALWAYS HIDDEN ITS VARIOUS MANIFESTATIONS FROM ALL EYES BUT YOURS.

AND NOW... YOU'VE SEEN IT!

YES! AND I'M WONDERING IF THAT MEANS I'M NOW TO BE INCLUDED WITH YOU AS A TARGET FOR FUTURE ATTACKS!

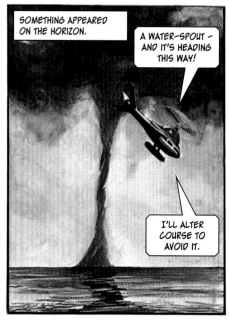

SOMETHING APPEARED ON THE HORIZON.

A WATER-SPOUT – AND IT'S HEADING THIS WAY!

I'LL ALTER COURSE TO AVOID IT.

BUT...

JANNO! IT'S STILL COMING AT US – IT'S CHASING US!

AAAAAAAH! WE'RE GOING TO SMASH INTO IT!

IT'S ANOTHER ATTACK, ZACCO! BOTH OF US THIS TIME!

NEXT INSTANT – DISASTER!

AFTER THE BREATH-ROBBING IMPACT, JANNO FELT HIMSELF FALLING... FALLING...

I WAS RIGHT! THE ALIEN FORCE IS GOING TO DESTROY ME, TOO!

THE TWO FLYERS ACTIVATED THEIR ESCAPE GEAR – IN TIME TO SEE THE MASSIVE COLUMN OF WATER COMING AT THEM AGAIN!

THE THING IS DIRECTED BY AN ALIEN INTELLIGENCE... AND IT'S DETERMINED TO WIPE US OUT!

SUDDENLY... A BLAST OF HEAVY GUNFIRE! A TRIGAN DESTROYER-CRAFT!

A SALVO OF WELL-PLACED PROJECTILES BROKE UP THE KILLER WATER-SPOUT!

SOON, THEY WERE BEING HELPED ABOARD THEIR RESCUER.

YOU JUST DON'T KNOW HOW CLOSE, LIEUTENANT!

GOOD THING WE HAPPENED TO BE AROUND. THAT WAS A CLOSE THING FOR YOU!

THEY'VE DESTROYED THE WATER-SPOUT... BUT NOTHING ON THIS PLANET COULD DESTROY THE MIND THAT DIRECTED IT!

PRESENTLY, THEY WERE ENTERING TRIGAN CITY HARBOUR. AND ONE THOUGHT BURNED IN JANNO'S MIND...

WE'VE GOT TO GET RID OF THIS EVIL FORCE... AT ANY COST!

THE TWO COMRADES WENT STRAIGHT TO PERIC'S LABORATORY. ELEKTON'S TOP SCIENTIST HEARD ALL THEIR EVIDENCE. THEN HE MADE A PRONOUNCEMENT.

THE FORCE IS MALIGNANT AND ALMOST INDESTRUCTIBLE. YOU HAVE BOTH BEEN EXTRAORDINARILY LUCKY TO ESCAPE IT SO FAR. I DO NOT, HOWEVER, CONSIDER THAT YOUR LUCK WILL LAST MUCH LONGER...

THE FORCE APPEARS TO HAVE A WIDE SPECTRUM OF MANIFESTATIONS... IT CAN TAKE OVER PLANT LIFE, INANIMATE OBJECTS... IT CAN EVEN INFLUENCE NATURAL PHENOMENA SUCH AS TEMPERATURE...

THIS THING MUST BE TAKEN BACK FROM WHENCE IT CAME... BEFORE IT EXTENDS ITS MALIGNANCY FROM YOU TWO TO THE REMAINDER OF THIS PLANET'S INHABITANTS!

YOU MEAN...?

I MEAN ONE OR BOTH OF YOU HAS GOT TO TAKE THE ACCURSED THING BACK TO THE MOON TARRON!

THEY WENT STRAIGHT TO THE HUGE CRAFT THAT WAS SCHEDULED TO MAKE THE NEXT FLIGHT TO TARRON.

IT'S THE ONLY ANSWER! THIS CRAFT MUST TAKE THE EVIL THING AND NEVER RETURN. AND NEVER AGAIN MUST WE LAND ON THE LESSER MOON TARRON – IT WILL BE OUTLAWED FOR ETERNITY!

IT'S THE ONLY ANSWER, AS YOU SAY, PERIC

I'LL GO. YOU'RE YOUNG. YOUR WHOLE LIFE'S AHEAD OF YOU!

RUBBISH! WE'LL DRAW LOTS FOR IT!

AND SO...

THERE ARE TWO DISCS IN THIS BAG, ONE PLAIN, THE OTHER MARKED WITH A STAR. THE ONE WHO TAKES THE STAR IS... HIM!

ZACCO DREW A DISC. THEN JANNO... AND...

I AM TAKING THE ONE-WAY TRIP TO THE LESSER MOON TARRON – WITH THE MALIGNANT FORCE AS PASSENGER!

BY DAWN NEXT DAY, JANNO HAD TAKEN HIS PLACE IN THE NOSE OF THE GIANT CRAFT THAT WAS TO TAKE HIM ON THE ONE-WAY JOURNEY TO TARRON. HE HAD SAID FAREWELL TO HIS FAMILY, HIS FRIENDS...

ZACCO AND KEREN HAD VOLUNTEERED TO ASSIST IN THE FINAL STAGES OF DEPARTURE.

DON'T FORGET, JANNO. AS SOON AS YOU'RE SATISFIED THAT THE EVIL FORCE HAS MANIFESTED ITSELF INSIDE THE CAPSULE WITH YOU, YOU WILL CALL FOR THE HATCHWAY TO BE CLOSED AND FOR BLAST-OFF TO COMMENCE. GOT IT?

I UNDERSTAND PERFECTLY, ZACCO.

GOODBYE, LAD. I'M PROUD TO HAVE KNOWN YOU. *YOU'RE A HERO!*

FAREWELL, ZACCO... AND YOU, KEREN.

JANNO ENTERED THE CAPSULE AND SPOKE WITH THE CONTROL.

THE INANIMATE OBJECT AND THE PLANT SPECIMEN SHOW NO CHANGE. THE FORCE HAS NOT YET MANIFESTED ITSELF IN THE CAPSULE. PERHAPS IT HAS REMAINED OUTSIDE WITH ZACCO...

AND THEN...

IT'S TAKEN OVER THE PLANT! IT'S HERE IN THE CAPSULE! SHUT THE HATCHWAY AND BEGIN BLAST-OFF PROCEDURE!

AN INSTANT LATER, ZACCO PLUNGED IN THROUGH THE HATCHWAY, KNIFE IN HAND.

GET OUT OF HERE! SHUT THE HATCHWAY!

OH, NO... JANNO!

HIS KNIFE SLASHED... AND HIS FIST CONNECTED WITH JANNO'S JAW!

I'VE GOT OTHER PLANS FOR YOU, LAD!

UUUUGH!

WHILE THE DEADLY TENDRILS CLUTCHED AT HIM, ZACCO PASSED JANNO'S LIMP FORM TO KEREN, OUTSIDE.

GET HIM OUT OF HERE!

KEREN HEARD ONE LAST DESPAIRING CRY FROM THE SPACE-VOYAGER...

SHUT THE HATCHWAY! I CAN'T HOLD THE THING AT BAY MUCH LONGER!

LATER, JANNO RECOVERED CONSCIOUSNESS WITH A GREAT BLAST OF SOUND DINNING IN HIS EARS. HE SAW THE HUGE CRAFT RISING SKYWARDS.

BUT... WHO?

ZACCO!

HE PLANNED IT ALL ALONG – TO TAKE YOUR PLACE! SAID HE BROUGHT THE EVIL THING HERE AND IT WAS HIS JOB TO TAKE IT BACK!

HE GAVE HIS LIFE FOR ME... AND PERHAPS FOR ALL ELEKTON!

JANNO'S WORDS WERE CARVED ON THE BASE OF A STATUE THAT WAS RAISED TO THE GREAT SPACE-VOYAGER IN TRIGAN CITY PARK. THE FINGER POINTED UPWARDS TO THE ORBIT OF TARRON – THE LESSER MOON THAT WAS OUTLAWED FOR ETERNITY.

THE TRIGAN EMPIRE
THE SUN WORSHIPPERS
Originally published in *Look and Learn* 621 - 629
8th December 1973 - 2nd February 1974
Story by Mike Butterworth
Art by Don Lawrence

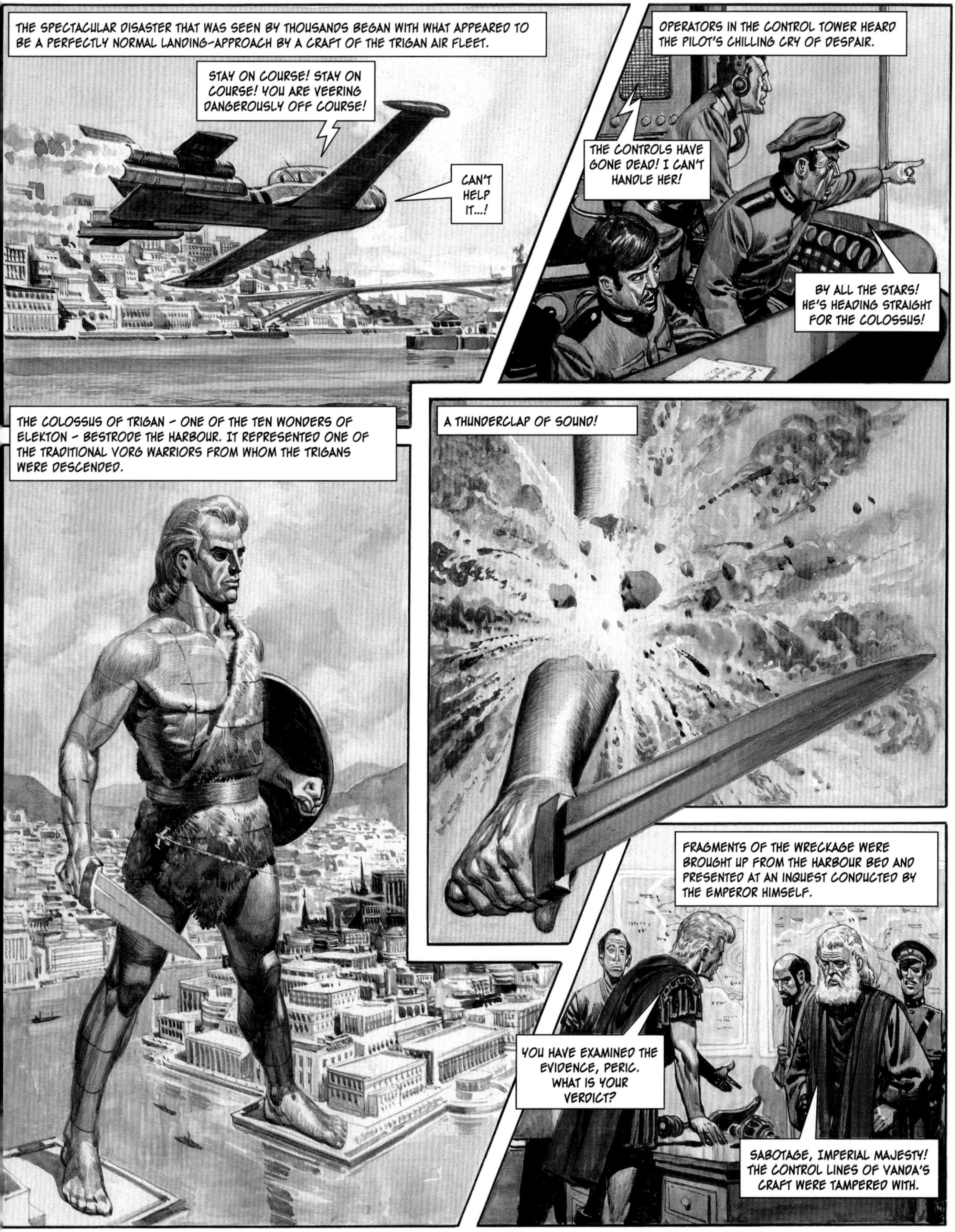

THE SPECTACULAR DISASTER THAT WAS SEEN BY THOUSANDS BEGAN WITH WHAT APPEARED TO BE A PERFECTLY NORMAL LANDING-APPROACH BY A CRAFT OF THE TRIGAN AIR FLEET.
STAY ON COURSE! STAY ON COURSE! YOU ARE VEERING DANGEROUSLY OFF COURSE!
CAN'T HELP IT...!
OPERATORS IN THE CONTROL TOWER HEARD THE PILOT'S CHILLING CRY OF DESPAIR.
THE CONTROLS HAVE GONE DEAD! I CAN'T HANDLE HER!
BY ALL THE STARS! HE'S HEADING STRAIGHT FOR THE COLOSSUS!
THE COLOSSUS OF TRIGAN - ONE OF THE TEN WONDERS OF ELEKTON - BESTRODE THE HARBOUR. IT REPRESENTED ONE OF THE TRADITIONAL VORG WARRIORS FROM WHOM THE TRIGANS WERE DESCENDED.
A THUNDERCLAP OF SOUND!
FRAGMENTS OF THE WRECKAGE WERE BROUGHT UP FROM THE HARBOUR BED AND PRESENTED AT AN INQUEST CONDUCTED BY THE EMPEROR HIMSELF.
YOU HAVE EXAMINED THE EVIDENCE, PERIC. WHAT IS YOUR VERDICT?
SABOTAGE, IMPERIAL MAJESTY! THE CONTROL LINES OF VANDA'S CRAFT WERE TAMPERED WITH.

ELEKTON'S TOP SCIENTIST SPOKE GRAVELY.

CAPTAIN VANDA IS MERELY THE LATEST VICTIM OF A WICKED AGENDA! THERE IS AN EVIL POWER AT WORK IN OUR MIDST THAT IS GNAWING AT THE HEART OF THE TRIGAN EMPIRE! I WILL GIVE YOU FURTHER INSTANCES.

"WHEN THE MILLIONAIRE HURRI RASS REFUSED TO HAND OVER HIS FORTUNE AND SUBMIT HIMSELF TO THIS POWER, MEANS WERE FOUND TO DISPOSE OF HIM IN HIS OWN HOME!"

"AN INFLUENTIAL PROVINCIAL GOVERNOR NAMED HAZZOR BETRAYED CERTAIN SECRETS TO THE POLICE," PERIC WENT ON. "AND HE MET WITH A TRAGIC BOATING ACCIDENT."

EEEEAAAAAAHHH!

TRIGO CUT IN.

AND THIS POWER OF WHICH YOU SPEAK... IS WHAT?

A CULT OF SUN-WORSHIPPERS, IMPERIAL MAJESTY! THE ANCIENT SUPERSTITION OF SUN WORSHIP HAS NOT BEEN PRACTISED ON THIS PLANET SINCE PRE-HISTORIC TIMES, BUT IT HAS BEEN REVIVED WITH ALL ITS EVIL! CAPTAIN VANDA, WHO WAS WORKING AS AN UNDERCOVER AGENT, WAS ABLE TO PASS ON SOME VITAL INFORMATION BEFORE THEY GOT HIM...!

DAWN BROKE OVER THE VORG HILLS. THE FIRST RAYS OF ELEKTON'S TWIN SUNS TOUCHED THE STONES OF AN ANCIENT, RUINED TEMPLE.

ALL HAIL, O RIDERS OF THE SKY! MAKE THY FOLLOWERS MIGHTY! BRING DESTRUCTION TO THE UNBELIEVERS!

SUDDENLY – A RUDE INTERRUPTION!

LINE UP OVER THERE! BY ORDER OF THE EMPEROR, YOU'RE ALL UNDER ARREST!

THE CHIEF PRIEST'S VOICE ECHOED HARSHLY IN THE STILL AIR...

THE EMPEROR! THE CURSE OF THE SUNS UPON THE SO-CALLED EMPEROR OF THE TRIGANS! FROM THIS DAY FORTH, EVERYTHING HE TOUCHES SHALL FALL TO RUIN – AND IN THE END HE WILL BE SWALLOWED UP!

HAVING DELIVERED HIS TERRIBLE UTTERANCE, THE CHIEF PRIEST VANISHED!

BY ALL THE DEMONS IN DAVELI! HE'S DISAPPEARED!

MY PEOPLE, I THANK YOU FROM THE BOTTOM OF MY HEART!

LONG LIVE THE EMPEROR!

LONG LIVE THE EMPEROR!

IT WAS FOUNDING DAY – THE GREATEST FEAST DAY IN THE CALENDAR, WHEN PEOPLES OF THE EMPIRE ASSEMBLED TO CELEBRATE THE FOUNDING OF TRIGAN CITY.

THE CAPTAIN OF THE IMPERIAL GUARD HANDED TRIGO A CEREMONIAL SPADE AND THE EMPEROR FORMALLY "PLANTED" A COMMEMORATIVE TREE.

BUT, OF COURSE, IT IS PERFECTLY OBVIOUS TO EVEN THE MOST STUPID THAT THE TREE IS ALREADY PLANTED.

QUITE SO, MAJESTY – BUT YOUR SYMBOLIC SPADEFUL MAKES ALL THE DIFFERENCE!

WHEN IT WAS DONE...

WHEN THIS YOUNG TREE IS OLDER THAN LIVING MEMORY, MAY TRIGAN CITY AND THE EMPIRE STILL THRIVE AND FLOURISH!

WELL SPOKEN, IMPERIAL MAJESTY!

HEAR, HEAR!

DISASTER!

BY ALL THE STARS! WHAT'S HAPPENING TO IT? IT'S DYING BEFORE OUR VERY EYES!

THERE WERE ALARMED AND AWESTRUCK MURMURS IN THE WATCHING MULTITUDE.

THE CURSE! THE CURSE OF THE HIGH-PRIEST IS BEING FULFILLED!

THEY SHOULD NEVER HAVE INTERFERED WITH THE SUN-WORSHIPPERS!

'TIS AN EVIL OMEN!

WE HAVEN'T SEEN THE END OF THIS YET – YOU MARK MY WORDS!

LATER THAT DAY, PERIC CONSULTED WITH THE EMPEROR.

THE WITHERED TREE? REALLY, PERIC, DO YOU HAVE TO BOTHER ME WITH SUCH A TRIVIALITY? CAN'T YOU SEE I'M BUSY?

IT MAY BE TRIVIAL, SIRE, BUT THE PEOPLE ARE WORRIED. THE OLD SUPERSTITIONS DIE HARD AMONG THE PEASANTS. THEY ARE CONVINCED YOU ARE DOOMED.

THE HIGH-PRIEST'S CURSE, EH? WHAT WAS IT HE SAID? "FROM THIS DAY FORTH, EVERYTHING TRIGO TOUCHES SHALL FALL TO RUIN – AND IN THE END HE WILL BE SWALLOWED UP!"

RUBBISH!

RUBBISH IT MAY BE, MAJESTY, TO OUR SOPHISTICATED MINDS. BUT THE COMMON PEOPLE...

SOME OTHER TIME, PERIC! I HAVE TO LAUNCH BATTLE-SHIP THIS AFTERNOON, AND IM' BEHIND SCHEDULE ALREADY...

NOW, WHERE'S THAT CONFOUNDED REPORT FROM LOKA?

THE BATTLE-SHIP "VORG WARRIOR", THE LARGEST VESSEL EVER BUILT, WAS DESIGNED TO WAGE SINGLE HANDED WAR AGAINST ANY POWER ON ELEKTON. BESIDES ITS MASSIVE ARMAMENT OF GUNS, IT CARRIED TWELVE SQUADRONS OF FIGHTING-CRAFT.

THE FATEFUL AFTERNOON, IT STOOD READY FOR LAUNCHING.

THE EMPEROR GAVE A STIRRING SPEECH.

I GIVE THIS VESSEL THE PROUD NAME OF "VORG WARRIOR"! MAY GOOD FORTUNE GO WITH ALL WHO TREAD "VORG WARRIOR'S" STOUT DECKS.

GRANDLY, THE SPLENDID SHIP DESCENDED THE SLIPWAY...

THEN — SUDDEN AND AWFUL DISASTER!

JANNO, THE EMPEROR'S NEPHEW, WAS PILOTING THE SOLE FIGHTER-CRAFT TO ESCAPE THE DISASTER. LOOKING BACK HE SAW THE CAPSIZED HULL OF THE "VORG WARRIOR"

BY ALL THE STARS! IT'S GHASTLY... UNBELIEVABLE!

WHEN ELEKTON'S TWIN SUNS ROSE IN THE DAWN SKY, A GATHERING OF MASKED FIGURES WAS WAITING ON A MOUNTAIN-TOP.

O RIDERS OF THE SKY – BRING DESTRUCTION TO ALL UNBELIEVERS, ESPECIALLY THE CREATURE WHO CALLS HIMSELF EMPEROR OF THE TRIGANS!

THE CHIEF PRIEST'S VOICE WAS VIBRANT WITH TRIUMPH.

MY FOLLOWERS! WE ARE INDESTRUCTIBLE! THEY WILL NEVER CRUSH US! FURTHERMORE, THE ACCURSED TRIGO IS ALREADY TUMBLING DOWN THE STEEP SLOPE TO ANNIHILATION!

I MUST REPORT THIS IMMEDIATELY!

THE SECRET CEREMONY OVER, ONE OF THE WORSHIPPERS MADE HASTE BACK IN THE DIRECTION OF TRIGAN CITY.

HE STOPPED AT THE FIRST PUBLIC CALL BOX.

GIVE ME POLICE HEADQUARTERS... SECTION Z...

TOO LATE, HE SAW HIS DANGER!

THAT'S ALL THE INFORMATION I HAVE AT THE MOMENT BUT... AAAAAAAH! WHAT'S HAPPENING?

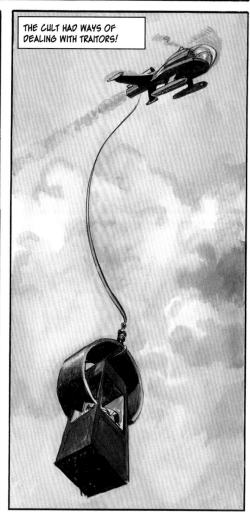

THE CULT HAD WAYS OF DEALING WITH TRAITORS!

LATER THAT MORNING, PERIC CALLED UPON THE EMPEROR WITH THE NEWS.

BY THE STARS! I THOUGHT WE HAD STAMPED OUT THAT EVIL! I WAS TOLD THAT THE CHIEF PRIEST HAD DISAPPEARED!

HE DISAPPEARED, IMPERIAL MAJESTY, BY THE SIMPLE MEANS OF A SECRET TRAPDOOR. AND, THIS MORNING, HE WAS GLOATING ABOUT YOUR IMPENDING DOWNFALL!

THE PERIL FROM THESE PEOPLE IS VERY REAL, MAJESTY. I FEAR THAT MY INFORMANT HAS ALREADY PAID DEARLY!

YOU REFER TO THE SO-CALLED CURSE LAID UPON ME... THAT EVERYTHING I TOUCH SHALL FALL TO RUIN...

FROM THE PALACE WINDOW, THEY COULD SEE THE HUGE, OVERTURNED HULK OF WHAT HAD ONCE BEEN THE PRIDE OF THE TRIGAN NAVY.

WHAT HAPPENED TO THE "VORG WARRIOR" WAS REAL ENOUGH, MAJESTY!

I TOUCHED THE GREAT SHIP... AND IT IMMEDIATELY FOUNDERED!

HOW COULD IT HAVE HAPPENED, PERIC? HOW COULD IT?

WE DON'T KNOW, JANNO – BUT WE'LL FIND OUT!

SOME DAYS LATER, TRIGO PERFORMED ANOTHER OFFICIAL CEREMONY IN THE PROVINCIAL TOWN OF ZARCUS.

THE PEACE AND PROGRESS THAT ATTENDS THE TRIGAN EMPIRE IS WELL EXEMPLIFIED BY THIS SPLENDID MODERN WATER FILTRATION AND PURIFICATION PLANT, WHICH I HAVE GREAT PLEASURE IN OPENING...

THE GOOD FOLK OF ZARCUS WERE PLEASED WITH THE NEW WATER.

CLEAR AS CRYSTAL... AND DELICIOUS TO THE PALATE, I SHOULDN'T WONDER!

BY THE FOLLOWING MORNING, THE TOWN WAS A PLACE OF SILENCE. NOT A LIVING THING STIRRED.

THE BUSIEST TIME OF THE DAY, AND NO ONE ABOUT... AM I DREAMING?

THE EMPEROR WAS TAKING HIS DAILY SWIM WHEN THE MESSAGE ARRIVED.

IMPERIAL MAJESTY!

WELL, WHAT IS IT, FELLOW?

ZARCUS, MAJESTY – THE TOWN WHERE YOU OPENED THE NEW WATER FILTRATION AND PURIFICATION PLANT YESTERDAY – HAS HAD A DISASTER!

THAT MORNING, THE ENTIRE POPULACE OF ZARCUS HAD BEEN FOUND UNCONSCIOUS! AT THAT MOMENT, LIMP FIGURES WERE BEING CARRIED AWAY TO THE OVERCROWDED HOSPITALS.

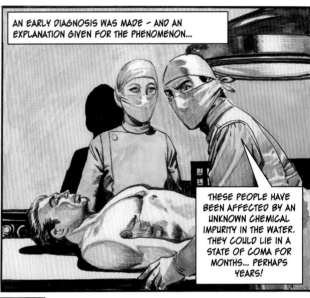

AN EARLY DIAGNOSIS WAS MADE – AND AN EXPLANATION GIVEN FOR THE PHENOMENON...

THESE PEOPLE HAVE BEEN AFFECTED BY AN UNKNOWN CHEMICAL IMPURITY IN THE WATER. THEY COULD LIE IN A STATE OF COMA FOR MONTHS... PERHAPS YEARS!

YOU HAVE TO ADMIT, IMPERIAL MAJESTY, THAT A PATTERN OF DISASTER IS BEGINNING TO EMERGE!

I DO NOT SAY THAT THE HIGH PRIEST'S CURSE IS BEHIND IT ALL. I MERELY POINT TO THE FACTS...

AM I TO UNDERSTAND, PERIC, THAT YOU – REPUTED TO POSSESS THE FINEST BRAIN ON THIS PLANET – ARE FALLING FOR THAT LOAD OF MUMBO-JUMBO?

I'LL LISTEN TO NO MORE, DO YOU HEAR? THE IMPERIAL LEADERS ARRIVE TODAY – AND I'LL HAVE NO TALK OF DISASTER WHILE THEY'RE IN TRIGAN CITY!

AS PART OF THE EVENTS CELEBRATING THE FOUNDING OF TRIGAN CITY, RULERS FROM ALL OF THE VARIOUS STATES THAT MADE UP THE EMPIRE WERE TO ATTEND A SUMMIT. TRIGO HIMSELF GREETED THE DISTINGUISHED VISITORS.

YOUR MAJESTY OF DAVELI. THIS IS BOTH AN HONOUR AND A PLEASURE.

IMPERIAL MAJESTY!

THE FIRST ITEM ON THE AGENDA WAS THE OPENING OF THE MASSIVE NEW IMPERIAL CONFERENCE HALL — THE TALLEST BUILDING ON ELEKTON AND AN ARCHITECTURAL MASTERPIECE.

TRIGO TOOK A PAIR OF CEREMONIAL CUTTERS FROM THE CAPTAIN OF THE IMPERIAL GUARD AND PROCEEDED TO CUT THE TAPE ACROSS THE ENTRANCE.

I DEDICATE THIS GREAT BUILDING TO THE CAUSE OF IMPERIAL PEACE AND BROTHERHOOD.

AND THEN...

LOOK!

NO!

IT CAN'T...

IT WAS ALL OVER IN LESS TIME THAN IT TAKES TO TELL. TRIGO WAS LEFT STANDING — LOOKING UPON A SEA OF BROKEN MASONRY AND TANGLED METAL!

DID... I... DO THAT?

THE INEXPLICABLE DESTRUCTION OF THE NEW IMPERIAL CONFERENCE HALL LAY LIKE A DARK SHADOW ACROSS THE ASSEMBLED GUESTS IN THE PALACE THAT EVENING.

YOUR MAJESTIES, EXCELLENCIES, CHIEFS! I GIVE YOU THE TOAST – TO THE FUTURE OF THE TRIGAN EMPIRE!

A SOUR, THOUGHTLESS REMARK...

DOES THE TRIGAN EMPIRE HAVE A FUTURE?

...DREW A VIOLENT REACTION!

WITHDRAW THOSE TREASONABLE WORDS, ANIMAL!

AAAAAAAAAGH!

BRIGHT BLADES FLASHED IN THE LAMPLIGHT! TABLES WERE OVERTURNED! IN A MATTER OF MOMENTS, THE DINING HALL WAS AN INFERNO OF BATTLING FIGURES!

THE EMPEROR HIMSELF WAS STRUCK DOWN FROM BEHIND BY A FLYING CHAIR!

UUUUUUGH!

IMPERIAL MAJESTY!

ONLY THE INTERVENTION OF RULLI, HIS CAPTAIN OF THE GUARD, PREVENTED TRIGO FROM FURTHER, AND PROBABLY FATAL, HARM!

STAY YOUR HAND, FOOL! THAT'S THE EMPEROR HIMSELF!

WHAT'S THIS? ANOTHER TREACHEROUS ANIMAL?

103

PRESENTLY, THE IMPERIAL GUARDS RESTORED ORDER AND DROVE THE RIOTERS FROM THE HALL AT GUN-POINT.

IT IS AN OUTRAGE!

IS THIS HOW TRIGO TREATS HIS GUESTS?

I SHALL NEVER SET FOOT IN TRIGAN CITY AGAIN!

LATER, CAPTAIN RULLI REPORTED TO HIS EMPEROR.

THE DISTINGUISHED GUESTS HAVE RETURNED HOME TO THEIR OWN COUNTRIES, SIRE. ALMOST WITHOUT EXCEPTION THEY ARE ANGRY, FRIGHTENED AND PUZZLED ABOUT WHAT HAS HAPPENED!

IT IS THE BEGINNING OF THE END OF THE TRIGAN EMPIRE!

IT IS ALL MY FAULT! EVERYTHING I TOUCH FALLS TO RUIN! THE CURSE OF THE HIGH PRIEST IS COMING TRUE IN EVERY DETAIL!

WISE OLD PERIC ANSWERED HIS FRIEND AND MASTER.

TRUE OR FALSE, THE PEOPLE OF THE EMPIRE BELIEVE IN THE CURSE. YOUR IMPERIAL MAJESTY MUST DEMONSTRATE TO THE PEOPLE THAT THE CURSE IS TO BE LIFTED — YOU MUST MAKE PEACE WITH THE SUN-WORSHIPPERS!

GLADLY! BUT — HOW?

NEAR THE REMOTE NORTHERN POLE OF THIS PLANET OF OURS, IN REGIONS SELDOM VISITED IN LIVING MEMORY, A STRANGE ISLAND JUTS OUT OF A SEA OF SWAMP. IT WAS ON THIS ISLAND, COUNTLESS AEONS AGO, THAT ELEKTON'S FIRST INHABITANTS RAISED THE FIRST TEMPLE TO THE SUNS...

"THE SUN-TEMPLE STILL STANDS," CONTINUED PERIC. "IN MY OPINION, YOUR IMPERIAL MAJESTY SHOULD TRAVEL THERE AND MAKE A SACRIFICE TO THE SUNS."

I WILL DO IT! AND YOU, MY TRUSTY CAPTAIN RULLI, SHALL ACCOMPANY ME!

AT YOUR ORDERS, SIRE!

THE NEWS WAS RELAYED TO THE PEOPLE OF TRIGAN CITY FROM THE GREAT PUBLIC SCREENS.

AS A DEMONSTRATION OF GOODWILL TOWARDS THE SUN-WORSHIPPERS, HIS IMPERIAL MAJESTY WILL JOURNEY TO THE ANCIENT TEMPLE NEAR THE NORTHERN POLE, AND MAKE AN ACT OF SACRIFICE TO THE SUNS. HE WILL BE ACCOMPANIED BY CAPTAIN RULLI OF THE GUARDS.

THE SUPERSTITIOUS PEOPLE REJOICED.

I ALWAYS SAID HE NEVER SHOULD HAVE BANNED SUN-WORSHIP!

FIRST SENSIBLE IDEA TRIGO'S HAD IN YEARS!

NOW WE'LL BE ABLE TO SLEEP PEACEFULLY – AT LAST!

NEXT DAWN, AN ALL-PURPOSE CRAFT STOOD READY FOR TAKE-OFF ON THE ROOF OF THE IMPERIAL PALACE.

FAREWELL, UNCLE. AND A SAFE VOYAGE!

JANNO, YOU SPEAK AS IF WE WERE GOING AWAY FOR YEARS! WHY, WE SHALL BE BACK IN NO TIME!

THE CRAFT ZOOMED SKYWARDS, WITH CAPTAIN RULLI AT THE CONTROLS.

SET COURSE FOR THE NORTHERN POLE, PILOT!

THE NORTHERN POLE IT IS, SIRE!

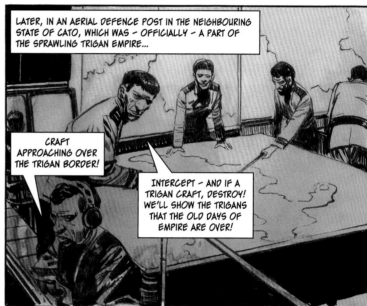

LATER, IN AN AERIAL DEFENCE POST IN THE NEIGHBOURING STATE OF CATO, WHICH WAS – OFFICIALLY – A PART OF THE SPRAWLING TRIGAN EMPIRE...

CRAFT APPROACHING OVER THE TRIGAN BORDER!

INTERCEPT – AND IF A TRIGAN CRAFT, DESTROY! WE'LL SHOW THE TRIGANS THAT THE OLD DAYS OF EMPIRE ARE OVER!

IT WAS TRIGO WHO SPOTTED THE CATON INTERCEPTOR.

THE CATONS ARE JUST CHECKING. NOTHING TO WORRY ABOUT...

AND THEN... IT HAPPENED!

TRIGO AND HIS PILOT WERE SAVED BY THE ALL-PURPOSE CRAFT'S HOVER CAPABILITY. RULLI BROUGHT THEM TO A JARRING HALT – AND THE CATON INTERCEPTOR FLASHED PAST.

AS THE CATON CAME IN FOR A SECOND RUN, RULLI SPUN HIS CRAFT... AIMED... AND FIRED!

GOT HIM!

THE TRIGANS RESUMED THEIR JOURNEY. LATER, RULLI'S WARNING LIGHT FLASHED RED.

WE'RE LOSING FUEL!

THE FUEL POD'S BEEN HIT ON THAT SIDE. UNLESS WE PLUG IT, WE'LL LAST NO MORE TIME AT ALL!

PUT DOWN ON TO THE SEA, RULLI!

DOWN ON THE SURFACE, THE EMPEROR CLIMBED OUT ON TO THE YAWING WING...

CAREFUL, MAJESTY!

I'LL SOON HAVE THAT HOLE PLUGGED!

SUDDENLY, A NIGHTMARE SHAPE AROSE FROM THE DEEP!

OH, NO!

SHUTTING HIS MIND TO THE MENACE THAT LOOMED ABOVE HIM, TRIGO PLUGGED THE HOLE IN THE FUEL POD.

NEXT INSTANT, A MIGHTY WAVE TIPPED THE EMPEROR FROM HIS SLIPPERY PERCH!

AAAAAAGH!

TRIGO SANK DEEPLY... AND THE CREATURE CAME AFTER HIM, JAWS AGAPE!

BUT HELP WAS AT HAND. RULLI TOOK THE ALL-PURPOSE CRAFT INTO A CRASH DIVE!

BLA-A-A-AMMM! ONE CLOSE PROJECTILE RENDERED THE BEAST UNCONSCIOUS!

OTHER DENIZENS OF THE DEEP WERE SWARMING IN AS TRIGO SEIZED HOLD OF THE CRAFT'S WING – AND WAS BORNE TOWARDS THE SURFACE.

NOT A SECOND TOO LATE, THE CRAFT BROKE SURFACE!

RULLI HELPED TRIGO TO CLAW HIS WAY INTO THE COCKPIT.

THAT WAS A CLOSE THING, SIRE!

NEVER CLOSER, CAPTAIN!

I SHALL NEVER FORGET THAT YOU SAVED MY LIFE!

THEY JOURNEYED ON, EVER NORTHWARDS. PRESENTLY, THEY CAME TO THE FARTHEST OUTPOST OF THE TRIGAN CIVILISATION – A LONELY TOWER JUTTING OUT OF THE ICY SEA.

THE LAST REFUELLING BASE. WE'LL FILL OUR TANKS HERE, SIRE.

THERE WAS NO SIGN OF LIFE ABOARD THE BASE.

BUT NO SOONER HAD THEY ALIGHTED FROM THE CRAFT...

HANDS ON HEADS!

BY ALL THE STARS!

LOKANS! TREACHEROUS ANIMALS!

THE MENACING PRESENCE OF THESE SOLDIERS – HIS SUBJECTS – WAS A BITTER REMINDER TO TRIGO THAT HIS PROUD EMPIRE WAS FALLING APART!

WE HAVE BEEN WAITING FOR YOU, IMPERIAL MAJESTY – TO TAKE YOU BACK TO LOKA IN CHAINS!

THE LOKAN LEADER RASPED A HARSH ORDER.

MANACLE THE PRISONERS!

RULLI SAW HIS CHANCE – AND ACTED!

HAAH!

UUUUUUUUH!

TRIGO SWIFTLY FOLLOWED HIS COMPANION'S EXAMPLE.

AAAAAAAAGH!

TWO OF THEIR ENEMY WERE UNCONSCIOUS. THE OTHER PAIR PLUMMETED FROM THE HIGH PLATFORM.

AAAAAAAAAHHH!

NEVER MIND THE REFUELLING, RULLI. WE CAN DO THAT ON THE JOURNEY BACK FROM THE TEMPLE. THE CRAFT THAT BROUGHT THOSE LOKANS HERE WILL SHORTLY RETURN!

THE EMPEROR GUESSED CORRECTLY. EVEN AS THEY ROSE SKYWARDS, A BIG LOKAN BATTLE-CRAFT CAME INTO SIGHT, CANNONS BLAZING.

DIVE, RULLI! DIVE FOR OUR LIVES!

THE ALL-PURPOSE CRAFT PLUNGED BENEATH THE SURFACE OF THE ICY OCEAN WITH PROJECTILES BURSTING ALL ROUND IT!

TRIGO AND RULLI CONTINUED THE REST OF THEIR VOYAGE TO THE NORTHERN POLE IN THE SAME SUBMERGED STATE AND SUFFERED NO FURTHER ATTACKS.

THEY SURFACED ON THE EDGE OF THE ICY SWAMP THAT MARKED THE NORTHERNMOST LAND ON THE PLANET ELEKTON.

THE ARCTIC NIGHT WAS FALLING WHEN THEY CAME TO THE FORBIDDING TEMPLE OF THE SUN.

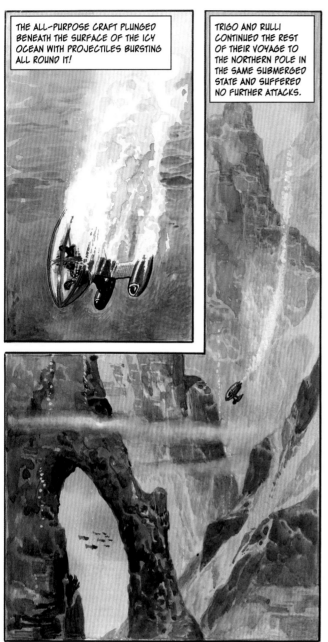

ACCORDING TO THE CHART, SIRE, THE TEMPLE STANDS ON AN ISLAND IN THAT DIRECTION.

THERE IS NO DENYING THAT THE PLACE HAS AN AWESOME ATMOSPHERE, RULLI.

IT WAS HERE THAT OUR FOREFATHERS FIRST WORSHIPPED THE SUNS OF ELEKTON.

I HAVE BROUGHT WINE AND DRIED FRUIT TO MAKE A SYMBOLIC SACRIFICE TO THE SUNS. A LOAD OF MUMBO-JUMBO, RULLI. BUT IT MIGHT – JUST MIGHT – SAVE THE TRIGAN EMPIRE.

YOU THINK SO?

TRIGO TURNED IN SURPRISE AT THE STRANGE TONE OF HIS COMPANION'S VOICE. THE BLOOD-RED RAYS OF THE DYING SUNS GLINTED ON THE MUZZLE OF A GUN.

YOUR CONTEMPTIBLE SACRIFICE OF WINE AND DRIED FRUIT WON'T DO, TRIGO.

WHAT DO YOU MEAN, RULLI? WHAT DEVILRY IS THIS, HEY?

FOOL! WHY DO YOU THINK I PRESERVED YOUR LIFE AT THE RISK OF MY OWN?

IT IS YOU, MIGHTY EMPEROR, WHO WILL BE SACRIFICED TO THE RIDERS OF THE SKY!

TRIGO JUDGED HIS DISTANCE FROM RULLI'S GUN MUZZLE AND TOOK A DEEP BREATH...

WHO ARE YOU?

NOT MERELY THE CAPTAIN OF YOUR IMPERIAL GUARD, I ASSURE YOU.

I AM ALSO THE HEREDITARY CHIEF PRIEST OF THE SUN-WORSHIPPERS!

SMALL WONDER THAT YOUR CURSE CAME TRUE WITH SUCH FREQUENCY!

YES! THE KILLING OF THE COMMEMORATIVE TREE, THE SINKING OF THE "VORG WARRIOR", THE POISONING OF THE WATER SUPPLY AT ZARCUS... I WAS WELL-PLACED TO ASSIST THE WORKINGS OF THE MYSTICAL CURSE!

SUN-WORSHIP, AS WE BOTH KNOW, IS SUPERSTITIOUS RUBBISH DEVISED TO ENTRAP THE IGNORANT – THE SAME IGNORANT FOOLS WHO ARE WAITING FOR ME TO RETURN WITH THE NEWS THAT I HAVE SACRIFICED YOU UPON THE ALTAR!

FAREWELL, EMPEROR. BEFORE THE LUNAR YEAR IS OUT, I EXPECT THE SUN-WORSHIPPERS TO PLACE YOUR CROWN UPON MY HEAD!

RULLI'S GUN BLAZED. TRIGO DUCKED AND THE DISINTEGRATING CHARGE SMASHED INTO THE ANCIENT ALTAR.

THE EMPEROR DIVED.

AAAAAGH!

RULLI WRITHED FREE OF TRIGO'S GRASP, TURNED AND...

EEEEEEEEGH!

MOMENTS LATER, THE TREACHEROUS GUARD CAPTAIN PLUNGED HEADLONG INTO THE ICY MORASS BELOW.

TRIGO SCRAMBLED TO THE RESCUE, BUT RULLI NEVER RESURFACED.

THE TRIGAN EMPIRE – AND ALL ELEKTON – IS SAFE AGAIN!

THE EMPEROR LANDED IN THE GREAT SQUARE OF TRIGAN CITY SOME DAYS LATER.

YOU HAVE MADE A SACRIFICE, IMPERIAL MAJESTY?

THE HEREDITARY CHIEF PRIEST HAS HIMSELF FALLEN VICTIM TO HIS OWN EVIL PLOT TO ENSLAVE OUR PLANET.

THAT NIGHT, HE BROADCAST TO HIS PEOPLE...

I GRANT AN UNCONDITIONAL AMNESTY TO THE SUN-WORSHIPPERS. AND I ASK THOSE AMONG YOU WHO ARE WILLING TO JOIN ME IN WORKING FOR THE GOOD OF THE EMPIRE AND THE PLANET TO EACH PLACE ONE SMALL STONE IN THE GREAT SQUARE THIS NIGHT...

IN THE DAWN, TRIGO LOOKED ACROSS THE GREAT SQUARE, WHERE A SMALL MOUNTAIN OF STONES GLISTENED IN THE LIGHT OF ELEKTON'S TWIN SUNS.

THEY WERE MANY IN NUMBER. MORE THAN WE EVER GUESSED.

THEY COULD HAVE DESTROYED EVERYTHING THE TRIGAN EMPIRE STANDS FOR. BUT NOW THEY'RE ON OUR SIDE.

XLV

THE TRIGAN EMPIRE
THE ROGUE PLANET
Originally published in *Look and Learn* 630 - 634
9th February 1974 - 9th March 1974
Story by Mike Butterworth
Art by Miguel Quesada

IT HAPPENED SUDDENLY AND WITHOUT WARNING. ALL ELEKTON WAS SMITTEN BY A SURFACE TREMOR. BUILDINGS FELL IN THE BROAD STREETS OF TRIGAN CITY.

AAAAAGH! EVERYTHING IS COMING TO AN END!

WE ARE DOOMED!

THE EMPEROR TRIGO BARELY MANAGED TO LEAP FROM HIS BED FOR THE SAFETY OF THE BALCONY, BEFORE THE CEILING OF HIS BEDCHAMBER FELL IN!

IS THIS AN ERUPTION OF THE PLANET?

THE EMPEROR REACHED THE PALACE GARDENS, WHERE HE WAS JOINED BY MEMBERS OF HIS HOUSEHOLD, INCLUDING THE GREAT SCIENTIST PERIC.

WHAT IS IT, PERIC? WHAT'S GOING ON?

IT IS SOME SORT OF DISTURBANCE IN THE UPPER ATMOSPHERE, IMPERIAL MAJESTY! SOMETHING ENTIRELY NEW AND UNIQUE IN MY EXPERIENCE!

DAWN BROUGHT THE SOLUTION TO THE MYSTERY. COUNTLESS MILLIONS LOOKED UP – TO SEE THAT THE SKY ABOVE THEIR PLANET WAS DOMINATED BY A STRANGE NEW SHAPE!

IT IS A NEW WORLD!

IT CAME IN THE NIGHT!

IT IS A MIRACLE!

THAT SAME DAY, PERIC ADDRESSED THE IMPERIAL COUNCIL IN THEIR RUINED CHAMBER.

THIS STRANGE PLANET IS VOLCANIC AND HIGHLY UNSTABLE, WHICH ACCOUNTS FOR ITS UNPREDICTABILITY. IT MAY STAY WITH US FOR EVER – OR IT MAY BE GONE TOMORROW. MY OBSERVATIONS LEAD ME TO SUPPOSE THAT IT MAY BE INHABITED!

THE EMPEROR ASKED THE QUESTION THAT WAS IN EVERY MIND...

CAN THIS PLANET BE REACHED BY ANY MEANS OF OUR TECHNOLOGY?

UNDOUBTEDLY, IMPERIAL MAJESTY! OUR PRESENT ATMOSPHERE CRAFT, SUITABLY MODIFIED, COULD CROSS THE VOID.

WITHIN A MONTH, A LARGE TRANSPORTER CRAFT WAS FITTED WITH BOOSTER ROCKETS FOR THE JOURNEY THROUGH SPACE.

THE ROCKETS WILL CARRY THE CRAFT OUT OF OUR ATMOSPHERE AND ACROSS THE VOID. ON ARRIVAL AT THE NEW PLANET, IT WILL DECELERATE...

THEN WE SHALL VISIT OUR NEW NEIGHBOUR!

THE EMPEROR HIMSELF WAS CAPTAIN OF THE GREAT ADVENTURE. HE LEFT HIS BROTHER BRAG IN CHARGE OF THE EMPIRE.

BE CAREFUL! WE DON'T WANT TO LOSE YOU FOREVER!

HAVE NO FEAR, BRAG. PERIC WILL GIVE US WARNING IF THE NEW PLANET SHOWS SIGNS OF DEPARTING INTO THE WILDERNESS OF SPACE!

THE GREAT ADVENTURE BEGAN!

MAY YOU COME BACK TO US, BROTHER! FOR MY SHOULDERS ARE NOT BROAD ENOUGH TO BEAR YOUR EMPIRE!

IT WAS A COMPARATIVELY SHORT JOURNEY. THEY CROSSED THE VOID THAT SEPARATED THE TWO PLANETS.

STAND BY TO DECELERATE...

AND SOON THEY WERE FLYING OVER AN ALIEN LANDSCAPE.

LOOK OUT FOR ANY SIGNS OF HABITATION!

AND THEN, TRIGO AND HIS COMPANIONS SAW...*IT!*

BY ALL THE STARS! DO YOU SEE THAT?

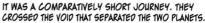

JANNO BROUGHT THE TRIGAN CRAFT LOW. AND THEY FLEW OVER A VAST TENTED ENCAMPMENT. A MULTITUDE OF FACES WERE TURNED TO LOOK AT THEM.

THE EMPEROR AND HIS COMPANIONS LOOKED DOWN.

ARE MY EYES DECEIVING ME, OR?...

IT'S A VORG ENCAMPMENT! ONE OF THE PRIMITIVE KINDS YOU USED TO SEE ON ELEKTON!

TRIGO ORDERED JANNO TO LAND. THEY CLIMBED DOWN FROM THEIR CRAFT.

ARE THEY PEACEFUL, UNCLE – OR SHALL WE HAVE TROUBLE?

BE PREPARED TO START SHOOTING!

THEN, TO THE FIVE TRIGANS' UTTER ASTONISHMENT; THEY WERE ADDRESSED IN THE COMMON LANGUAGE OF THEIR OWN PLANET!

I AM GARRON, CHIEFTAIN OF THE ZOOTHA VORGS! I WELCOME YOU TO PLANET ZOOTHA!

YOU ARE ONE OF US...FROM ELEKTON?

THAT IS SO! IN A TIME LONG PAST, WHEN ZOOTHA LAST CAME CLOSE TO ELEKTON, SOME OF OUR PEOPLE VENTURED ACROSS THE WILDERNESS OF SPACE TO THIS PLANET, AS YOU HAVE DONE!

GARRON SHOWED THEM THE CRUMBLING RUINS OF AN ANCIENT FLYING CRAFT.

THIS IS THE CRAFT IN WHICH OUR ANCESTORS CAME. IT IS A TREASURED RELIC OF OUR PEOPLE!

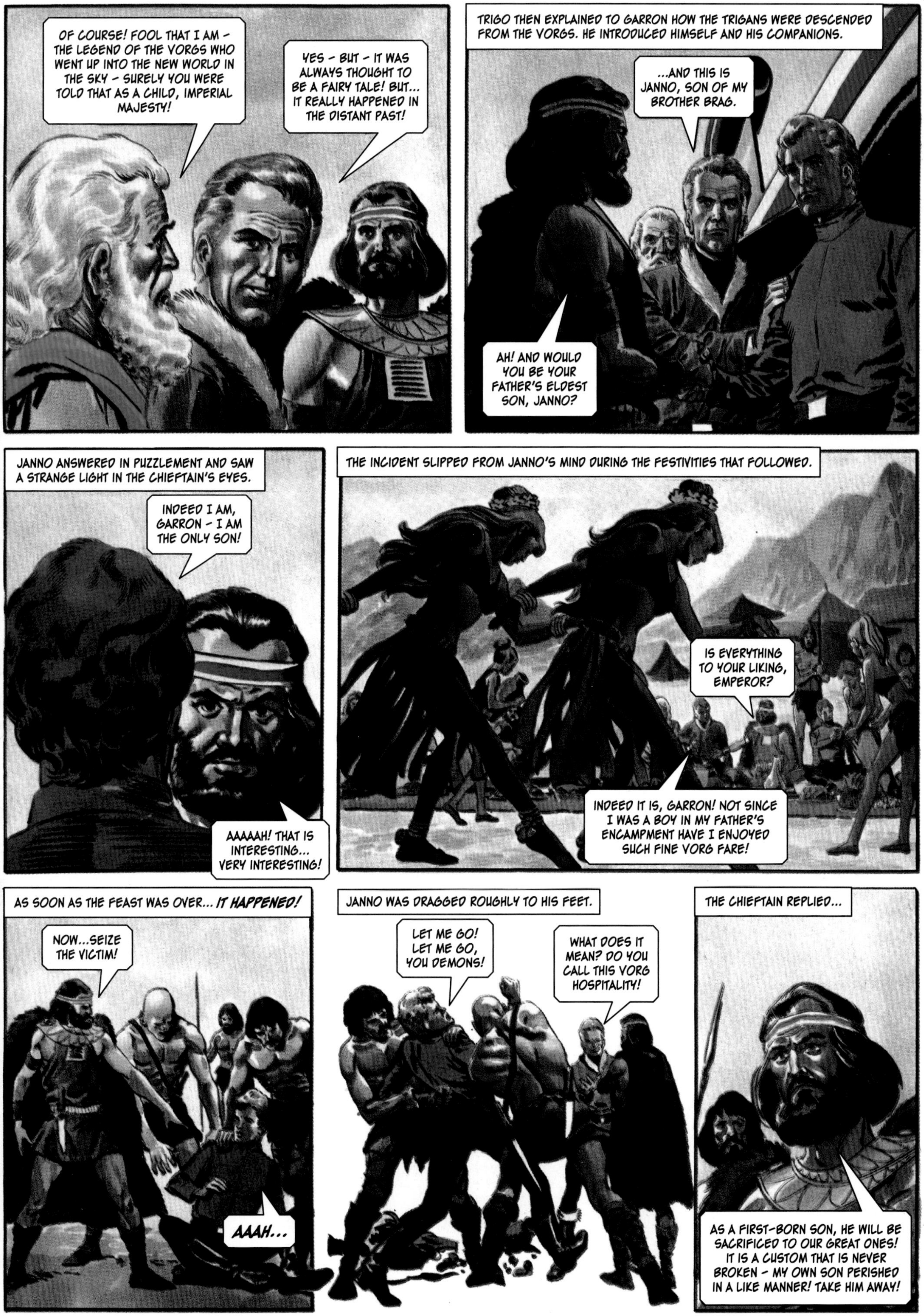
OF COURSE! FOOL THAT I AM – THE LEGEND OF THE VORGS WHO WENT UP INTO THE NEW WORLD IN THE SKY – SURELY YOU WERE TOLD THAT AS A CHILD, IMPERIAL MAJESTY!
YES – BUT – IT WAS ALWAYS THOUGHT TO BE A FAIRY TALE! BUT... IT REALLY HAPPENED IN THE DISTANT PAST!
TRIGO THEN EXPLAINED TO GARRON HOW THE TRIGANS WERE DESCENDED FROM THE VORGS. HE INTRODUCED HIMSELF AND HIS COMPANIONS.
...AND THIS IS JANNO, SON OF MY BROTHER BRAG.
AH! AND WOULD YOU BE YOUR FATHER'S ELDEST SON, JANNO?
JANNO ANSWERED IN PUZZLEMENT AND SAW A STRANGE LIGHT IN THE CHIEFTAIN'S EYES.
INDEED I AM, GARRON – I AM THE ONLY SON!
AAAAAH! THAT IS INTERESTING... VERY INTERESTING!
THE INCIDENT SLIPPED FROM JANNO'S MIND DURING THE FESTIVITIES THAT FOLLOWED.
IS EVERYTHING TO YOUR LIKING, EMPEROR?
INDEED IT IS, GARRON! NOT SINCE I WAS A BOY IN MY FATHER'S ENCAMPMENT HAVE I ENJOYED SUCH FINE VORG FARE!
AS SOON AS THE FEAST WAS OVER... IT HAPPENED!
NOW...SEIZE THE VICTIM!
AAAH...
JANNO WAS DRAGGED ROUGHLY TO HIS FEET.
LET ME GO! LET ME GO, YOU DEMONS!
WHAT DOES IT MEAN? DO YOU CALL THIS VORG HOSPITALITY!
THE CHIEFTAIN REPLIED...
AS A FIRST-BORN SON, HE WILL BE SACRIFICED TO OUR GREAT ONES! IT IS A CUSTOM THAT IS NEVER BROKEN – MY OWN SON PERISHED IN A LIKE MANNER! TAKE HIM AWAY!

BEHOLD — THE GREAT ONES!

TRIGO WAS DEEPLY IMPRESSED.

THEY LOOK LIKE GODS! DO SUCH CREATURES LIVE?

THEY LIVE! AND THEY DEMAND THE SACRIFICE OF THE BEST THINGS WE HAVE — OUR BEST FLOCKS, FINEST FOODSTUFFS, AND OUR FIRST-BORN SONS. IN RETURN, THEY ALLOW US TO LIVE AND PROSPER!

GARRON POINTED TO JANNO.

THAT ONE WILL BE SACRIFICED TO THE GREAT ONES THIS DAY! OPPOSE THIS AT YOUR PERIL, MIGHTY EMPEROR!

JANNO WAS BROUGHT TO A GREAT CAVE MOUTH...

HE WAS TIED THERE...

SOON, NOBLE YOUTH, YOU WILL HAVE THE HONOUR OF PERISHING AT THE HANDS OF THE GREAT ONES!

AAAH...

TRIGO, ON THE PRETEXT OF SAYING FAREWELL TO HIS NEPHEW, WHISPERED AS ASSURANCE IN HIS EAR.

I WILL SAVE YOU, JANNO! NEVER FEAR - YOU WILL NOT BE ABANDONED! DO YOU UNDERSTAND?

YES, UNCLE.

A MIGHTY HORN WAS SOUNDED. ITS MOURNFUL NOTE ECHOED AND RE-ECHOED IN THE DEEP FASTNESSES OF THE GREAT CAVERN.

THEN JANNO WAS LEFT STANDING ALONE, IN THE GROWING DARKNESS.

HOW... HOW LONG DO I HAVE TO WAIT?

HE WAS NOT ALONE FOR LONG!

AAAAAAH!

OUT OF THE DARKNESS OF THE GREAT CAVERN... *THEY* CAME!

SOME DISTANCE AWAY, IN THE VORG CAMP, WHEN ALL WAS SILENT, TRIGO ROSE TO HIS FEET.

FIRST - TO DEAL WITH THAT SENTRY!

THE TRIGAN EMPEROR SET OFF TO KEEP HIS PROMISE.

I HOPE I AM NOT TOO LATE!

TRIGO REACHED THE CAVE MOUTH.

GONE! JANNO HAS GONE!

HE GAZED UP AT THE STAKE WHERE HIS NEPHEW HAD BEEN TIED.

THEY'VE TAKEN HIM! IT MAY BE THAT ALL I CAN DO NOW IS TO EXACT VENGEANCE!

ENTERING THE VAST CAVE MOUTH, HE SAW...

THERE'S LIGHT DOWN THERE!

HE DESCENDED INTO THE GLOOM. PRESENTLY, THE TRIGAN EMPEROR WAS GAZING UPON A SCENE THAT STAGGERED THE IMAGINATION.

BY ALL THE STARS! IT IS A WORLD WITHIN A WORLD!

THERE WAS A VAST UNDERGROUND CITY, ALL BATHED IN A PHOSPHORESCENT GLOW THAT WAS BRIGHTER THAN DAYLIGHT.

AS TRIGO STARED IN AWE, A GROUP OF SLAVES TOILED PAST, GUARDED BY HIDEOUS, SQUAT CREATURES.

AT A CURT ORDER FROM THEIR GUARDS, THE WEARY SLAVES STOPPED TO REST.

IF I COULD GET CLOSER AND SPEAK TO ONE OF THOSE POOR WRETCHES...

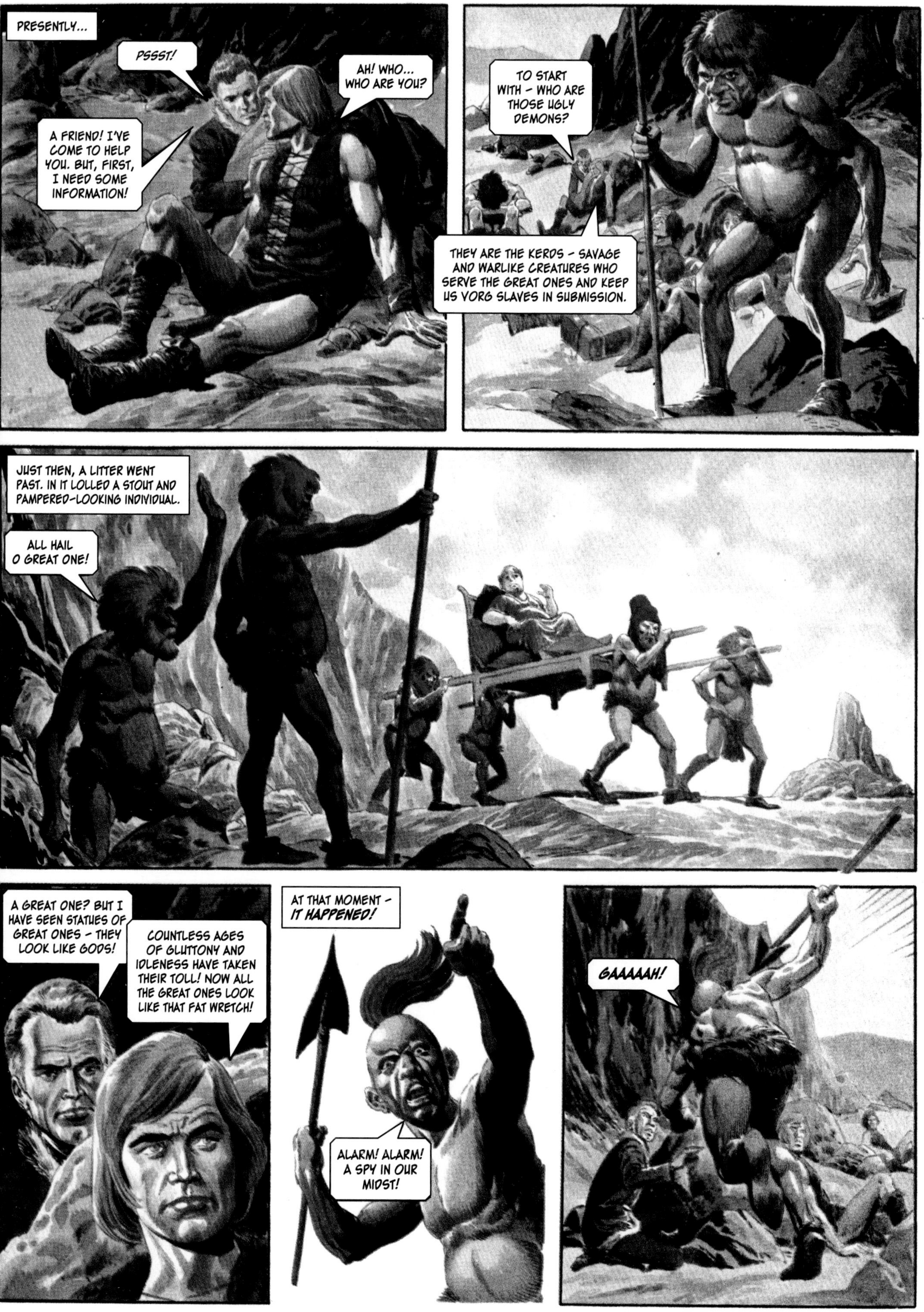
PRESENTLY...
PSSST!
AH! WHO... WHO ARE YOU?
A FRIEND! I'VE COME TO HELP YOU. BUT, FIRST, I NEED SOME INFORMATION!
TO START WITH - WHO ARE THOSE UGLY DEMONS?
THEY ARE THE KEROS - SAVAGE AND WARLIKE CREATURES WHO SERVE THE GREAT ONES AND KEEP US VORG SLAVES IN SUBMISSION.
JUST THEN, A LITTER WENT PAST. IN IT LOLLED A STOUT AND PAMPERED-LOOKING INDIVIDUAL.
ALL HAIL O GREAT ONE!
A GREAT ONE? BUT I HAVE SEEN STATUES OF GREAT ONES - THEY LOOK LIKE GODS!
COUNTLESS AGES OF GLUTTONY AND IDLENESS HAVE TAKEN THEIR TOLL! NOW ALL THE GREAT ONES LOOK LIKE THAT FAT WRETCH!
AT THAT MOMENT - IT HAPPENED!
ALARM! ALARM! A SPY IN OUR MIDST!
GAAAAAH!

AN INSTANT BEFORE CERTAIN DESTRUCTION, TRIGO ROLLED SIDEWAYS – AND THE KERD'S SPEAR SHATTERED AGAINST THE ROCK CLOSE TO THE EMPEROR'S HEAD!

UUUGH!

PICKING UP THE SMALL, MUSCULAR FORM, TRIGO HURLED THE KERD INTO THE FACES OF HIS ONCOMING COMRADES.

AAAAGH!

UUUUUGH!

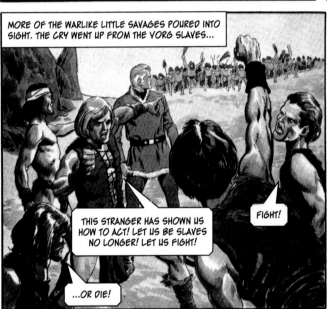

MORE OF THE WARLIKE LITTLE SAVAGES POURED INTO SIGHT. THE CRY WENT UP FROM THE VORG SLAVES...

THIS STRANGER HAS SHOWN US HOW TO ACT! LET US BE SLAVES NO LONGER! LET US FIGHT!

FIGHT!

...OR DIE!

THE SLAVES FOUGHT, AND TRIGO FOUGHT WITH THEM. BUT THEY WERE OVERPOWERED BY SHEER WEIGHT OF NUMBERS.

TAKE THEM ALIVE! THE GREAT ONES SHALL DECIDE THEIR FATE!

THEY WERE DRAGGED TO THE CITY, AND BROUGHT BEFORE THE STOUT AND PAMPERED CREATURES WHO RULED THE PLANET BY FEAR.

NO-ONE DEFIES THE LAW OF THE GREAT ONES! YOU SHALL PERISH!

THEN – IT HAPPENED!...

TAKE THEM AWAY AND...

AAAAAAAAH!

THE GROUND TREMBLED! A MIGHTY ROARING FILLED THE AIR! THE GREAT BUILDING COLLAPSED!

IT IS HAPPENING AGAIN! THE PLANET IS MOVING!

VORGS! RALLY TO ME! LET US GAIN THE UPPER WORLD!

TRIGO LED THE VORGS THROUGH THE TUNNEL AND OUT OF THE VAST CAVE MOUTH ON THE SURFACE OF THE PLANET. GREAT WAS THE EMPEROR'S JOY TO FIND THAT HIS NEPHEW WAS AMONG THOSE WHOM HE HAD BROUGHT OUT.

JANNO! THANK THE STARS YOU'RE ALIVE!

I WAS CONDEMNED TO A LIFETIME OF SLAVERY, UNCLE - BUT I NEVER DOUBTED THAT YOU'D KEEP YOUR PROMISE AND SAVE ME!

THEY REJOINED THE OTHERS IN THE VORG CAMP. IT WAS A TIME OF JOYFUL REUNIONS.

MY SON! MY FIRST-BORN! WHEN I DELIVERED YOU TO THE GREAT ONES AS A SACRIFICE, I NEVER THOUGHT TO SEE YOU AGAIN!

THE GREAT ONES ARE NOT GODS, FATHER. NOW THE MYTH IS DESTROYED, WE SHALL NEVER SACRIFICE TO THEM AGAIN!

WHERE ARE THE GREAT ONES NOW, MY SON?

IN THE NETHER-WORLD, TOGETHER WITH THEIR MINIONS THE KERDS. THEY FEAR TO SET FOOT UP HERE. WE SHALL NEVER BE BOTHERED WITH THEM AGAIN.

THE VOLCANIC DISTURBANCE DROVE THEM INTO A STATE OF TERROR.

THE GREAT SCIENTIST PERIC BROKE IN...

SPEAKING OF VOLCANIC DISTURBANCE, THE SIGNED ARE THAT THIS PLANET IS IN A HIGHLY UNSTABLE STATE AND WILL SHORTLY BE CHANGING ITS ORBIT AGAIN! WE MUST RETURN TO ELEKTON BEFORE IT IS TOO LATE!

TRIGO ADDRESSED THE CHIEFTAIN, POINTING TO THE VAST BULK OF ELEKTON ABOVE THEM.

GARRON! THERE MAY BE TIME, YET, TO SEND SPACE-CRAFT TO TAKE YOU AND YOUR PEOPLE TO THE PLANET OF YOUR FOREFATHERS. WHAT DO YOU SAY?

ZOOTHA IS OUR HOME, MIGHTY EMPEROR. HERE WE WILL STAY. THANKS TO YOU, LIFE WILL BE INFINITELY SWEETER FROM NOW ON!

THAT EVENING, THE TRIGANS TOOK OFF FOR THEIR RETURN VOYAGE ACROSS THE WILDERNESS OF SPACE.

FAREWELL!

FAREWELL!

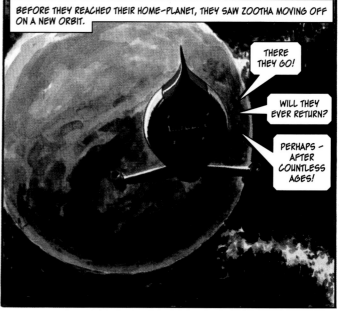

BEFORE THEY REACHED THEIR HOME-PLANET, THEY SAW ZOOTHA MOVING OFF ON A NEW ORBIT.

THERE THEY GO!

WILL THEY EVER RETURN?

PERHAPS - AFTER COUNTLESS AGES!

XLVI

THE TRIGAN EMPIRE
THE MELTING ICE CAPS
Originally published in *Look and Learn* 635 - 644
16th March 1974 - 18th May 1974
Story by Mike Butterworth
Art by Philip Corke

WHAT IS IT, DAD?

SON! WE'RE GOING TO LEAVE THIS TO THE COPS!

THE CRAFT AND ITS DEAD CREW WERE SUBJECTED TO THE MOST DETAILED SCRUTINY...

IT IS CLEAR THAT THESE QUASI-HUMAN CREATURES ARE NOT OF OUR GALAXY, AND THAT THEIR INTELLIGENCE IS EQUAL – OR MORE – OF OUR OWN...

THE HEART OF THE MYSTERY LAY IN THE PRINTED BOOKS THAT WERE CARRIED ABOARD THE CRAFT. IT TOOK PROFESSOR P.R. HADDON OF BOSTON, MASSACHUSETTS A LIFETIME OF WORK TO DECIPHER THE ALIEN WRITINGS.

I'VE DONE IT AT LAST!

THE BOOKS TOLD OF ANOTHER WORLD IN DEEP SPACE: THE PLANET ELEKTON IN THE GALAXY OF YARNA. THE GREATEST POWER ON ELEKTON IS THE TRIGAN EMPIRE, RULED OVER BY ITS FOUNDER, THE EMPEROR TRIGO. MUCH OF THE STORY OF THE TRIGAN EMPIRE HAS ALREADY BEEN RECOUNTED. WE NOW CONTINUE WITH THE BEGINNING OF THE SEVENTH BOOK.

IT WAS IN THE SECOND YEAR OF SERTH (BEGINS THE SEVENTH BOOK) THAT DWELLERS IN THE RIVER VALLEYS BEYOND THE PLAIN OF VORG NOTICED A STRANGE BEHAVIOUR.

LOOK! WATER'S COMING UP OUT OF THE FLOOR!

THE RIVER'S NEVER BEEN SO HIGH IN LIVING MEMORY!

AND THERE HASN'T BEEN A DROP OF RAIN ALL THIS LONG, HOT SUMMER!

THE AIR FLEET CARRIER 'DAVELI' WAS CRUISING IN THE SOUTHERN OCEAN AND THE CREWS WERE PRACTISING LANDINGS.

JANNO, THE EMPEROR'S NEPHEW RECEIVED A FATEFUL SUMMONS THAT DAY.

LIEUTENANT, THERE'S A MESSAGE FROM TRIGAN CITY. YOU'RE TO RETURN THERE AT ONCE, TO ATTEND AN IMPERIAL CONFERENCE.

AN IMPERIAL CONFERENCE? - ABOUT WHAT, I WONDER?

THE FOLLOWING DAY, JANNO TOOK HIS PLACE IN THE VAST AUDIENCE CHAMBER OF THE IMPERIAL PALACE. PRESENT WERE THE MEMBERS OF THE IMPERIAL FAMILY, HEADS OF STATES, AND MILITARY CHIEFS OF THE EMPIRE. ELEKTON'S TOP SCIENTIST, PERIC, ROSE TO ADDRESS THEM. HIS OPENING WORDS STUNNED THEM INTO SILENCE...

MY FRIENDS!... THIS PLANET IS FACED WITH DISASTER!

PERIC TOUCHED A BUTTON - AND A LARGE MODEL WAS UNVEILED.

THIS, AS YOU WILL RECOGNISE, IS THE PLAIN OF VORG AND THE MOUNTAINS THAT FLANK IT ON EACH SIDE. AT THE FAR END OF THE PLAIN, ON THE RIVER VORG, IS TRIGAN CITY...

IT HAS BEEN OBSERVED IN ALL PARTS OF THE EMPIRE - AS YOU ALL KNOW WELL - THAT WATER LEVELS ARE RISING, DESPITE THE SUMMER'S DROUGHT. THIS IS CAUSED BY THE MELTING OF THE ICE CAPS AT OUR POLES, WHICH, IN ITS TURN, IS CAUSED BY THE PRESENT PROXIMITY OF OUR SUN.

HE TOUCHED ANOTHER BUTTON. INSTANTLY, THERE WAS A RUSHING OF WATERS... A DEVASTATING INUNDATION!

WATCH CLOSELY! - TRIGAN CITY IS BEING CARRIED AWAY!

THIS, MY FRIENDS, IS WHAT WILL HAPPEN IN THREE LUNAR MONTHS' TIME! BY THAT TIME, ALL THE REST OF THE PLANET WILL BE UNDER WATER! THE DESTRUCTION OF TRIGAN CITY WILL SPELL THE END OF LIFE ON THE PLANET OF ELEKTON!

WITHIN ANOTHER LUNAR MONTH (CONTINUES THE SEVENTH BOOK), THE SURFACE OF THE WATERS ROSE ALL OVER ELEKTON, ENGULFING THE HOMES OF THE POOR...

COURAGE! WE MUST BE BRAVE! THE EMPEROR WILL SEE TO IT THAT WE COME TO NO HARM!

...AND THE RICH, ALIKE!

WHAT'S TO BECOME OF US? NO ONE CAN AID US...EVEN THE EMPEROR IS HELPLESS!

WOULD IT WORK?... WOULD IT, I WONDER?

IN HIS PRIVATE LABORATORY AT THE IMPERIAL PALACE IN TRIGAN CITY, ELEKTON'S TOP SCIENTIST, PERIC, WORKED DAY AND NIGHT ON THE PROBLEM.

FROM TIME TO TIME, HE WOULD CALL UPON HIS YOUNG FRIEND JANNO.

JANNO - I WOULD LIKE TO SEE THE PLAIN OF VORG AGAIN - AT LOW LEVEL.

IT WAS A SHORT FLIGHT FROM THE CITY TO THE PLAIN AND ITS FLANKING MOUNTAIN RANGES. PERIC ASKED, AGAIN AND AGAIN, TO BE TAKEN UP AND DOWN THE LENGTH OF THE WIDE PLAIN.

I HAVE A PLAN TO SAVE THE PLAIN OF VORG AND TRIGAN CITY - BUT TIME IS FAST RUNNING OUT!

PERIC PRESENTED HIS PLAN TO THE EMPEROR TRIGO AND HIS MINISTERS THAT SAME DAY.

A WALL?

A DAM, SIRE! - STRETCHING ACROSS THE NARROWEST PART OF THE VALLEY!

AS ON PREVIOUS OCCASION, PERIC TOUCHED A BUTTON THAT BROUGHT A TORRENT OF WATER RUSHING DOWN THE VALLEY. BUT, THIS TIME, IT REACHED NO FURTHER THAN THE WALL!

THE WALL HAS SAVED THE PLAIN AND THE CITY!

AS I TOLD YOU, MAJESTY, THIS WILL BE THE LAST AREA OF LAND TO BE INUNDATED...AND THE WALL COULD SAVE IT, IF WE CAN BUILD IN TIME!

TRIGO'S VOICE RANG OUT, COMMANDINGLY.

THE TOTAL RESOURCES OF THE EMPIRE WILL BE POURED INTO THE BUILDING OF THE WALL! WHEN IT IS DONE, EVERY MAN, WOMAN AND CHILD ON ELEKTON WHO CHOOSES TO SHELTER BEHIND IT WILL BE WELCOMED WITH OPEN ARMS!

THE VAST PROJECT BEGAN. WITHIN A LUNAR MONTH (WHEN MORE THAN HALF THE PLANET WAS UNDER WATER), THE WALL TOWERED HIGH ABOVE THE PLAIN OF VORG.

A CONSTANT STREAM OF REFUGEES SWARMED IN FROM THE SUBMERGED PARTS OF ELEKTON. THE ONLY REQUIREMENTS FOR ADMITTANCE WERE THE GIVING-UP OF ALL OFFENSIVE WEAPONS - AND THE PROMISE TO OBEY THE LAWS OF THE TRIGAN EMPIRE.

ONE LARGE PARTY GAVE SOME CAUSE FOR ANXIETY. THESE WERE LOKANS - A SUBJECT RACE OF THE TRIGAN EMPIRE.

WEAPONS?

IT IS DEATH FOR A LOKAN TO BEAR ARMS - THAT IS TRIGAN LAW. AS YOU WELL KNOW!

BUT WE LOKANS WILL BE AVENGED - IF WE HAVE TO WIPE OUT THE WHOLE PLANET IN THE PROCESS, AND OURSELVES WITH IT!

CAME A FATEFUL DAWN, WHEN THE SOUND OF TOIL CEASED. THE LAST STONE WAS PLACED UPON ANOTHER, MILLIONS OF TOILERS LAID DOWN THEIR TOOLS — AND THE GREAT WALL WAS FINISHED!

FROM THE TOWERING TOP, THE EMPEROR AND HIS COMPANIONS LOOKED DOWN AT THE APPROACHING WATERS.

NOT A DAY TOO SOON! BY NIGHTFALL, THE PLAIN WILL BE COVERED!

TRIGAN CITY ON ITS FIVE HILLS, AND ALL THE PLAIN SURROUNDING IT, WAS COVERED BY THE DENSE MASSES OF REFUGEES FROM ALL OVER THE PLANET.

THE LOKANS KEPT THEMSELVES APART.

THE WALL IS FINISHED AND THE WATERS HAVE COME. WE WILL STRIKE BEFORE SUNSET!

THE DAY OF VENGEANCE HAS COME!

ONLY ONE DISSENTING VOICE WAS RAISED.

WHAT SORT OF VENGEANCE IS IT — WHEN WE DESTROY EVERYONE, INCLUDING OURSELVES?

SILENCE! WHAT DO YOU KNOW OF THE WRONGS WE HAVE SUFFERED AT THE HANDS OF TRIGANS?

PASS IT BACK!

LOAD IT ABOARD THE CART!

EVERY LOKAN MAN, WOMAN AND CHILD PRODUCED A PIECE OF GREY MATERIAL.

ENOUGH EXPLOSIVE TO TEAR A HOLE IN THE WALL AND DESTROY TRIGAN CITY!

THE MATERIAL WAS LOADED INTO THE CART AND COVERED WITH A LAYER OF FRUIT.

LATE THAT AFTERNOON, JANNO WENT DOWN TO THE QUAYSIDE BELOW THE CITY. HIS SHIP, THE 'DAVELI', TOGETHER WITH OTHER UNITS OF THE FLEET, HAD JUST ARRIVED.

SUDDENLY...

MY LORD! I MUST SPEAK WITH YOU!

WHAT DO YOU WANT, LOKAN?

MY PEOPLE! — THEY ARE GOING TO BLOW UP THE WALL!

BY THAT TIME, THE SURGING WATERS HAD CLIMBED ALMOST TO THE VERY TOP OF THE PROTECTIVE WALL.

TRIGAN GUARDS, PARCHED IN THE RAYS OF THE DYING SUNS, WERE GLAD TO SEE THE ARRIVAL OF THE LOKANS AND THEIR CART.

MELONS! LOVELY, JUICY MELONS!

HOW MUCH, YOU LOKANS?

FOR OUR FRIENDS, THE TRIGANS, WHO HAVE SAVED US FROM THE TERROR OF THE WATERS — NOTHING!

HUH?

THAT IS THE LAST MOUTHFUL EVER TO PASS YOUR LIPS TRIGAN ANIMAL!

MOMENTS LATER...

IT WAS AT THE HOUR OF SUNSET, JUST AS ELEKTON'S TWIN SUNS WERE DIPPING BELOW THE HORIZON, THAT A MIGHTY EXPLOSION RIPPED A GASH IN THE GREAT WALL!

AAAAAAH!

THERE'S NO ESCAPE!

THE TIDAL WAVE OF DESTRUCTION BURST DOWN THE GATES OF TRIGAN CITY AND THE BUILDINGS BEYOND.

JANNO, FLYING TO INVESTIGATE THE REPORTED SABOTAGE, LOOKED DOWN AND SAW A WALL OF WATER TEAR DOWN THE PLAIN OF VORG.

I WAS TOO LATE TO STOP THE ACCURSED LOKANS!

THE SHIPS OF THE TRIGAN FLEET WERE CAUGHT LIKE STRAWS IN A WHIRLPOOL. EVEN THE HUGE AIR FLEET CARRIER 'DAVELI' WAS ALL BUT SUNK!

LATER, WHEN JANNO PUT HIS CRAFT DOWN UPON THE ROOF OF THE IMPERIAL PALACE, NOTHING REMAINED OF THE CITY BUT THE FIVE HILLS AND THE BUILDINGS THAT CROWNED THEM.

HIS UNCLE, THE EMPEROR TRIGO, GREETED THE YOUNG PILOT.

I WAS TOO LATE!

NOT TOO LATE TO SAVE MOST OF THE PEOPLE, JANNO. THANKS TO YOUR WARNING, WE WERE ABLE TO GET THEM TO HIGHER GROUND IN TIME.

THERE WAS SOMEONE ELSE – THE LOKAN YOUTH WHO HAD BETRAYED THE PLOT TO JANNO...

LORD, JANNO, MY NAME IS ZARO. THERE IS NOTHING I CAN DO TO WIPE OUT MY PEOPLE'S CRIME – BUT I SHOULD LIKE TO SERVE WITH YOU!

I SHALL BE PROUD TO HAVE YOU AS A COMRADE, ZARO!

THE FOLLOWING DAWN, THE WATERS CONTINUED TO RISE. SO GREAT WAS THE PRESS OF PEOPLE THAT MANY WERE TRANSFERRED TO THE MOUNTAIN TOPS THAT WERE NOW A STRING OF ISLANDS.

PERIC ADDRESSED THE IMPERIAL COUNCIL AT THE END OF THE FIRST DAY OF THE INUNDATION.

IMPERIAL MAJESTY...LORDS... OUR SMALL STRING OF ISLANDS CAN KEEP ALIVE THE SURVIVORS WHO WILL REPOPULATE THE PLANET WHEN THE WATER'S SUBSIDE!

ONE PERIL THAT PERIC HAD OVERLOOKED WAS...*THEM!* *THEY* HAD NEVER BEEN SEEN BEFORE THE GREAT FLOOD – BUT *THEY* SOON MADE THEIR PRESENCE KNOWN!

FOOD BECAME A PROBLEM. DAY AND NIGHT, FISHING BOATS TOILED AT THEIR TASK OF PROVIDING FOR THE TEEMING MULTITUDES.

SUDDENLY, THE HELMSMAN SAW...

AAAAAH!

...THE FACE OF EVIL!

THE BOAT WAS FROM ONE OF THE ISLANDS THAT WAS POPULATED BY PEOPLE FROM THE FORMER PROVINCE OF THARV. NEXT MORNING, THEY FOUND IT DRIFTING...

WHAT COULD HAVE HAPPENED?

THAT'S EASY TO ANSWER! SOMEONE ATTACKED THEM, THREW OUR LADS OVERBOARD AND STOLE THEIR CATCH!

WHO WOULD DO SUCH A THING?

THE PEOPLE FROM OVER THERE - WHO ELSE? THE ANIMALS FROM CATO!

ACCURSED CATONS! NEVER TRUST A CATON, MY FATHER USED TO SAY!

ANCIENT HATREDS HAVING BEEN AROUSED, THE THARVS SET OUT TO AVENGE THE IMAGINED CRIME!

LONG LIVE THARV! DOWN WITH THE CATON MURDERERS!

THROW THEM BACK INTO THE SEA!

SOON, A BATTLE WAS RAGING!

SHARE THAT BETWEEN YOU, THARVS!

AAAAAGH!

EEEEEEGH!

THE TURMOIL WAS ONLY ENDED BY THE ARRIVAL OF A TRIGAN AIRCRAFT.

CEASE FIGHTING! OR WE OPEN FIRE ON YOU ALL!

THE EMPEROR TRIGO HIMSELF ARRIVED.

YOU'VE LOST YOUR HOMELANDS AND YOUR POSSESSIONS! HAVE YOU ALSO TAKEN LEAVE OF YOUR SENSES!

THE CATONS RAIDED ONE OF OUR FISHING BOATS!

THAT IS A LIE!

SILENCE! IF THIS KIND OF MADNESS CONTINUES, THERE WILL BE NO ONE LEFT TO REBUILD THIS PLANET OF OURS! FROM NOW ON, ALL SURVIVORS WILL LIVE IN MIXED GROUPS – NO MORE TRIBAL WARFARE!

THE FOLLOWING DAWN, ABOARD THE AIR FLEET CARRIER 'DAVELI'.

AAAAAAAHHHHH!

IN THE EARLY LIGHT, IT WAS SEEN THAT THE 'DAVELI' WAS SINKING!

ONE SHATTERING EXPLOSION AND THE 'DAVELI' PLUNGED INTO THE DEPTHS!

THE EMPEROR CONDUCTED AN ENQUIRY INTO THE DISASTER.

HOW DID IT HAPPEN?

NONE OF THE SURVIVORS WERE ABLE TO TELL, IMPERIAL MAJESTY! ALL WE KNOW IS THAT, SHORTLY AFTER DAY BREAK, THE SHIP SUDDENLY BEGAN TO SINK!

THE EMPEROR'S OWN NEPHEW WAS THE FIRST TO RESPOND.

I'LL GO!

AND I!

TO LOSE MORE VESSELS, IN OUR PRESENT PLIGHT, WOULD BE A DOUBLE DISASTER! I CALL FOR TWO VOLUNTEERS TO EXAMINE THE WRECK!

THE SECOND VOLUNTEER WAS THE LOKAN YOUTH, ZARO. LATER...

STRANGE TO THINK OF YOU - A LOKAN - IN THE SERVICE OF THE EMPEROR!

I HAVE TO MAKE SOME AMENDS FOR THE TERRIBLE WRONGS THAT MY PEOPLE DID UNDER THE EVIL LEADERSHIP OF YORRI-ZIM.

YORRI-ZIM WAS A SON OF THE TYRANT ZORTH, LAST KING OF THE LOKANS. BY OUR TRADITIONS OF OBEDIENCE, WE WERE BOUND TO FOLLOW HIM!

I DISOBEYED HIM AND BETRAYED HIM! I THANK THE STARS THAT HE PERISHED IN THE DELUGE!

BUT ZARO WAS WRONG! DAY AND NIGHT, A PAIR OF HATE-FILLED EYES WATCHED THE IMPERIAL PALACE, FROM A ROOFTOP NEARBY.

IT WAS...YORRI-ZIM!

ONCE TRIGO SHOWS HIMSELF, I WILL DESTROY HIM! WHEN HE IS GONE, THE REST OF THEM WILL TURN AND TEAR EACH OTHER APART! I SHALL BE THE LAST MAN ALIVE ON ELEKTON!

ALL EYES WERE UPON JANNO AND ZARO AS THEY PLUNGED INTO THE FLOOD WATERS.

GOOD LUCK!

DOWN...DOWN...DOWN... PAST FAMILIAR, SUBMERGED LANDMARKS.

THERE'S THE GREAT GATE OF THE CITY!

PRESENTLY...

THE 'DAVELI'!

AS THEY DREW NEAR THE SUNKEN CRAFT, JANNO HAD A PREMONITION OF PERIL. TURNING, HE SAW...THEM!

ZARO! BEHIND YOU!

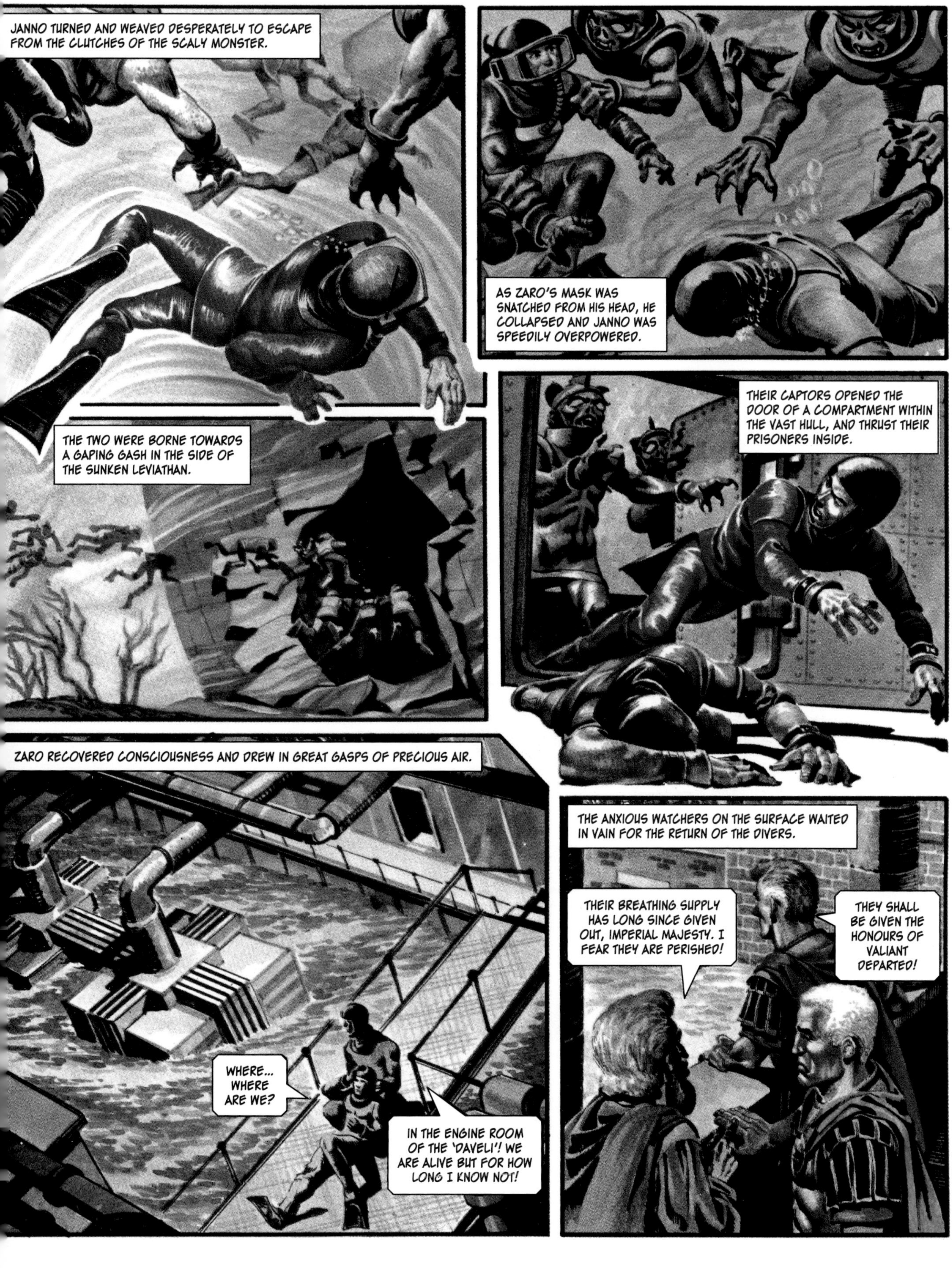
JANNO TURNED AND WEAVED DESPERATELY TO ESCAPE FROM THE CLUTCHES OF THE SCALY MONSTER.
AS ZARO'S MASK WAS SNATCHED FROM HIS HEAD, HE COLLAPSED AND JANNO WAS SPEEDILY OVERPOWERED.
THE TWO WERE BORNE TOWARDS A GAPING GASH IN THE SIDE OF THE SUNKEN LEVIATHAN.
THEIR CAPTORS OPENED THE DOOR OF A COMPARTMENT WITHIN THE VAST HULL, AND THRUST THEIR PRISONERS INSIDE.
ZARO RECOVERED CONSCIOUSNESS AND DREW IN GREAT GASPS OF PRECIOUS AIR.
WHERE... WHERE ARE WE?
IN THE ENGINE ROOM OF THE 'DAVELI'! WE ARE ALIVE BUT FOR HOW LONG I KNOW NOT!
THE ANXIOUS WATCHERS ON THE SURFACE WAITED IN VAIN FOR THE RETURN OF THE DIVERS.
THEIR BREATHING SUPPLY HAS LONG SINCE GIVEN OUT, IMPERIAL MAJESTY. I FEAR THEY ARE PERISHED!
THEY SHALL BE GIVEN THE HONOURS OF VALIANT DEPARTED!

SALUTES WERE FIRED OVER THE SPOT. A FLIGHT OF TRIGAN FIGHTING CRAFT DIPPED OVERHEAD, AS THE EMPEROR THREW A CHAPLET OF FLOWERS INTO THE WATER.

THE EMPIRE WILL NEVER FORGET!

LATER, A WEBBED HAND TOOK THE CHAPLET AND DREW IT BENEATH THE SURFACE!

ON HIS WAY BACK UP TO THE IMPERIAL PALACE, TRIGO SUDDENLY FELT HIS BROTHER'S HAND ON HIS SHOULDER...

TRIGO! THROW YOURSELF FLAT!

EH?

THE EMPEROR OBEYED – IN THE NICK OF TIME!

SOMEONE FIRING... FROM THAT ROOFTOP!

BY ALL THE STARS!

THE ROOFTOP WAS SEARCHED, BUT THE WOULD-BE ASSASSIN HAD GONE.

HE MUST HAVE DROPPED THIS IN HIS HURRY TO ESCAPE!

CAPTAIN! SEARCH THE VICINITY!

YORRI-ZIM THE LOKAN WAS NOT FAR AWAY!

THERE IS MORE THAN ONE WAY OF DESTROYING AN EMPEROR!

"TO JANNO AND ZARO – FROM A GRATEFUL EMPEROR AND HIS SORROWING PEOPLE!"

A FUNERARY CHAPLET... OURS!

AT ABOUT THAT SAME TIME, JANNO AND ZARO WERE STARING DOWN AT SOMETHING THAT HAD SLIPPED INTO THEIR UNDERWATER TOMB.

FROM THE ROOF OF THE IMPERIAL PALACE, TRIGO AND PERIC GAZED OUT OVER THE INUNDATION.

YOU HAVE EXAMINED THE SITUATION?

YES, IMPERIAL MAJESTY. MY CALCULATIONS TELL ME THAT THE WATERS HAVE CEASED TO RISE.

IT MAY BE THAT THEY WILL BEGIN TO RECEDE, IN WHICH CASE – UNLESS NO OTHER ADVERSE FACTOR ENTERS INTO THE SITUATION – WE MAY SURVIVE.

WHAT ADVERSE FACTOR DO YOU HAVE IN MIND, PERIC?

PERIC ANSWERED HIS EMPEROR...GRAVELY.

YOUR ASSASSINATION, MAJESTY!

THE MAN WHO HAD ALREADY MADE ONE ATTEMPT TO DESTROY TRIGO WAS, AT THAT MOMENT, WATCHING THE PALACE GATES.

TONIGHT... I ACT!

AT NIGHTFALL YORRI-ZIM, THE LOKAN, OVERPOWERED THE GUARD AT THE GATES!

AAAAAAHHH...

A HIDING-PLACE...I NEED A HIDING PLACE!

MEANWHILE, BACK IN THE VAST ENGINE ROOM OF THE SUNKEN 'DAVELI', JANNO AND ZARO WERE AWARE OF THE PRESENCE OF...THEM!

JANNO! - LOOK!

A GROUP OF THE SCALY DENIZENS OF THE DEEP STOOD BEFORE THEM!

THAT ONE THERE...WITH THE MORE ELABORATE TRAPPINGS...HE COULD BE THEIR LEADER!

TO JANNO'S SURPRISE, THE STRANGE LEADER LAID HIS WEBBED HAND HIS BROW, AND PLACED JANNO'S ON HIS OWN. INSTANTLY THE YOUNG TRIGAN SENSED...*COMMUNICATION!*

JANNO! — WHAT IS IT?

I—I CAN TELL WHAT HE'S THINKING!

A MESSAGE CAME CLEARLY INTO JANNO'S MIND. IT WAS AS IF THE STRANGE CREATURE WAS ADDRESSING HIM...

YOU—WILL—TAKE—ME—TO—HE—WHO—COMMANDS—YOUR—PEOPLE!

SIMILARLY, HE WAS ABLE TO COMMUNICATE BACK!

YES! — I—WILL—DO—IT—GLADLY!

THE FOLLOWING MORNING, THE IMPERIAL PALACE WAS IN AN UPROAR.

SEARCH EVERYWHERE! SOMEONE OVERPOWERED A GUARD AND STOLE HIS WEAPON! THAT SOMEONE MAY STILL BE HERE!

YORRI-ZIM HAD FOUND HIS HIDING PLACE!

THEY WILL NEVER FIND ME HERE — AND HERE I WILL REMAIN TILL TRIGO APPEARS BELOW! AND THEN...FAREWELL, EMPEROR!

JANNO AND ZARO HEADED FOR THE SURFACE, ACCOMPANIED BY THE WEIRD, UNDERWATER MEN.

THEY ROSE INTO THE SUNLIGHT OF AN ELEKTON DAY.

THE SIGHT OF THEM SPREAD PANIC AMONG THE PEOPLE.

AAAAH! JANNO AND ZARO ARE BACK FROM THE DEAD!

AND LOOK WHAT THEY'VE BROUGHT WITH THEM!

NEWS WAS BROUGHT TO THE EMPEROR, TRIGO.

MY NEPHEW, YOU SAY, AND ZARO?

YES, IMPERIAL MAJESTY! AND WITH THEM ARE FOUR CREATURES, THE LIKE OF WHOM I HAVE NEVER SET EYES ON BEFORE!

JANNO! ZARO! WE HAD NEVER THOUGHT TO SEE YOU BOTH ALIVE AGAIN!

AND THESE PEOPLE... PERSONS... CREATURES?

WE DON'T KNOW WHO THEY ARE OR FROM WHENCE THEY CAME, UNCLE, BUT I HAVE COMMUNICATED WITH THIS ONE... THEIR LEADER... AND HE WANTED TO MEET YOU!

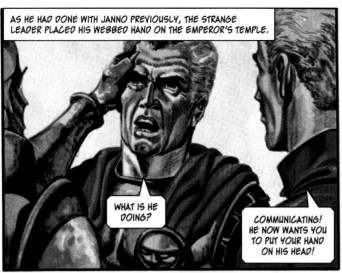

AS HE HAD DONE WITH JANNO PREVIOUSLY, THE STRANGE LEADER PLACED HIS WEBBED HAND ON THE EMPEROR'S TEMPLE.

WHAT IS HE DOING?

COMMUNICATING! HE NOW WANTS YOU TO PUT YOUR HAND ON HIS HEAD!

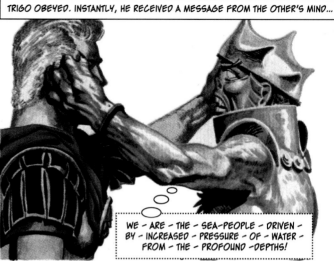

TRIGO OBEYED. INSTANTLY, HE RECEIVED A MESSAGE FROM THE OTHER'S MIND...

WE – ARE – THE – SEA-PEOPLE – DRIVEN – BY – INCREASED – PRESSURE – OF – WATER – FROM – THE – PROFOUND –DEPTHS!

FURTHERMORE, TRIGO WAS ABLE TO SEND BACK HIS OWN THOUGHTS!

YOU – HAVE – SEEN – OUR – POWER! DO – YOU – WANT – PEACE – OR – DO – YOU – WANT – WAR?

PEACE! WE – WANT – PEACE – WITH – YOU!

FROM – NOW – ON – WE – ARE – FRIENDS!

I – DO – NOT – UNDERSTAND! WHAT – IS – FRIENDS?

AND THEN...

MY LONG VIGIL IS OVER! NOW, MIGHTY EMPEROR, YOU SHALL PERISH!

AS THE ASSASSIN FIRED...

...TRIGO SAW THE GUN-FLASH. HE HURLED HIMSELF FORWARD TO SHIELD THE STRANGE CREATURE WITH HIS OWN BODY.

AAAAAAGHH!

...HE HIMSELF WAS HIT!

ONE OF THE BODYGUARDS TURNED AND A VIVID STREAK OF FLAME LEAPT TOWARDS THE GUNMAN.

THE ASSASSIN TOPPLED TO HIS DOOM!

EEEEEEEH–H–H! AAAAAH!

THEY EXAMINED THE STRICKEN EMPEROR.

HIS IMPERIAL MAJESTY IS GRAVELY HURT, BUT HE WILL LIVE!

THANK THE STARS!

AFTER HIS RECOVERY, SOME LUNAR MONTHS LATER, TRIGO MADE A MOMENTOUS ANNOUNCEMENT TO THE IMPERIAL COUNCIL.

NOW – I – UNDERSTAND – WHAT – IS – FRIENDS! – YOU – SAVED – MY – LIFE! – THAT – IS – FRIENDS!

WHEN TRIGO'S EYES FLICKERED OPEN, HE "COMMUNICATED" WITH THE LEADER OF THE SEA PEOPLE.

PERIC HAS DEVISED A PLAN TO RID THE PLANET OF THE FLOOD WATERS! IT WILL BE ONE OF THE MOST ASTONISHING FEATS OF GEOPHYSICAL ENGINEERING EVER ACCOMPLISHED – IF IT SUCCEEDS! WE SHALL DO IT IN COLLABORATION WITH OUR FRIENDS, THE SEA PEOPLE!

THE SCHEME CALLED FOR THE PENETRATION OF THE PROFOUND DEPTHS OF THE GREAT OCEAN BY UNDERWATER CRAFT OF THE TRIGAN FLEET.

DESPITE THE TERRIBLE PRESSURES OF THE SWOLLEN OCEAN, THE SEA-PEOPLE VENTURED OUT AND LAID A MASSIVE EXPLOSIVE CHARGE.

THE EXPLOSION THAT FOLLOWED WAS SEEN IN FAR-OFF TRIGAN CITY.

IF ALL GOES WELL, A FISSURE WILL BE OPENED UP IN THE OCEAN BED. THE EXCESS WATER WILL BE DRAINED AWAY INTO THE MOLTEN CORE OF OUR PLANET. AND THE NIGHTMARE OF THE FLOOD WILL BE OVER!

IN A FEW DAYS, THE NEAR-MIRACLE BEGAN TO HAPPEN...

THREE LUNAR MONTHS LATER, TRIGAN CITY STOOD AGAIN!

THE EMPEROR TRIGO SPOKE FOR THE SURVIVORS OF THE GREAT DISASTER.

NOW WE CAN BEGIN TO REBUILD OUR PLANET!

XLVII

THE TRIGAN EMPIRE

THE ELIXIR OF ETERNAL YOUTH

Originally published in *Look and Learn* 645 - 652

25th May 1974 - 13th July 1974

Story by Mike Butterworth

Art by Philip Corke

THEY CAME FROM ALL OVER THE SPRAWLING TRIGAN EMPIRE, TO WITNESS THE IMPERIAL GAMES IN THE CAPITAL'S MAMMOTH AMPHITHEATRE.

WE BRING YOU A REPORT ON THE TEN THOUSAND TELLAR FOOT RACE! COMING UP FOR THE LAST LAP, ZAMPHA OF THARV IS IN THE LEAD...

THE HIGH SPOT OF THE GAMES WAS THE CLASSIC VORG WRESTLING. FINALISTS WERE A TRIGAN NAMED MALLO AND A DAVELI NAMED HELLER.

YOU HAVE HIM, HELLER!

DO SOMETHING, MALLO!

MALLO TURNED THE TABLES ON HIS BIGGER OPPONENT, WITH A THROW THAT THRILLED THE CROWD AND WON HIM THE CROWN!

THE EMPEROR CROWNED THE YOUNG VICTOR, AND SPOKE KINDLY TO HIM.

I HEAR THAT YOU ARE A PROMISING SCIENTIST, MALLO. YOU MUST COME AND BE PERIC'S ASSISTANT.

I WOULD COUNT THAT A GREAT HONOUR, IMPERIAL MAJESTY!

I SHALL BE DELIGHTED.

THAT DODDERING OLD FOOL CAN'T LAST FOR LONG, THEN I SHALL BE HEAD OF THE IMPERIAL RESEARCH LABORATORY - WITH PLENTY OF CHANCES TO LINE MY PURSE!

AND SO, THE SCHEMING YOUTH WENT TO WORK WITH PERIC, ELEKTON'S TOP SCIENTIST.

WHAT IS THIS EXPERIMENT?

MERELY A FORLORN ATTEMPT TO REJUVENATE THIS POOR RORN, WHO HAS GIVEN SO MANY YEARS' GOOD SERVICE AS A LABORATORY ANIMAL...

POOR OLD FELLOW. HE'S LIKE ME...TOO MANY GREY HAIRS AND NOT ENOUGH TEETH. NATURE MUST TAKE ITS COURSE.

MAY NATURE SWIFTLY TAKE ITS COURSE WITH YOU, MUMBLING OLD HAS-BEEN!

THAT NIGHT, WHILE PERIC WAS WORKING ON HIS EXPERIMENT, THERE WAS A SHATTERING EXPLOSION.

AAAAAAGHHH!

NO ONE HEARD THE CRASH AND THE OLD SCIENTIST LAY UNCONSCIOUS UNTIL DAWN.

WHAT HAPPENED? I REMEMBER! THERE WAS A FLASH...

HE CROSSED OVER TO INSPECT THE DAMAGE.

WHAT A MESS!

WHAT HAPPENED TO THAT POOR OLD RORN?

BY ALL THE STARS!

THE CREATURE'S TAKEN ON A NEW LEASE OF LIFE! IT HASN'T EXERCISED ON ITS TREADMILL FOR YEARS!

IT WAS THEN THAT PERIC SAW HIS OWN REFLECTION...

CAN THAT BE...ME?

I LOOK TWENTY YEARS YOUNGER! MY HAIR'S REGAINED ITS COLOUR AND... AND THAT ISN'T ALL!

IN THE COURTYARD OF A TRIGAN CITY APARTMENT, TWO YOUTHS WERE PRACTISING THE CLASSIC ART OF VORG WRESTLING.

HOW WAS THAT?

WELL DONE, JANNO!

JANNO WAS DELIGHTED TO BE TAKING LESSONS FROM MALLO, THE WRESTLING EXPERT.

DID I HURT YOU, MY FRIEND?

IT'S ALL RIGHT, JANNO.

THE EMPEROR'S NEPHEW CALLS ME "FRIEND"! MY, YOU'VE COME A LONG WAY FROM BEING THE SON OF A SHOE-MENDER, MALLO!

AT THAT MOMENT, A MESSENGER ARRIVED.

SOMETHING IMPORTANT?

A SUMMONS FROM MY UNCLE. I AM TO GO IMMEDIATELY TO THE PALACE. AND YOU ARE TO COME WITH ME, MALLO.

THE TWO YOUTHS ARRIVED IN THE IMPERIAL APARTMENTS, WHERE THE EMPEROR TRIGO AWAITED THEM.

YOU WANTED TO SEE ME, UNCLE?

YES! JANNO AND MALLO, I WANT YOU BOTH TO MEET AN OLD FRIEND...

GOOD DAY TO YOU, SIRS!

PERIC!

THE VERY SAME, AND TO PROVE IT...

EEEEEEH!

IN MY YOUNG DAYS, JANNO, I WAS SOMETHING OF A WRESTLER! AND SUDDENLY IT ALL COMES BACK TO ME!

ELEKTON'S TOP SCIENTIST – NOW MUCH CHANGED – GRINNED AT HIS COMPANIONS.

BUT, YOU'RE... YOU'RE...

YOUNGER! BETWEEN TWENTY AND THIRTY LUNAR YEARS YOUNGER! WITH SCARCELY ANY GREY HAIRS, ALL MY TEETH, AND WITH THE PULSE AND BLOOD PRESSURE OF A MAN IN HIS PRIME!

I ABSORBED THAT GREEN LIQUID AND IT TOOK YEARS OFF MY LIFE! IT HAS ALL GONE, BUT WE WILL FIND MORE OF IT, MALLO! YOU AND I WILL WORK, DAY AND NIGHT, TO RE-DISCOVER THE SECRET OF YOUTH!

BUT... HOW?

IT HAPPENED LAST NIGHT! AS MALLO KNOWS, I HAVE BEEN SEARCHING FOR A REJUVENATING AGENT. LAST NIGHT, A STRANGE GREEN LIQUID APPEARED IN THE TEST TUBE. ALMOST IMMEDIATELY, IT EXPLODED...

YES, PERIC!... YES!

IN THE DAYS AND NIGHTS THAT FOLLOWED, PERIC AND HIS ASSISTANT NEVER LEFT THE IMPERIAL RESEARCH LABORATORY.

THE MIXTURE OF INGREDIENTS IS VERY CRITICAL, I MUST TAKE A SHORT REST. YOU CARRY ON, MALLO. BUT BE VERY CAREFUL – THE TRUE MIXTURE IS HIGHLY UNSTABLE!

ALONE, THE AMBITIOUS YOUNG SCIENTIST GREW RECKLESS.

THE SECRET OF YOUTH! IT WOULD MAKE ME THE RICHEST MAN ON ELEKTON, AND MORE POWERFUL THAN ANY EMPEROR!...

TO BLAZES WITH CAUTION! I WILL INCREASE THE INGREDIENTS A HUNDREDFOLD!

THE SECRET OF ETERNAL YOUTH IS MINE! ALL MINE!

SUDDENLY, THE LIQUID IN HIS TEST TUBE TURNED INTO A LUMINOUS GREEN!

THE COMPETITION TRACK NEAR TRIGAN CITY.

ONE MORE LAP AT THAT SPEED AND HE'S BROKEN THE RECORD!

DO YOU HEAR THAT NARROD? YOU'RE NEARLY THERE! WATCH OUT ON THAT NEXT CORNER!

THE SCREAMING RACER BRIEFLY TOUCHED THE BARRIER WALL AND...

HE'S GOING TO CRASH!

EJECT, NARROD!

THE DRIVER EJECTED FROM HIS COCKPIT – AN INSTANT BEFORE THE RACE-AUTO TURNED INTO A FIREBALL!

NARROD, ARE YOU ALL RIGHT?

YOU'RE LUCKY TO BE ALIVE. I CAN TELL YOU!

MY SIGHT FAILED ME, AND MY REACTIONS WERE TOO SLOW AT THAT CORNER! I'M FINISHED! I SHALL NEVER GET INTO A RACE-AUTO AGAIN!

ONCE HE HELD EVERY SPEED RECORD ON ELEKTON!

WELL, OLD AGE GETS US ALL IN THE END!

A LIFETIME OF RECORD-BREAKING HAD MADE NARROD A PLANET-WIDE CELEBRITY AND A MILLIONAIRE. BUT HE WENT BACK TO HIS LUXURIOUS VILLA IN BLACK DESPAIR.

MY LIFE IS FINISHED. I MAY STILL LIVE ON FOR YEARS...

...IF YOU CAN CALL IT LIVING. WHY NOT END IT ALL NOW?

A VISITOR IS REQUESTING TO SEE YOU, MASTER. HIS NAME IS MALLO.

NOT THE MALLO WHO WON THE VORG WRESTLING CROWN AT THE IMPERIAL GAMES? SHOW HIM IN, ZAPP.

MY, HOW I ENVY YOU, MY BOY. DO YOU KNOW I WON THE VORG WRESTLING CROWN THREE TIMES WHEN I WAS YOUR AGE! WHAT WOULDN'T I GIVE TO BE YOUNG AGAIN!

YOU CAN BE YOUNG AGAIN, NARROD! YOUTH LIES WITHIN THIS PHIAL AND IT CAN BE YOURS!...

...FOR A MILLION THULLARS! — CASH!

AT MALLO'S PROPOSITION, NARROD THREW BACK HIS HEAD AND LAUGHED TILL THE TEARS RAN DOWN HIS LINED CHEEKS.

A MILLION THULLARS IN CASH? – HA, HA, HA! – YOU REALLY HAVE TAKEN LEAVE OF YOUR SENSES!

THE OLD MAN'S MOOD CHANGED. SUDDENLY, MALLO SAW SOMETHING OF WHAT NARROD MUST HAVE BEEN IN THE DAYS OF HIS YOUTH AND STRENGTH.

YOU INSOLENT YOUNG ANIMAL! A MILLION THULLARS IS HALF OF MY FORTUNE, WHICH I EARNED BY THE SWEAT OF MY BROW AND BY RISKING MY LIFE...

I WILL SHOW YOU HOW I CAME TO BE A MILLIONAIRE, MY LAD!...

NARROD TOUCHED A SWITCH...

WATCH!...AND LEARN!

NARROD WINNING THE ELEKTON WATER-SPEED RECORD!!

NARROD GAINING THE ELEKTON ALL-SPEED TITLE!!

NARROD WINNING THE VORG WRESTLING CROWN AT THE IMPERIAL GAMES – FOR THE THIRD TIME!!

THERE WAS MORE – MUCH MORE. WHEN IT WAS OVER, THE VETERAN GRABBED HIS COMPANION IN A CLASSIC VORG WRESTLING GRIP.

I CAN STILL DO IT! I CAN STILL THROW YOU ACROSS THE ROOM, OLD AS I AM!

THINK SO?

UUUUUHH...

YOU WILL NEVER THROW AN OPPONENT AGAIN, YOU OLD WRECKAGE OF A CREATURE! NO MORE CROWNS... NO MORE TITLES... NO MORE SPEED RECORDS... YOU ARE FINISHED! FINISHED!

NARROD ANSWERED WHININGLY – BROKENLY...

MAKE ME YOUNG AGAIN...IF IT'S IN YOUR POWER, MALLO!

FIRST – THE MONEY!

THAT MORNING, IN THE BANK OF TRIGAN, A MILLION THULLARS WERE COUNTED OUT FOR THE YOUNG SCIENTIST-ATHLETE.

THREE HUNDRED AND FIFTY THOUSAND... THREE HUNDRED AND SIXTY THOUSAND...

AND NOW... THE ELIXIR!

TAKE IT! DRINK IT DOWN!

...BUT LATER, WHEN YOU'RE ALONE!

A STORM BROKE OVER TRIGAN CITY THAT NIGHT. IT ILLUMINATED THE LUXURIOUS LIVING ROOM OF NARROD'S VILLA, AS THE OLD MAN RAISED THE PHIAL TO HIS LIPS AND DEVOURED THE STRANGE BREW IN ONE GULP!

EARLY NEXT MORNING, WITH A SCREECH OF HIGH-POWERED ENGINES, A SLEEK RACE-CRAFT STREAKED ROUND A MEASURED COURSE IN THE TRIGAN RIVER ESTUARY.

HE'S TOO OLD FOR THAT GAME!

IT WAS ONLY THE OTHER DAY HE NEARLY KILLED HIMSELF TRYING TO BREAK THE AUTO-TRACK RECORD!

ON THE LAST LAP OF THE COURSE, WITH THE FINISHING POST IN SIGHT – *TROUBLE!*

ONE OF HIS ENGINES HAS OVERHEATED! IT'S GOING TO BLOW UP!

BAIL OUT, NARROD! BAIL OUT!

THE PILOT STAYED WITH HIS BLAZING CRAFT AND TOOK IT PAST THE FINISH!

WITH GREAT SKILL, HE BROUGHT THE CRAFT TO THE GROUND AND LEAPT FOR SAFETY AS IT EXPLODED!

NARROD! THAT WAS MAGNIFICENT!

CONGRATULATIONS, NARROD!

IT WAS NOTHING, WAIT TILL I'VE BUILT A FASTER, BETTER, RACE-CRAFT, THEN YOU'LL REALLY SEE SOMETHING!

NOT TILL HE WAS ALONE DID NARROD REMOVE HIS CONCEALING HELMET – TO REVEAL THE FACE OF A MAN TWENTY YEARS YOUNGER THAN HIS TRUE AGE!

YES! I SHALL BETTER ALL MY OLD RECORDS! NOW THAT I'VE REGAINED MY YOUTH, NOTHING CAN STOP ME!

MEANWHILE, BACK IN HIS LABORATORY, PERIC WAS STILL TRYING TO REPEAT THE EXPERIMENT THAT HAD LED TO HIS OWN DRAMATIC REJUVENATION.

NO LUCK, MASTER?

ONE HAS TO PROCEED CAREFULLY, MALLO. I'LL LEAVE YOU TO CONTINUE FOR A WHILE.

ALONE, MALLO PLUNGED RECKLESSLY...

LITTLE DOES PERIC REALISE THAT IT'S SIMPLY A MATTER OF USING LARGE QUANTITIES OF THE INGREDIENTS...

I NEED ANOTHER SUPPLY OF THE STUFF – AND ANOTHER RICH OLD MAN TO BUY IT!

THAT NIGHT, ON AN IMPULSE THAT GAVE HIM A FEELING OF LONG-FORGOTTEN PLEASURE, NARROD SEARCHED OUT AN OLD FAVOURITE OF HIS CHILDHOOD.

HELLO, OLD SOLDIER – IT'S BEEN A LONG TIME! HOW ARE YOU, EH?

IN THE MORNING, WHEN HIS MANSERVANT CAME TO WAKE HIM...

HEY! WHAT ARE YOU DOING HERE, BOY? WHO ARE YOU?

I'M YOUR MASTER – NARROD!

AND WHY ARE YOU CALLING ME "BOY"?

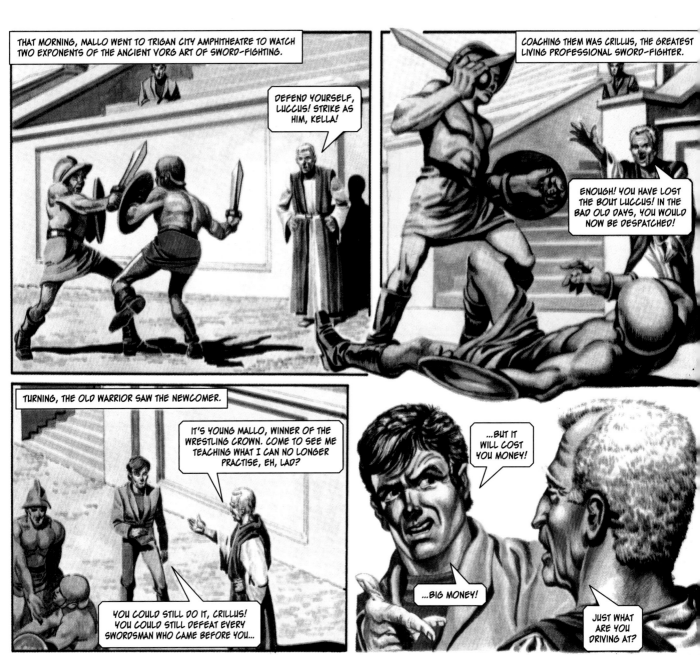

THAT MORNING, MALLO WENT TO TRIGAN CITY AMPHITHEATRE TO WATCH TWO EXPONENTS OF THE ANCIENT VORG ART OF SWORD-FIGHTING.

DEFEND YOURSELF, LUCCUS! STRIKE AS HIM, KELLA!

COACHING THEM WAS CRILLUS, THE GREATEST LIVING PROFESSIONAL SWORD-FIGHTER.

ENOUGH! YOU HAVE LOST THE BOUT LUCCUS! IN THE BAD OLD DAYS, YOU WOULD NOW BE DESPATCHED!

TURNING, THE OLD WARRIOR SAW THE NEWCOMER.

IT'S YOUNG MALLO, WINNER OF THE WRESTLING CROWN. COME TO SEE ME TEACHING WHAT I CAN NO LONGER PRACTISE, EH, LAD?

YOU COULD STILL DO IT, CRILLUS! YOU COULD STILL DEFEAT EVERY SWORDSMAN WHO CAME BEFORE YOU...

...BUT IT WILL COST YOU MONEY!

...BIG MONEY!

JUST WHAT ARE YOU DRIVING AT?

YOU HEARD NARROD BROKE THE ALL-TIME AIR RACE-CRAFT RECORD YESTERDAY?

YES, A MAN MY OWN AGE! I COULD SCARCELY BELIEVE MY EARS! WHAT OF IT?

MALLO EXPLAINED...

ARE YOU TRYING TO TELL ME THAT ALL I HAVE TO DO IS DRINK THIS GREEN LIQUID AND – LIKE NARROO – I SHALL BE YOUNG AGAIN?

YES! DON'T TAKE MY WORD FOR IT. TAKE IT HOME AND TRY IT!

THE PRICE IS A MILLION THULLARS – THE SAME AS I CHARGED NARROD!

156

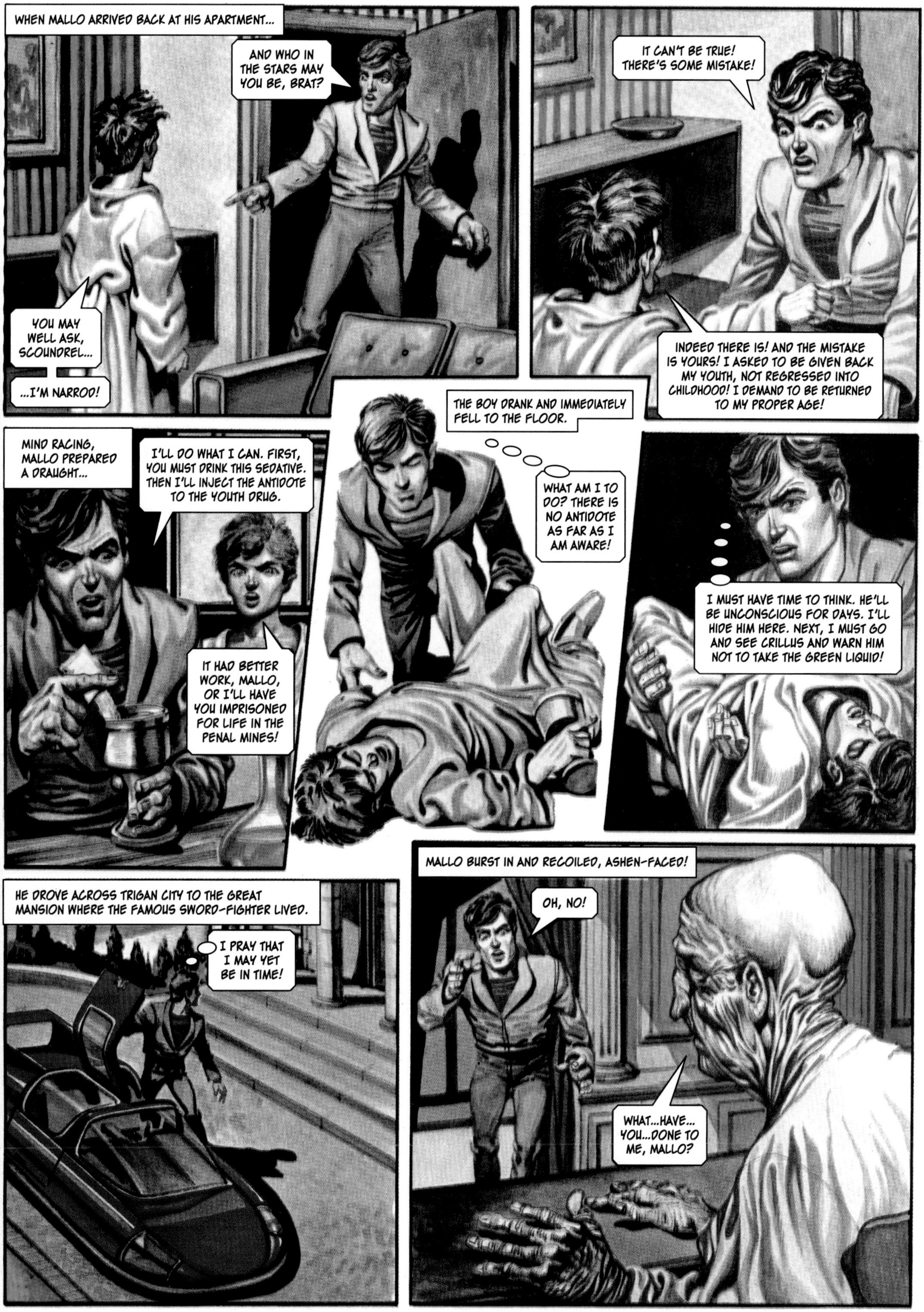
WHEN MALLO ARRIVED BACK AT HIS APARTMENT...
AND WHO IN THE STARS MAY YOU BE, BRAT?
YOU MAY WELL ASK, SCOUNDREL...
...I'M NARROO!
IT CAN'T BE TRUE! THERE'S SOME MISTAKE!
INDEED THERE IS! AND THE MISTAKE IS YOURS! I ASKED TO BE GIVEN BACK MY YOUTH, NOT REGRESSED INTO CHILDHOOD! I DEMAND TO BE RETURNED TO MY PROPER AGE!
MIND RACING, MALLO PREPARED A DRAUGHT...
I'LL DO WHAT I CAN. FIRST, YOU MUST DRINK THIS SEDATIVE. THEN I'LL INJECT THE ANTIDOTE TO THE YOUTH DRUG.
IT HAD BETTER WORK, MALLO, OR I'LL HAVE YOU IMPRISONED FOR LIFE IN THE PENAL MINES!
THE BOY DRANK AND IMMEDIATELY FELL TO THE FLOOR.
WHAT AM I TO DO? THERE IS NO ANTIDOTE AS FAR AS I AM AWARE!
I MUST HAVE TIME TO THINK. HE'LL BE UNCONSCIOUS FOR DAYS. I'LL HIDE HIM HERE. NEXT, I MUST GO AND SEE CRILLUS AND WARN HIM NOT TO TAKE THE GREEN LIQUID!
HE DROVE ACROSS TRIGAN CITY TO THE GREAT MANSION WHERE THE FAMOUS SWORD-FIGHTER LIVED.
I PRAY THAT I MAY YET BE IN TIME!
MALLO BURST IN AND RECOILED, ASHEN-FACED!
OH, NO!
WHAT...HAVE... YOU...DONE TO ME, MALLO?

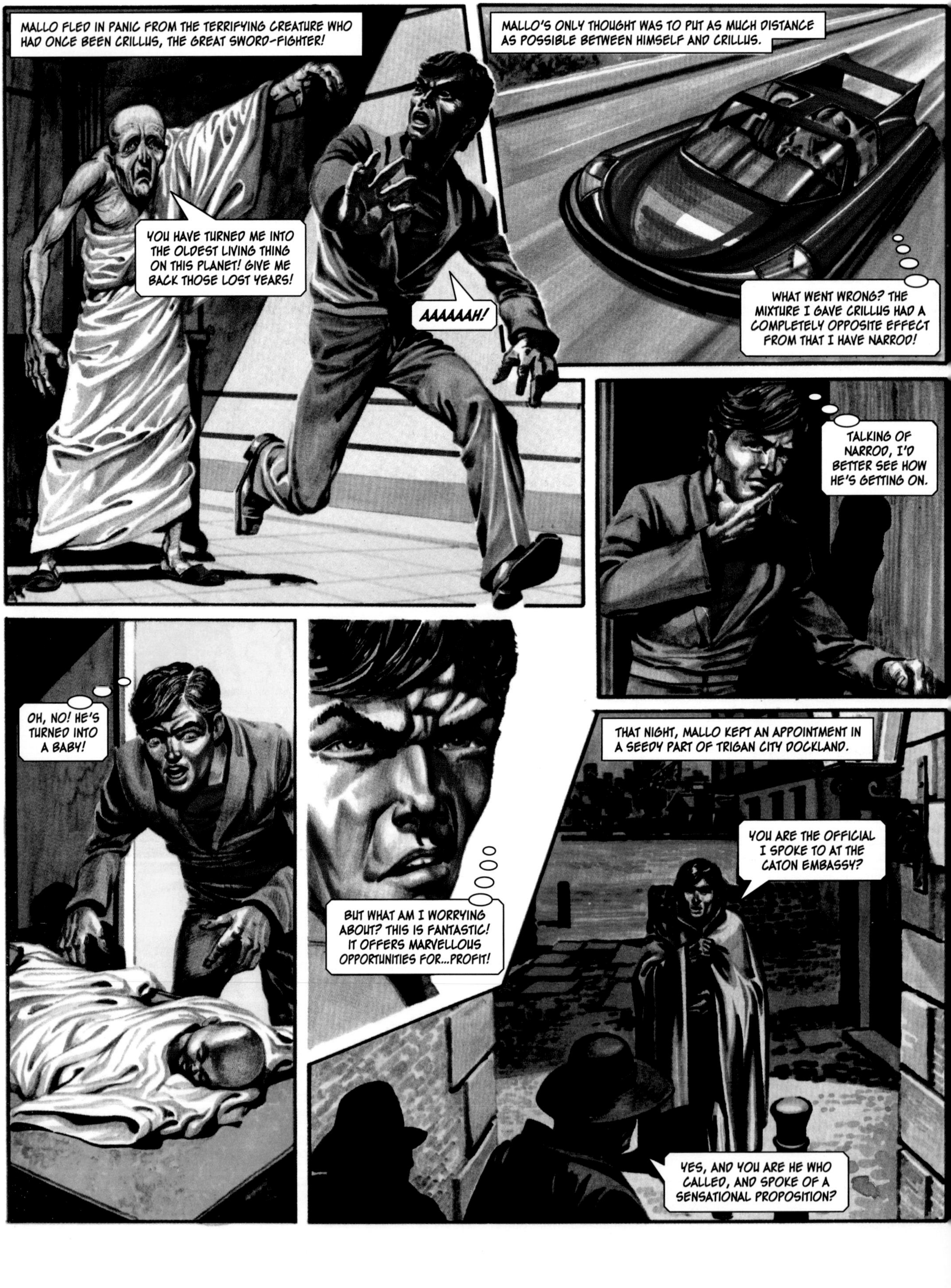
MALLO FLED IN PANIC FROM THE TERRIFYING CREATURE WHO HAD ONCE BEEN CRILLUS, THE GREAT SWORD-FIGHTER!
YOU HAVE TURNED ME INTO THE OLDEST LIVING THING ON THIS PLANET! GIVE ME BACK THOSE LOST YEARS!
AAAAAAH!
MALLO'S ONLY THOUGHT WAS TO PUT AS MUCH DISTANCE AS POSSIBLE BETWEEN HIMSELF AND CRILLUS.
WHAT WENT WRONG? THE MIXTURE I GAVE CRILLUS HAD A COMPLETELY OPPOSITE EFFECT FROM THAT I HAVE NARROD!
TALKING OF NARROD, I'D BETTER SEE HOW HE'S GETTING ON.
OH, NO! HE'S TURNED INTO A BABY!
BUT WHAT AM I WORRYING ABOUT? THIS IS FANTASTIC! IT OFFERS MARVELLOUS OPPORTUNITIES FOR...PROFIT!
THAT NIGHT, MALLO KEPT AN APPOINTMENT IN A SEEDY PART OF TRIGAN CITY DOCKLAND.
YOU ARE THE OFFICIAL I SPOKE TO AT THE CATON EMBASSY?
YES, AND YOU ARE HE WHO CALLED, AND SPOKE OF A SENSATIONAL PROPOSITION?

THOUGH NOT CURRENTLY AT WAR, CATO AND THE TRIGAN EMPIRE WERE - AS USUAL - IN A STATE OF MUTUAL LOATHING.

IN EITHER CASE, MY COUNTRY WOULD IMMEDIATELY INVADE! THE TRIGAN EMPIRE IS NOTHING WITHOUT THE GUIDING HAND OF TRIGO!

WHAT WOULD CATO GIVE TO A SCIENTIST WHO COULD TURN THE EMPEROR TRIGO INTO A DOTARD, OR PERHAPS, AN INFANT?

THEN, MY FRIEND, WE ARE IN BUSINESS! LISTEN...

MUCH LATER...

THE FOLLOWING EVENING, MALLO PRESENTED HIMSELF, BY INVITATION, AS A SPLENDID GATHERING IN THE IMPERIAL PALACE.

THERE'S TRIGO. I SLIP THE STUFF INTO HIS GOBLET WHILE HE ISN'T LOOKING, THEN STAND BY FOR QUICK RESULTS!

IT IS AGREED! YOU WILL FEED THE GREEN LIQUID TO TRIGO. WHEN WE HAVE PROOF THAT IT HAS TAKEN EFFECT, WE WILL ACT AND YOU WILL BE REWARDED!

I WILL GIVE IT TO HIM TOMORROW NIGHT - AT THE IMPERIAL RECEPTION!

MALLO WORKED TILL DAWN TO PREPARE MORE OF THE STRANGE GREEN FLUID.

WHICH WAY WILL THIS WORK, I WONDER?

'TIS AS EASY AS LYING!

I DO NOT FORESEE ANY IMMEDIATE TROUBLE FROM CATO, GENTLEMEN.

DRINK IT DOWN! DRINK IT!

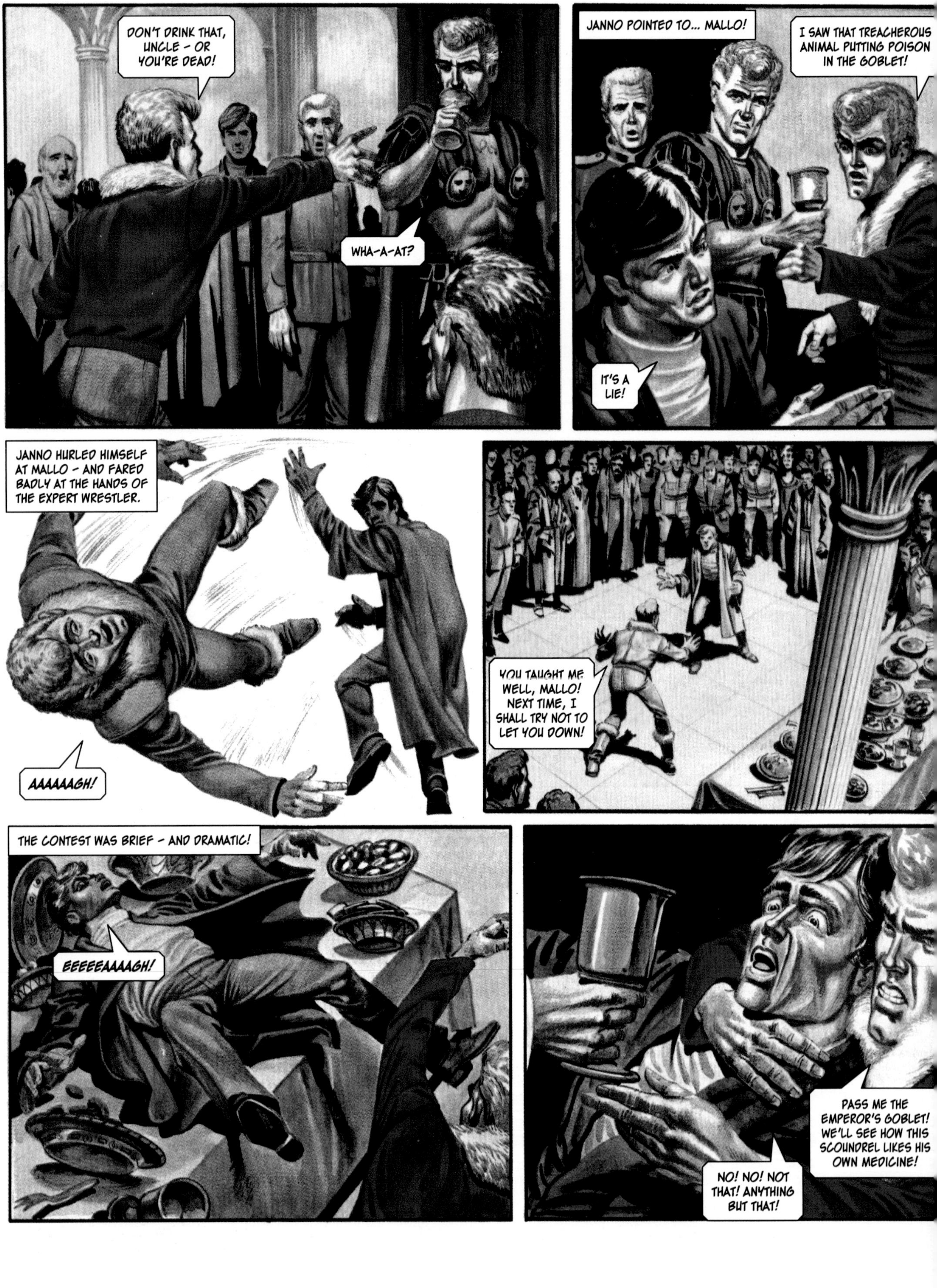

DON'T DRINK THAT, UNCLE - OR YOU'RE DEAD!
WHA-A-AT?
JANNO POINTED TO... MALLO!
I SAW THAT TREACHEROUS ANIMAL PUTTING POISON IN THE GOBLET!
IT'S A LIE!
JANNO HURLED HIMSELF AT MALLO - AND FARED BADLY AT THE HANDS OF THE EXPERT WRESTLER.
AAAAAAGH!
YOU TAUGHT ME WELL, MALLO! NEXT TIME, I SHALL TRY NOT TO LET YOU DOWN!
THE CONTEST WAS BRIEF - AND DRAMATIC!
EEEEEAAAAGH!
PASS ME THE EMPEROR'S GOBLET! WE'LL SEE HOW THIS SCOUNDREL LIKES HIS OWN MEDICINE!
NO! NO! NOT THAT! ANYTHING BUT THAT!

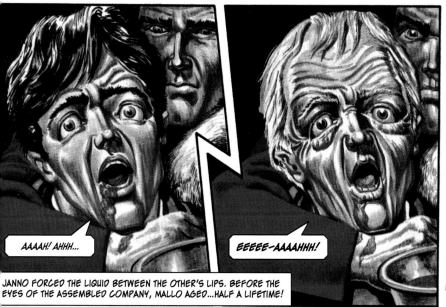

AAAAH! AHHH...

EEEEE-AAAAHHH!

JANNO FORCED THE LIQUID BETWEEN THE OTHER'S LIPS. BEFORE THE EYES OF THE ASSEMBLED COMPANY, MALLO AGED...HALF A LIFETIME!

MOMENTS LATER, AN INCREDIBLY AGED CREATURE SANK TO HIS KNEES.

IM-IMPERIAL MAJESTY...I WAS TEMPTED...THE CATONS WERE GOING TO PAY ME... TO DO THIS...TO YOU...

BY ALL THE STARS!

THE EMPEROR TURNED TO PERIC, HIS TOP SCIENTIST.

YOUR MAJESTY, I BLAME MYSELF! I ALLOWED THIS YOUTH TO TAMPER IN EXPERIMENTS FAR BEYOND IS INTELLECT!

THESE EXPERIMENTS WILL CEASE, PERIC! AND YOU WILL DEVOTE YOURSELF TO DEVISING AN ANTIDOTE FOR THIS EVIL THING!

SO IT WAS THAT PERIC WORKED, DAY AND NIGHT, IN HIS LABORATORY.

IS THIS THE ANTIDOTE?

THERE IS ONE SWIFT AND SURE WAY TO FIND OUT!

LATER...

I SEE, FROM YOUR CHANGED APPEARANCE, THAT YOU HAVE CARRIED OUT MY ORDER!

YES, IMPERIAL MAJESTY! I HAVE AGED - ONCE AGAIN! I HAVE ALSO DESTROYED ALL MY NOTES!

I SHALL NEVER FIND THE SECRET OF YOUTH AGAIN. BUT I CAN RESTORE TO THEIR NORMAL STATE THE OTHERS - INCLUDING MALLO - FOR WHOM THE EXPERIMENT WENT HIDEOUSLY WRONG!

THIS WAS DONE. SOME TIME LATER, OLD CRILLUS AND OLD NARROD WATCHED A RACE-CRAFT STREAKING ROUND THE MEASURED COURSE.

THERE GOES YOUNG JANNO - BREAKING YOUR RECORD!

GOOD LUCK TO THE LAD! I'VE LEARNED MY LESSON! FROM NOW ON, I'M LEAVING RECORD-BREAKING TO THE YOUNG - THE REALLY YOUNG!

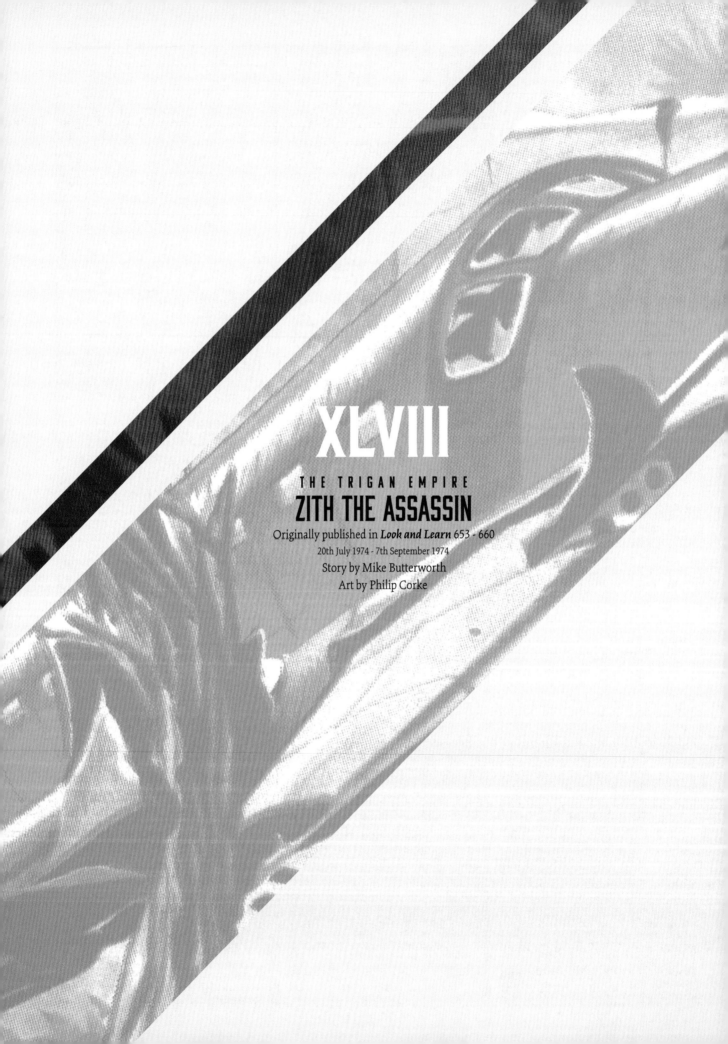

XLVIII

THE TRIGAN EMPIRE
ZITH THE ASSASSIN

Originally published in *Look and Learn* 653 - 660

20th July 1974 - 7th September 1974

Story by Mike Butterworth
Art by Philip Corke

IN THE TRANSLUCENT DEPTHS OF THE SEA OFF THARV, A LONE HUNTER WAS CLOSING ON HIS PREY.

ALL AT ONCE, THE HUNTER FOUND HIMSELF — THE HUNTED.

KNOCKED UNCONSCIOUS BY A SHOCK-PROJECTILE, THE VICTIM WAS CONNECTED TO A GRAB...

AND LIFTED ABOARD A WAITING SEA-CRAFT.

LATER, WHEN HE HAD RECOVERED CONSCIOUSNESS...

SEE HERE, YOU — WHOEVER YOU ARE!

WHO I AM IS OF NO IMPORTANCE TO YOU! I APOLOGISE FOR INTERRUPTING YOUR SPORT, BUT I HAVE NEED OF YOUR SPECIAL SERVICES!

WHO DO YOU WANT ME TO KILL — AND FOR HOW MUCH?

THE EMPEROR TRIGO! FOR HALF A MILLION THULLARS! CASH IN ADVANCE!

HOW DID YOU COME TO KNOW OF ME?

THAT IS IMMATERIAL! I KNOW YOU ARE THE TOP OPERATOR IN YOUR – ER – PROFESSION! THAT YOU KILL SILENTLY AND WITHOUT TRACE!

YOU WILL FLY TO TRIGAN CITY AND ASSASSINATE TRIGO DURING THE OPENING OF THE IMPERIAL ASSEMBLY IN TWO DAYS TIME! FAIL...AND YOU PERISH!

I NEVER FAIL!

IN ACCORDANCE WITH HIS INSTRUCTIONS, THE HIRED KILLER BOARDED A TRANS-PLANETARY AIR-CRUISER IN THARV.

THE AIR-CRUISER WAS SOON SKYBOUND.

NOT MANY PEOPLE FLYING TO TRIGAN CITY TODAY.

SUDDENLY, OVER THE DAVELI JUNGLE – IT HAPPENED!

ALARM! ALARM! THIS IS AN EMERGENCY! ALL PASSENGERS REMAIN SEATED! WE ARE GOING TO CRASH-LAND!

THE BIG CRUISER TORE A PATH OF FIRE AND WRECKAGE THROUGH THE DENSE JUNGLE...THEN THERE WAS SILENCE.

MUCH LATER, THE ASSASSIN CLAWED HIS WAY OUT.

AM I THE ONLY SURVIVOR?

A VOICE MADE THE ASSASSIN SPIN AROUND.

HEY! COME AND HELP ME WITH THE OTHERS! THEY'RE ALL HURT AND UNCONSCIOUS!

UNKNOWN TO THE ASSASSIN, HIS COMPANION WAS NONE OTHER THAN THE EMPEROR'S NEPHEW, JANNO.

THIS IS THE PILOT. HE'S IN A BAD WAY.

AS THEY TENDED TO THE OTHER SURVIVORS, THE ASSASSIN'S MIND TURNED TO HIS TERRIBLE PREDICAMENT.

THE OTHER TWO ARE ONLY CONCUSSED.

IF I DON'T CARRY OUT MY ORDERS AND DESTROY TRIGO AT THE OPENING OF THE IMPERIAL ASSEMBLY, THOSE PEOPLE WILL DESTROY ME!

I'VE GOT TO GET OUT OF HERE! I MUST GET TO TRIGAN CITY!

SO MUST I, MY FRIEND! IT'S A MATTER OF LIFE AND DEATH!

JANNO'S THOUGHTS FLED BACK A FEW HOURS...

THIS IS THE WAY TO SPEND ONE'S LEAVE - WINTER-SPORTING IN THARV!

YAAHHOOO!

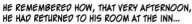

HE REMEMBERED HOW, THAT VERY AFTERNOON, HE HAD RETURNED TO HIS ROOM AT THE INN...

STRANGE! I DON'T REMEMBER LEAVING THE DOOR UNLOCKED!

AH!

NOT A SOUND, LORD JANNO!

WHAT DO YOU WANT?

LISTEN! YOU MUST WARN YOUR UNCLE, THE EMPEROR, THAT HE IS TO BE ASSASSINATED AT THE OPENING OF THE IMPERIAL ASSEMBLY!

BUT WHO ARE YOU?

A MEMBER OF THE CONSPIRACY, BUT I HAVE DECIDED IT HAS GONE TOO FAR!

DON'T TRANSMIT THIS INFORMATION, IT'S TOO RISKY. GO BACK TO TRIGAN CITY TODAY AND INFORM THE EMPEROR FROM YOUR OWN LIPS! GOOD LUCK!

JANNO RECALLED HOW HE HAD OBEYED THE MASKED STRANGER - AND HOW THE AIR-CRUISER HAD CRASHED IN FLAMES!

JANNO GAZED AT HIS COMPANION, UNAWARE THAT THIS WAS THE PAID ASSASSIN WHO ALSO HAD AN URGENT REASON TO REACH TRIGAN CITY.

HERE WE ARE - STUCK IN THIS CONFOUNDED JUNGLE!

WE'VE GOT TO WORK TOGETHER TO GET OUT!

SUDDENLY...

DOWN! DOWN, FOR YOUR LIFE!

AS JANNO BORE HIS COMPANION TO THE GROUND, AN EVIL HEAD FLASHED PAST ON THE END OF A WHIPLASH NECK!

AAAAAAGH!

IT'S A DAVELI DRAGON!

LIGHTNING-FAST, THE ASSASSIN LEAPT FOR HIS CASE...

JANNO RACED FOR COVER BUT TRIPPED AND SAW THE TERRIBLE HEAD LASHING TOWARDS HIM!

AND SECONDS LATER...

LUCKY FOR ME, YOU HAD THAT WITH YOU! WHAT A WEAPON! IT NEVER MADE A SOUND! I'VE NEVER SEEN ITS LIKE BEFORE...

MY OWN DESIGN...

I AM A... PROFESSIONAL HUNTER. MY TECHNIQUE IS TO STALK MY PREY UNSEEN, KILL IN SILENCE, AND THEN DISAPPEAR!

A GROAN ATTRACTED THEIR ATTENTION.

UUUUUUUH... MY HEAD!

ONE OF THEM HAS RECOVERED CONSCIOUSNESS.

THE SURVIVOR LOOKED ABOUT HIM. PUZZLEMENT TURNED TO ALARM.

I REMEMBER NOW! WE CRASHED!

BUT, I'VE GOT TO GET TO TRIGAN CITY TODAY! MY BEST FRIEND'S LIFE DEPENDS ON IT!

EVERYONE WANTS TO GET TO TRIGAN CITY ON A MATTER OF LIFE AND DEATH!

THE STRANGER'S NAME WAS KITTU. RAPIDLY, HE THOUGHT BACK TO A FATEFUL NIGHT, A LUNAR MONTH PREVIOUSLY, WHEN HE HAD SUPPED WITH HIS BEST FRIEND.

VAZLI, YOU LOOK WORN OUT. WHY DON'T YOU COME ON THIS FISHING HOLIDAY WITH ME TOMORROW?

I CAN'T, KITTU. TOMORROW, I MUST VISIT MY SKINFLINT UNCLE – NEVER A PLEASANT EXPERIENCE!

KITTU SPENT THE NEXT MONTH IN THE GREAT OCEAN, FAR FROM ALL COMMUNICATION WITH CIVILISATION.

ON HIS WAY HOME, CHANGING AIR-CRUISERS IN THARV, HE SAW THE SHOCKING NEWS ITEM...

OH, NO! IT CAN'T BE TRUE! I KNOW IT CAN'T BE TRUE!

MY FRIEND IS TO BE EXECUTED TOMORROW FOR THE MURDER OF HIS UNCLE, AND I AM THE ONLY ONE WHO CAN SAVE HIM! YOU SEE, HE WAS WITH ME AT THE TIME OF THE MURDER!

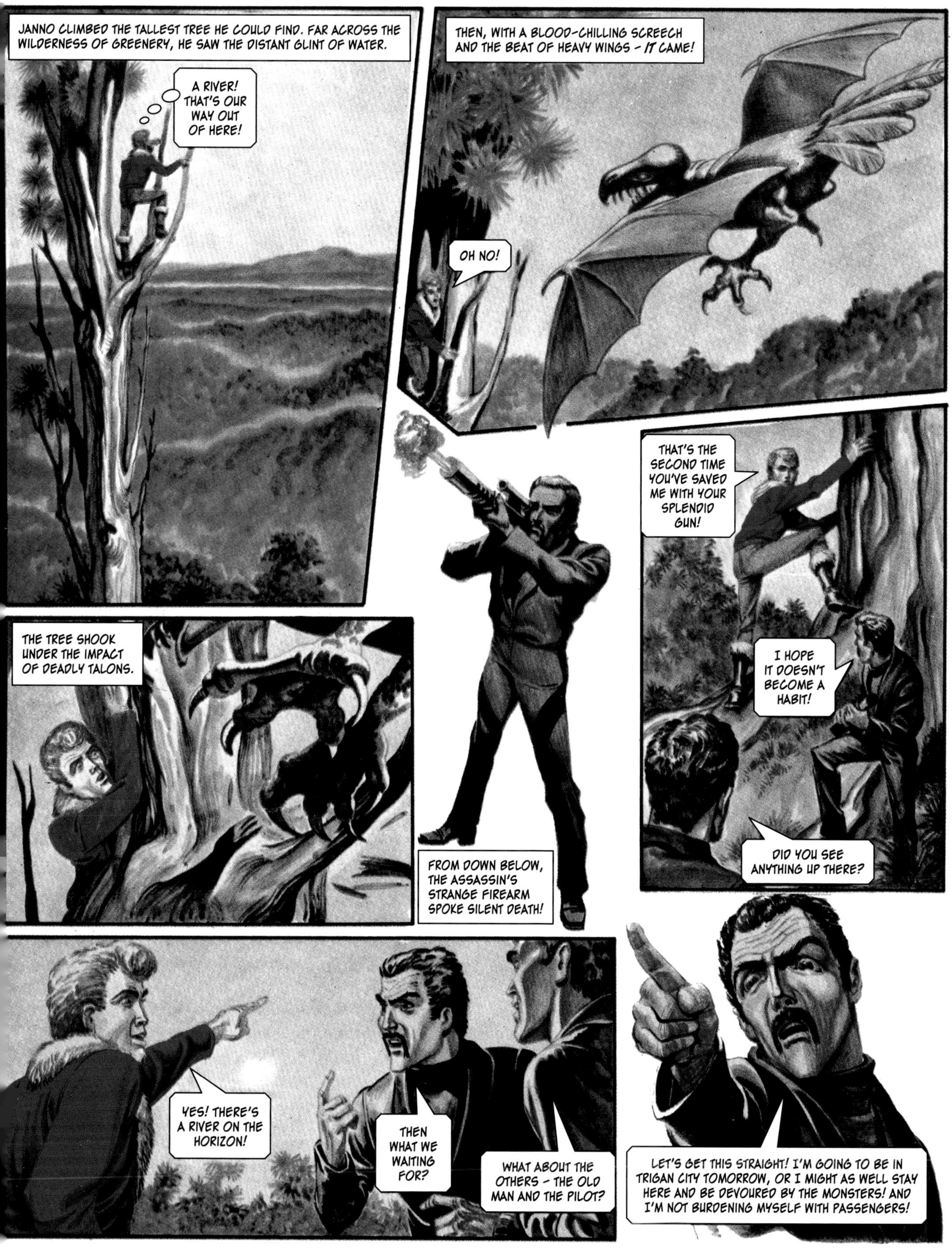

JANNO CLIMBED THE TALLEST TREE HE COULD FIND. FAR ACROSS THE WILDERNESS OF GREENERY, HE SAW THE DISTANT GLINT OF WATER.
A RIVER! THAT'S OUR WAY OUT OF HERE!
THEN, WITH A BLOOD-CHILLING SCREECH AND THE BEAT OF HEAVY WINGS - IT CAME!
OH NO!
THE TREE SHOOK UNDER THE IMPACT OF DEADLY TALONS.
FROM DOWN BELOW, THE ASSASSIN'S STRANGE FIREARM SPOKE SILENT DEATH!
THAT'S THE SECOND TIME YOU'VE SAVED ME WITH YOUR SPLENDID GUN!
I HOPE IT DOESN'T BECOME A HABIT!
DID YOU SEE ANYTHING UP THERE?
YES! THERE'S A RIVER ON THE HORIZON!
THEN WHAT WE WAITING FOR?
WHAT ABOUT THE OTHERS - THE OLD MAN AND THE PILOT?
LET'S GET THIS STRAIGHT! I'M GOING TO BE IN TRIGAN CITY TOMORROW, OR I MIGHT AS WELL STAY HERE AND BE DEVOURED BY THE MONSTERS! AND I'M NOT BURDENING MYSELF WITH PASSENGERS!

AAAAH!

THE OLD MAN'S COMING TO!

LOOK! WE'RE STUCK IN THE DAVELI JUNGLE AND OUR ONLY WAY OUT IS TO MARCH TO A RIVER. DO YOU THINK YOU CAN MANAGE A LONG WALK?

YES, I'M STRONGER THAN I LOOK, YOUNG FELLOW.

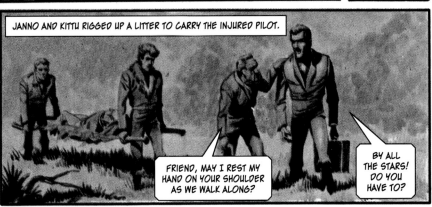

JANNO AND KITTU RIGGED UP A LITTER TO CARRY THE INJURED PILOT.

FRIEND, MAY I REST MY HAND ON YOUR SHOULDER AS WE WALK ALONG?

BY ALL THE STARS! DO YOU HAVE TO?

YES. YOU SEE, I AM BLIND!

THEY STRUCK OUT IN THE DIRECTION OF THE RIVER – THROUGH THE MOST HAZARDOUS COUNTRY ON ALL THE PLANET ELEKTON!

FOR THREE OF THEM, AT LEAST, THERE WAS AN URGENT REASON FOR HASTE. THREE MINDS, EACH WITH A SINGLE, BURNING DESIRE...

I MUST REACH TRIGAN CITY TOMORROW TO SAVE VAZLI FROM EXECUTION!

I'VE GOT TO WARN UNCLE TRIGO OF THE ASSASSINATION ATTEMPT!

UNLESS I DESTROY THE EMPEROR TRIGO AS ORDERED, THEY'LL DESTROY ME!

THEY PRESSED ON THROUGH THE HEAT OF THE DAY. AT LENGTH, THE OLD BLIND MAN STUMBLED AND FELL.

I...I MUST REST!

THEN REST AND ROT! WE'RE HALTING FOR NOTHING AND NO-ONE!

JANNO'S VOICES RASPED OUT, COMMANDINGLY...

I SAY WE HALT!

OH, YOU DO EH? WELL, JUST YOU LISTEN TO ME, MY FINE YOUNG...

THE SECRET ASSASSIN NEVER FINISHED WHAT HE HAD TO SAY.

EEEEAAAAGHH!

THE HIDEOUS ARMS WERE ALREADY SCRABBLING AT HIM, AS JANNO TOOK HURRIED AIM AND FIRED!

HE-E-E-ELP!

JANNO RACED FORWARD AND GRABBED THE FALLEN GUN-CASE. AS HE DID SO, HE SAW THE FACE OF THE THING IN THE HOLLOW TREE!

I'VE GOT TO GET THAT CREATURE BEFORE IT GETS ME, TOO!

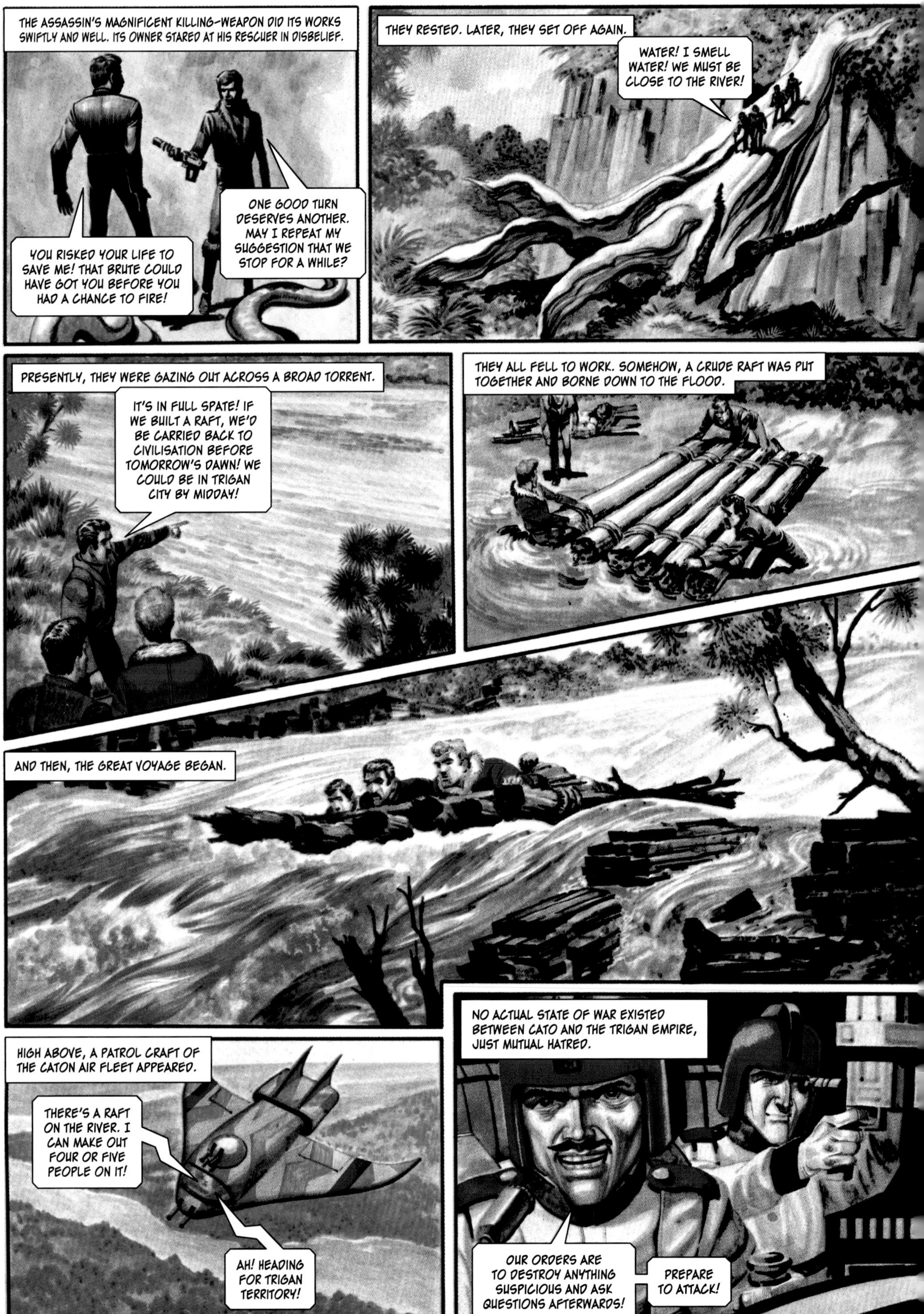
THE ASSASSIN'S MAGNIFICENT KILLING-WEAPON DID ITS WORKS SWIFTLY AND WELL. ITS OWNER STARED AT HIS RESCUER IN DISBELIEF.
YOU RISKED YOUR LIFE TO SAVE ME! THAT BRUTE COULD HAVE GOT YOU BEFORE YOU HAD A CHANCE TO FIRE!
ONE GOOD TURN DESERVES ANOTHER. MAY I REPEAT MY SUGGESTION THAT WE STOP FOR A WHILE?
THEY RESTED. LATER, THEY SET OFF AGAIN.
WATER! I SMELL WATER! WE MUST BE CLOSE TO THE RIVER!
PRESENTLY, THEY WERE GAZING OUT ACROSS A BROAD TORRENT.
IT'S IN FULL SPATE! IF WE BUILT A RAFT, WE'D BE CARRIED BACK TO CIVILISATION BEFORE TOMORROW'S DAWN! WE COULD BE IN TRIGAN CITY BY MIDDAY!
THEY ALL FELL TO WORK. SOMEHOW, A CRUDE RAFT WAS PUT TOGETHER AND BORNE DOWN TO THE FLOOD.
AND THEN, THE GREAT VOYAGE BEGAN.
HIGH ABOVE, A PATROL CRAFT OF THE CATON AIR FLEET APPEARED.
THERE'S A RAFT ON THE RIVER. I CAN MAKE OUT FOUR OR FIVE PEOPLE ON IT!
AH! HEADING FOR TRIGAN TERRITORY!
NO ACTUAL STATE OF WAR EXISTED BETWEEN CATO AND THE TRIGAN EMPIRE, JUST MUTUAL HATRED.
OUR ORDERS ARE TO DESTROY ANYTHING SUSPICIOUS AND ASK QUESTIONS AFTERWARDS!
PREPARE TO ATTACK!

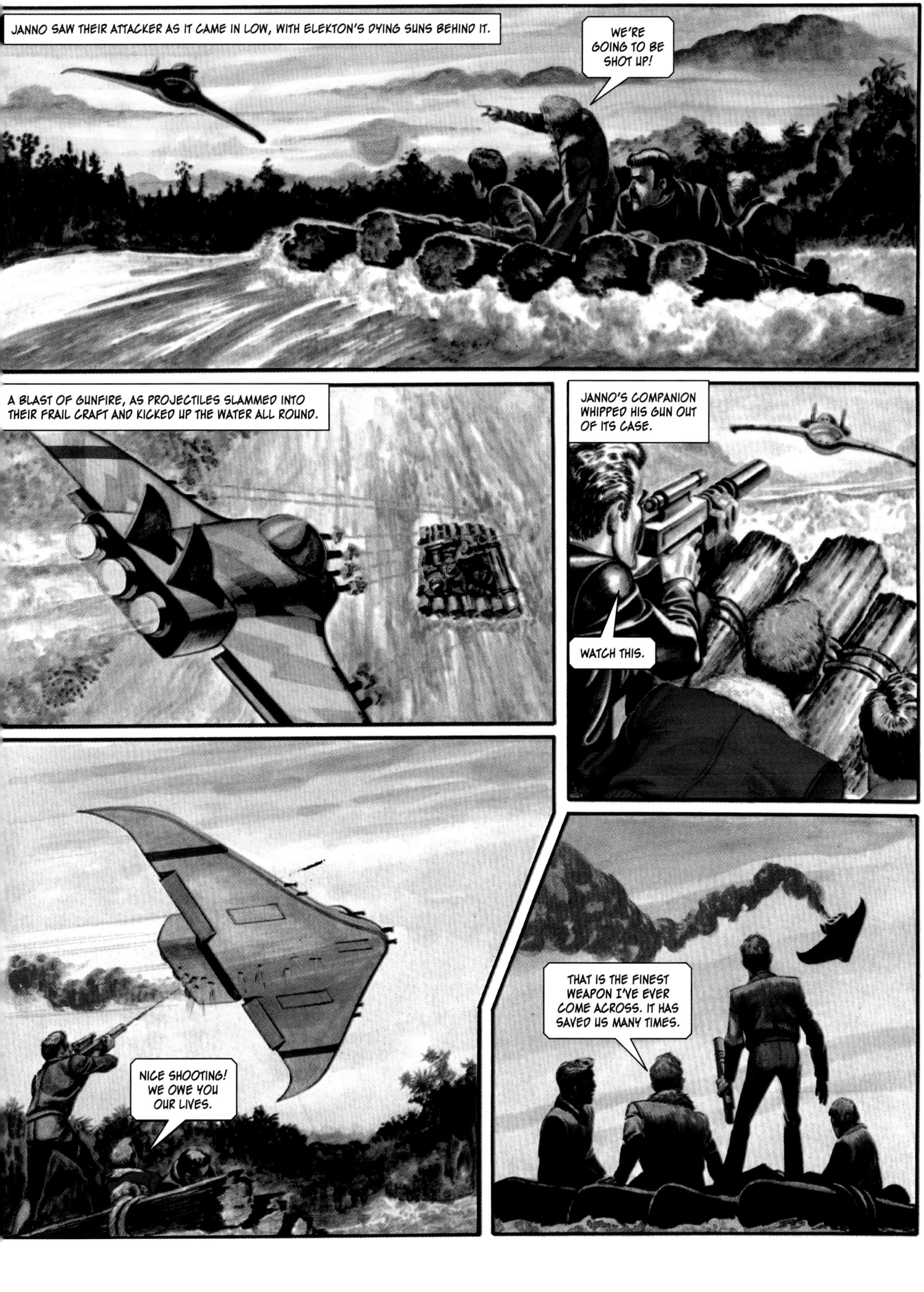
JANNO SAW THEIR ATTACKER AS IT CAME IN LOW, WITH ELEKTON'S DYING SUNS BEHIND IT.
WE'RE GOING TO BE SHOT UP!
A BLAST OF GUNFIRE, AS PROJECTILES SLAMMED INTO THEIR FRAIL CRAFT AND KICKED UP THE WATER ALL ROUND.
JANNO'S COMPANION WHIPPED HIS GUN OUT OF ITS CASE.
WATCH THIS.
NICE SHOOTING! WE OWE YOU OUR LIVES.
THAT IS THE FINEST WEAPON I'VE EVER COME ACROSS. IT HAS SAVED US MANY TIMES.

THE ASSASSIN SMILED.

IT WILL ALSO SERVER TO ELIMINATE THE EMPEROR TRIGO AND EARN ME A FORTUNE.

HE WOULD HAVE BEEN SURPRISED TO HAVE KNOWN JANNO'S THOUGHTS AT THAT MOMENT.

MAY WE REACH TRIGAN CITY IN TIME FOR ME TO WARN UNCLE TRIGO THAT SOMEONE IS PLANNING TO ASSASSINATE HIM TOMORROW.

A THIRD MEMBER OF THE PARTY – KITTU – HAD OTHER GRAVE REASONS FOR WANTING TO REACH CIVILISATION.

MY BEST FRIEND WILL BE EXECUTED UNLESS I'M THERE TOMORROW, TO PROVE HIS INNOCENCE.

ALL THROUGH THE LONG NIGHT, THE MAKESHIFT RAFT WAS BORNE ON THE TURBULENT WATERS OF THE BROAD RIVER. AT DAWN, THEY SAW LIGHTS AND KNEW THAT THEIR LONG VOYAGE WAS NEARLY OVER.

IT'S A FISHING VILLAGE.

THEY'LL HAVE COMMUNICATIONS WITH THE CAPITAL. I'LL HAVE AIR TRANSPORT HERE IN NO TIME.

JANNO SENT A MESSAGE TO TRIGAN CITY WHICH SWIFTLY BROUGHT A TRANSPORT CRAFT OF THE AIR FLEET.

YOU MUST HAVE PLENTY OF INFLUENCE, TO ORDER UP ONE OF THOSE THINGS SO SMARTLY.

WHO ARE YOU, ANYHOW? I NEVER THOUGHT TO ASK.

I'M THE EMPEROR'S NEPHEW, JANNO.

TO THINK I'VE TRAVELLED WITH A CLOSE RELATIVE OF THE VERY PERSON I'VE COME HERE TO ELIMINATE.

LATER, AS THE CRAFT TOOK OFF FOR TRIGAN CITY AND A DATE WITH DESTINY, THE ASSASSIN'S KEEN MIND HAD ARRIVED AT A DECISION.

WHAT A STROKE OF LUCK. I SHALL USE FRIEND JANNO'S INFLUENCE TO GET MYSELF CLOSE TO THE EMPEROR THIS AFTERNOON...FOR THE FATAL SHOT.

JANNO'S FATHER, BRAG, WAS FIRST TO GREET HIM ON HIS ARRIVAL AT TRIGAN CITY AIRPORT.

THANK THE STARS YOU'RE SAFE, LAD. BUT WHY THE SERIOUS FACE?

I HAVE GRAVE NEWS, FATHER, BUT IT MUST WAIT UNTIL WE ARE ALONE!

HE INTRODUCED HIS FELLOW TRAVELLERS.

KITTU MUST GO IMMEDIATELY TO THE COURT OF JUSTICE. HE HAS EVIDENCE WHICH WILL SAVE HIS BEST FRIEND FROM UNJUST EXECUTION.

HE SHALL BE ESCORTED THERE BY MY OWN PERSONAL BODYGUARDS.

LORD BRAG, THE THANKS OF AN OLD BLIND MAN ARE POURED UPON YOUR FINE SON, FOR HIS BRAVERY AND HIS KINDNESS.

I THANK YOU.

AND NO, FATHER, I WANT YOU TO MEET THE TRUE HERO OF THE ADVENTURE. WE NEVER WOULD HAVE GOT BACK WITHOUT HIM AND I DON'T EVEN KNOW HIS NAME!

CALL ME...ZITH.

I AM IN YOUR DEBT, ZITH. ANY FAVOUR YOU ASK WILL BE GRANTED.

I WOULD GREATLY LIKE TO SEE TODAY'S OPENING OF THE IMPERIAL ASSEMBLY, FROM A SEAT HIGH UP SO THAT I SHALL NOT MISS ANYTHING OF THE SPECTACLE.

THAT AFTERNOON, THE EMPEROR AND HIS FAMILY AND ENTOURAGE ENTERED THE VAST ASSEMBLY BUILDING.

LONG LIVE THE EMPEROR!

FOLLOWING JANNO'S GRAVE NEWS THAT THERE WOULD BE AN ASSASSINATION ATTEMPT, THE GREAT AMPHITHEATRE WAS RINGED WITH ARMED GUARDS.

ALONE, IN A FAVOURED PLACE NEAR THE ROOF, WAS ZITH. THERE WAS NO ONE TO SEE HIM PRODUCE HIS DEADLY GUN!

AND NOW, PROUD EMPEROR, WITH THE HELPFUL CONNIVANCE OF YOUR FAMILY, I WILL ELIMINATE YOU!

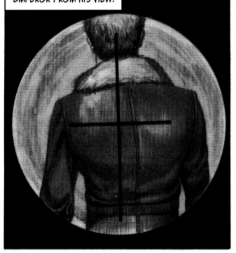

THE PROFESSIONAL ASSASSIN TOOK AIM AT THE SAME MOMENT THAT JANNO'S BROAD BACK OBSCURED THE EMPEROR FROM HIS VIEW.

MOVE, CURSE YOU, OR I'LL HAVE TO ELIMINATE YOU TO GET A SHOT AT YOUR UNCLE!

I CAN'T KILL JANNO IN COLD BLOOD...

NOT SOMEONE WHO SAVED MY LIFE AT THE RISK OF HIS OWN!

THEN, A VOICE BEHIND HIM, A MENACING, HISSING VOICE.

SHOOT THEM BOTH NOW!

YOU?

IT WAS THE OLD BLIND MAN! NOT BLIND, AND AT CLOSER INSPECTION, NOT SO VERY OLD!

YES! MY TASK WAS TO FOLLOW YOU AND MAKE SURE THAT YOU DID YOUR TASK!

TRIGO ROSE TO HIS FEET.

MY LORDS, CITIZENS OF THE EMPIRE! I DECLARE THE ASSEMBLY OPEN!

LONG LIVE THE EMPEROR!

LONG LIVE THE EMPEROR!

HIGH IN THE ROOF OF THE VAST DOME, ZITH GLARED INTO THE MENACING FACE OF HIS COMPANION.

SHOOT! DO YOUR DUTY AND DESTROY TRIGO. YOU'VE HAD YOUR FEE, NOW EARN IT!

I TAKE NO ORDERS FROM THE LIKES OF YOU. I'M A PROFESSIONAL ASSASSIN, PROUD OF HIS CRAFT. I NEED NO SNEAKING ANIMAL TO CHECK UP ON ME. GO BACK AND TELL YOUR MASTERS THEY CAN HAVE THEIR MONEY BACK AND GET SOMEONE ELSE TO KILL TRIGO.

ALL RIGHT, FOOL. IT WAS MY TASK TO ELIMINATE YOU AFTER YOU HAD ELIMINATED THE EMPEROR BUT NOW...

...I'LL DESTROY YOU FIRST AND KILL THE EMPEROR MYSELF!

THAT'S WHAT YOU THINK!

NEXT MOMENT, THE TWO WERE GRAPPLING WITH EACH OTHER.

AAAAGH!

THE SOUND OF A SHOT, ECHOING AND RE-ECHOING IN THAT HUGE ASSEMBLY, HAD SILENCED THE SOLEMN PROCEEDINGS.

SOMEONE'S UP THERE!

LOOK, UNCLE!

A FIGURE CAME CARTWHEELING DOWN TO DESTRUCTION.

EAAAAAA-A-A-AGGHH!

JANNO LED THE RUSH TO INVESTIGATE THE UPPER GALLERY. WHEN THEY REACHED THERE, ZITH HAD GONE.

I DISTINCTLY WAS TWO FIGURES FIGHTING UP HERE, JUST AFTER THE SHOT.

ONE OF THEM MUST HAVE BEEN ZITH. BUT WHERE IS HE?

COME TO THINK OF IT, WHO IS HE?

JANNO NEVER RECEIVED AN ANSWER TO HIS QUESTION. AT THAT VERY MOMENT, ZITH, THE ASSASSIN, WAS CROSSING THE BRIDGE OUT OF TRIGAN CITY. WITH HIM HE CARRIED THE CASE THAT HELD HIS DEADLY KILLING-WEAPON.

THE GAME ISN'T WHAT IT USED TO BE. TOO MANY AMATEURS AND BUSYBODIES SPOILING THE ARTISTRY OF THE DEDICATED PROFESSIONAL. I'LL GIVE IT UP, THAT'S WHAT I'LL DO, AND BECOME A FARMER INSTEAD.

WITH THAT THOUGHT, ZITH HURLED HIS BELOVED KILLING-WEAPON FAR OUT INTO THE WATERS OF TRIGAN RIVER...

...AND WENT ON HIS WAY, NEVER TO TAKE LIFE AGAIN.

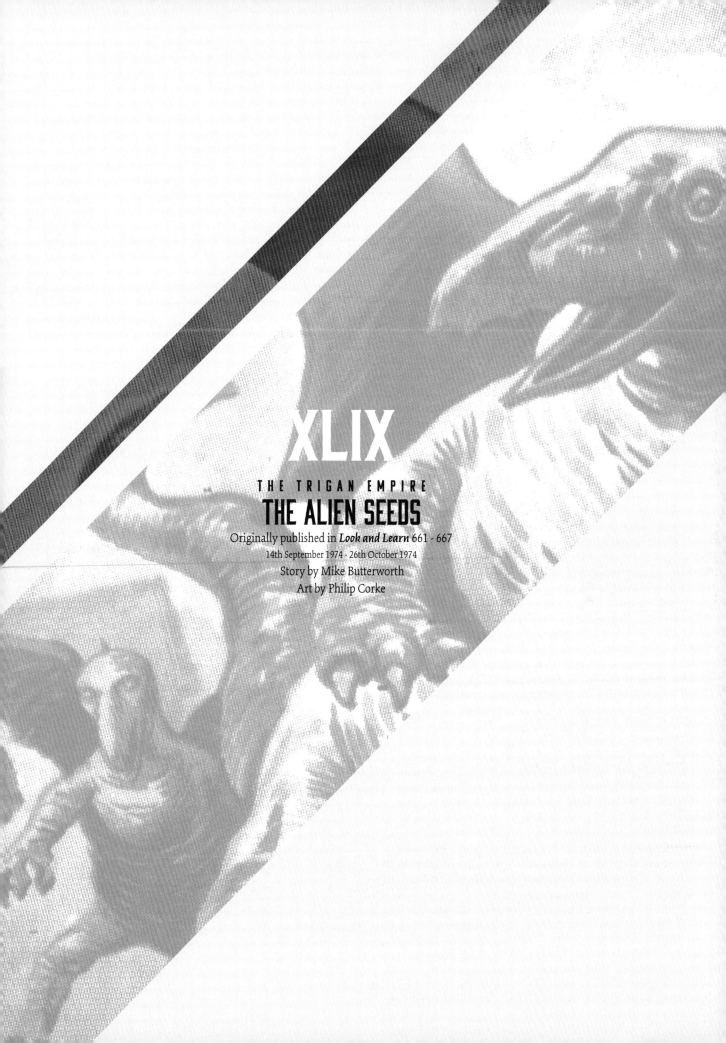

XLIX

THE TRIGAN EMPIRE
THE ALIEN SEEDS

Originally published in *Look and Learn* 661 - 667

14th September 1974 - 26th October 1974

Story by Mike Butterworth

Art by Philip Corke

IT WAS IN THE FOURTH LUNAR MONTH OF THE YEAR OF ZOOTH THAT AN ASTRAL PHENOMENON WAS OBSERVED IN THE SKY ABOVE ELEKTON.

COUNTLESS MULTITUDES SAW IT, WONDERING AT ITS BRIGHTNESS THAT TURNED THE NIGHT TO DAY.

IT'S A SHOOTING STAR!

I NEVER SAW SUCH A SHOOTING STAR BEFORE IN MY LIFE!

ELEKTON'S TOP SCIENTIST, PERIC, HAD THE ANSWER TO THE STRANGE OBJECT IN THE SKY.

IT IS AN EXPLODED WORLD!

SOMEWHERE OUT IN SPACE, A WORLD LIKE OURS BLEW UP INTO FRAGMENTS. THE THING THAT PASSED THROUGH OUR OUTER ATMOSPHERE WAS ONE OF THE PIECES OF THAT DESTROYED PLANET!

THE PHENOMENON PASSED ON ITS WAY INTO THE TRACKLESS WILDERNESS OF OUTER SPACE. BUT, HIGH IN THE UPPER ATMOSPHERE OF ELEKTON, A CLOUD OF STRANGE PARTICLES REMAINED AND SLOWLY DESCENDED.

THE PARTICLES WERE SEEDS. THEY FELL UPON THE SURFACE OF THE PLANET, WILDLY SCATTERED. PRESENTLY, THEY PUT FORTH SMALL WHITE FLOWERS...

SOME DISTANCE FROM TRIGAN CITY, A HERDSMAN PLAYED HIS PIPE AND IDLY WATCHED HIS FLOCK.

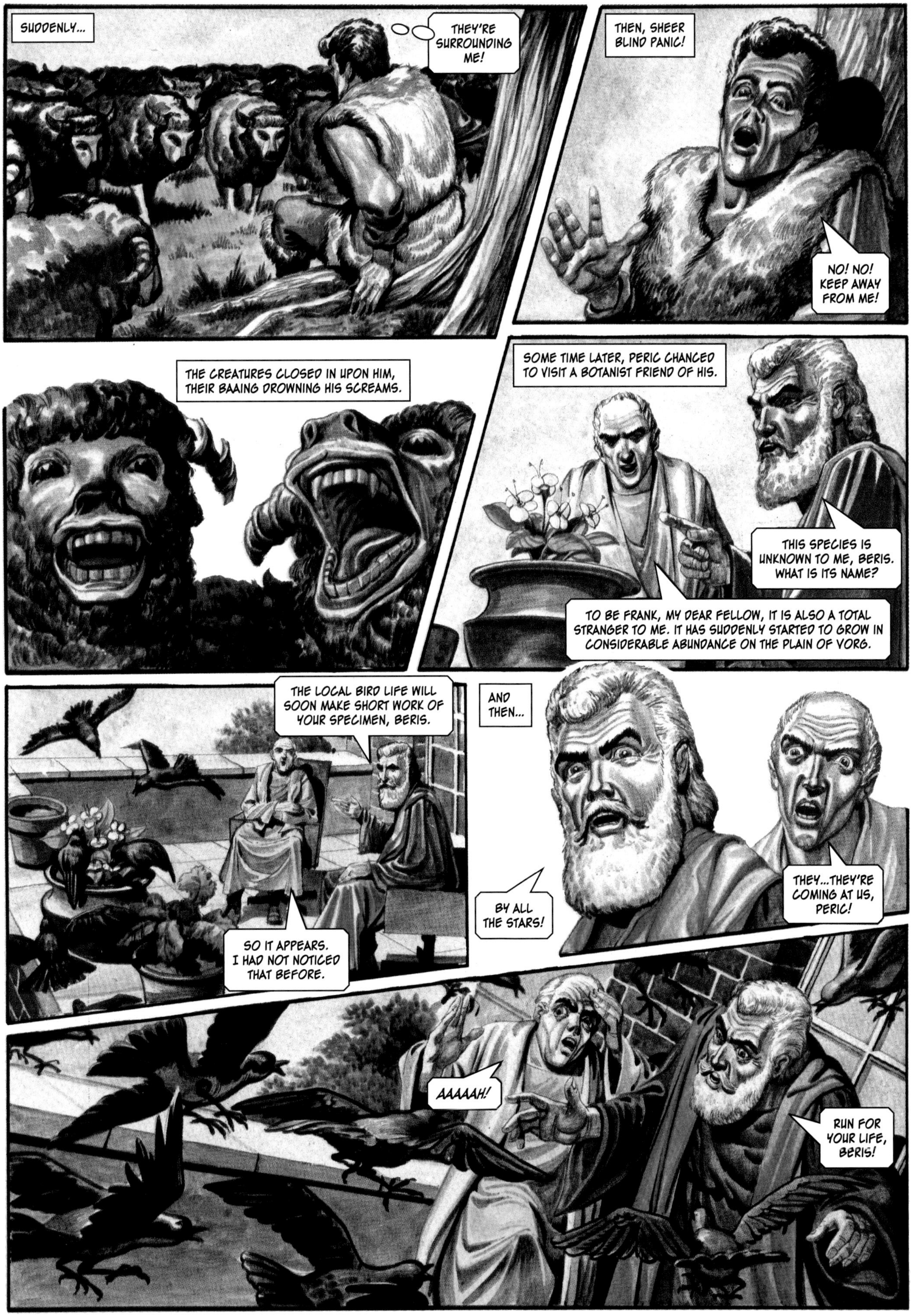
SUDDENLY...
THEY'RE SURROUNDING ME!
THEN, SHEER BLIND PANIC!
NO! NO! KEEP AWAY FROM ME!
THE CREATURES CLOSED IN UPON HIM, THEIR BAAING DROWNING HIS SCREAMS.
SOME TIME LATER, PERIC CHANCED TO VISIT A BOTANIST FRIEND OF HIS.
THIS SPECIES IS UNKNOWN TO ME, BERIS. WHAT IS ITS NAME?
TO BE FRANK, MY DEAR FELLOW, IT IS ALSO A TOTAL STRANGER TO ME. IT HAS SUDDENLY STARTED TO GROW IN CONSIDERABLE ABUNDANCE ON THE PLAIN OF VORG.
THE LOCAL BIRD LIFE WILL SOON MAKE SHORT WORK OF YOUR SPECIMEN, BERIS.
SO IT APPEARS. I HAD NOT NOTICED THAT BEFORE.
AND THEN...
BY ALL THE STARS!
THEY...THEY'RE COMING AT US, PERIC!
AAAAAH!
RUN FOR YOUR LIFE, BERIS!

THE TWO SCIENTISTS BACKED AWAY, BEATING OFF THE TINY FORMS AND THEIR SLASHING BEAKS AND TALONS.

CLOSE THE DOOR, OR WE'RE DONE FOR!

SAFE INSIDE, THEY STARED AT THEIR ASSAILANTS.

THEY'VE TURNED INTO FIGHTING MAD KILLERS!

BUT... WHY?... HOW?

IN THE LUNAR MONTHS THAT FOLLOWED, THE STRANGE PLANT GAVE FORTH A BERRY-LIKE FRUIT.

A PARTY OF SCHOOLBOYS FROM TRIGAN CITY WERE CAMPING IN THE FOREST OF VORG, UNDER THE CHARGE OF THEIR MASTER.

GO EXPLORING, BY ALL MEANS, BUT MIND YOU'RE ALL BACK IN CAMP BY THE TIME THE SUN SETS.

LATER...

THESE BERRIES LOOK GOOD.

I'M GOING TO TRY ONE!

WATCH IT. THEY MIGHT BE POISONOUS.

WHAT'S IT TASTE LIKE?

IT'S...IT'S... FANTASTIC! TRY SOME FOR YOURSELVES.

TOWARDS SUNSET...

WHERE ARE THOSE CONFOUNDED LADS? I TOLD THEM TO BE BACK BY NOW.

SO THERE YOU ARE. ABOUT TIME, TOO!

WHY ARE YOU LOOKING AT ME LIKE THAT? DON'T... DON'T PLAY GAMES.

GET HIM!

DESTROY HIM.

HE RAN FOR HIS LIFE AND THEY FOLLOWED, BAYING LIKE ANIMALS.

NO! NO!

GA–A–A–AH!

E–E–E–E–E–EAAAAAH!

AT DAWN THE NEXT DAY, THE BOYS APPROACHED A NEARBY TRIGAN ARMY OUTPOST.

THE SENTRY WAS ALL UNSUSPECTING...

HELLO, LADS. WHAT CAN I DO FOR YOU, EH?

HEY! WHAT'S COME OVER YOU?

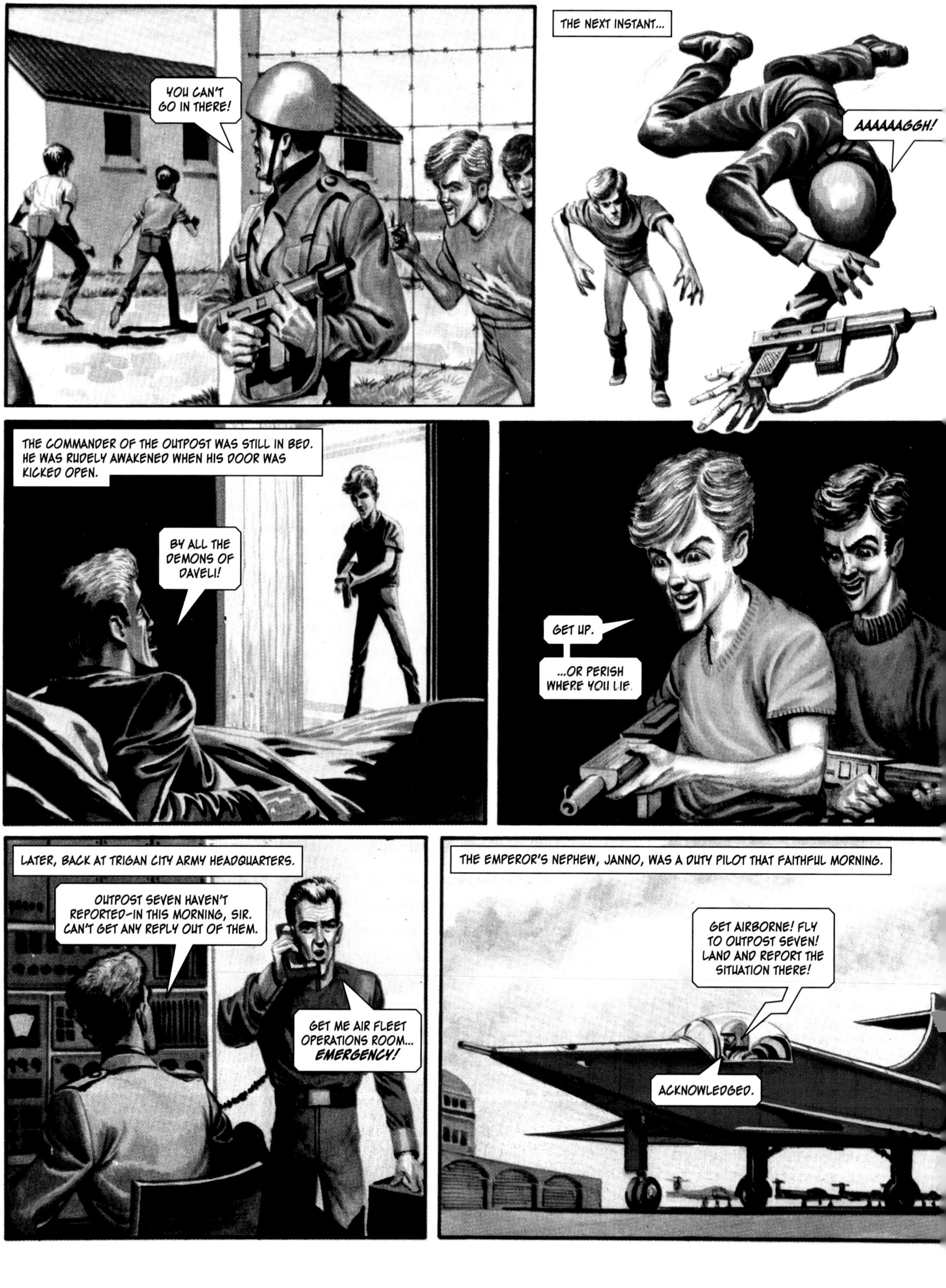
YOU CAN'T GO IN THERE!
THE NEXT INSTANT...
AAAAAAGGH!
THE COMMANDER OF THE OUTPOST WAS STILL IN BED. HE WAS RUDELY AWAKENED WHEN HIS DOOR WAS KICKED OPEN.
BY ALL THE DEMONS OF DAVELI!
GET UP.
...OR PERISH WHERE YOU LIE.
LATER, BACK AT TRIGAN CITY ARMY HEADQUARTERS.
OUTPOST SEVEN HAVEN'T REPORTED-IN THIS MORNING, SIR. CAN'T GET ANY REPLY OUT OF THEM.
GET ME AIR FLEET OPERATIONS ROOM... EMERGENCY!
THE EMPEROR'S NEPHEW, JANNO, WAS A DUTY PILOT THAT FAITHFUL MORNING.
GET AIRBORNE! FLY TO OUTPOST SEVEN! LAND AND REPORT THE SITUATION THERE!
ACKNOWLEDGED.

IT WAS A SHORT ULTRA-SONIC HOP TO THE CLEARING IN THE FOREST OF VORG WHERE THE OUTPOST LAY.

THE PLACE LOOKS PERFECTLY NORMAL FROM HERE.

HE LANDED AND CLIMBED OUT OF HIS CRAFT - TO BE IMMEDIATELY SURROUNDED.

WHAT ARE YOU LADS DOING HERE?

THE OUTPOST IS OURS. WE HAVE - *ELIMINATED* THE GARRISON!

YOU, HOWEVER, CAN BE OF SOME *USE* TO US!

LATER THAT MORNING, JANNO'S FIGHTING-CRAFT CAME IN FOR A TOUCH-DOWN AT ITS BASE.

HERE COMES JANNO. NOW WE'LL FIND OUT WHY HE HASN'T REPORTED-IN ABOUT THE SITUATION AT OUTPOST SEVEN.

AT THE LAST MOMENT, THE SIGHTING-CRAFT TURNED SHARPLY...

WHAT'S JANNO *DOING?*

...AND DIVED TO THE ATTACK!

AGAIN AND AGAIN, THE FIGHTING-CRAFT CAME IN WITH GUNS BLAZING.

OPEN FIRE ON HIM!

THE DEFENDERS NEVER HAD TIME TO STRIKE BACK.

THE ATTACKER STREAKED OFF.

YOU'LL PAY FOR THIS DAY'S WORK, JANNO – YOU FOUL TRAITOR!

THE NEWS WAS BROUGHT TO THE EMPEROR TRIGO.

MY OWN NEPHEW, YOU SAY? IS THERE NO POSSIBILITY OF A MISTAKE IN THE IDENTIFICATION OF THE CRAFT?

NONE AT ALL, IMPERIAL MAJESTY. IT WAS LORD JANNO'S CRAFT – AND HE HAS CAUSED HAVOC AT THE BASE!

YES, IMPERIAL MAJESTY.

THAT CRAFT – OR MY NEPHEW – ARE TO BE ATTACKED AND DESTROYED ON SIGHT!

ALONE, TRIGO COULD ONLY PONDER AND GRIEVE.

JANNO! WHY DID YOU DO IT, LAD? WHY?...WHY?

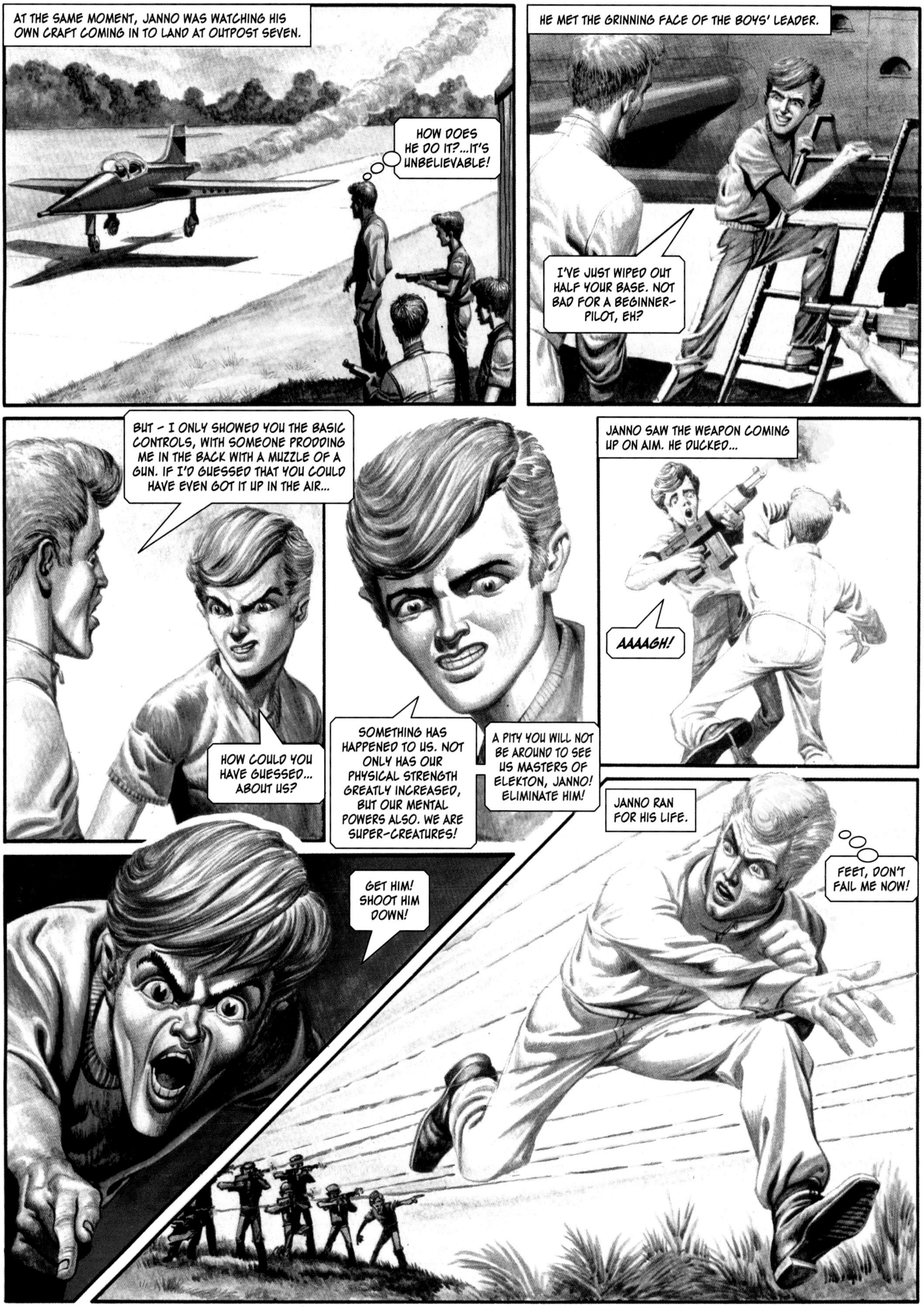
AT THE SAME MOMENT, JANNO WAS WATCHING HIS OWN CRAFT COMING IN TO LAND AT OUTPOST SEVEN.
HOW DOES HE DO IT?...IT'S UNBELIEVABLE!
HE MET THE GRINNING FACE OF THE BOYS' LEADER.
I'VE JUST WIPED OUT HALF YOUR BASE. NOT BAD FOR A BEGINNER-PILOT, EH?
BUT - I ONLY SHOWED YOU THE BASIC CONTROLS, WITH SOMEONE PRODDING ME IN THE BACK WITH A MUZZLE OF A GUN. IF I'D GUESSED THAT YOU COULD HAVE EVEN GOT IT UP IN THE AIR...
HOW COULD YOU HAVE GUESSED... ABOUT US?
SOMETHING HAS HAPPENED TO US. NOT ONLY HAS OUR PHYSICAL STRENGTH GREATLY INCREASED, BUT OUR MENTAL POWERS ALSO. WE ARE SUPER-CREATURES!
A PITY YOU WILL NOT BE AROUND TO SEE US MASTERS OF ELEKTON, JANNO! ELIMINATE HIM!
JANNO SAW THE WEAPON COMING UP ON AIM. HE DUCKED...
AAAAGH!
GET HIM! SHOOT HIM DOWN!
JANNO RAN FOR HIS LIFE.
FEET, DON'T FAIL ME NOW!

JANNO DIVED HEADLONG FOR THE UNDERGROWTH, WITH PROJECTILES SLASHING PAST HIM LIKE METEORITES.

HE LAY STILL, WHILE HIS MERCILESS PURSUERS SEARCHED THE FOREST ALL ROUND HIM.

NO SIGN OF HIM. HE'S ESCAPED US.

WHAT DOES IT MATTER? HE'S A NOBODY.

THE SELF-APPOINTED LEADER OF THE SUPER-CREATURES PRODUCED A HANDFUL OF DEADLY FRUIT.

WE WILL CONTINUE WITH OUR PLANS OF CONQUEST. BUT FIRST... WE WILL FEAST AGAIN OFF THE FOOD OF THE GODS.

JANNO STAYED HIDDEN TILL NIGHTFALL. HE THEN SET OFF FOR TRIGAN CITY, REACHING THERE BY DAYBREAK.

I'LL REPORT TO MY UNCLE AT ONCE. THOSE BOYS ARE A REAL DANGER AND MUST BE STOPPED IMMEDIATELY.

BUT...

LOOK! IT'S JANNO!

CUT HIM DOWN!

ONLY JANNO'S QUICK WITS AND LIGHTNING PHYSICAL REACTIONS SAVED HIM.

BY ALL THE STARS!

WHY ARE MY OWN PEOPLE SHOOTING AT ME ON SIGHT?

HE SOON LEARNED THE ANSWER...

DID WE GET HIM?

I HOPE SO! WE'LL BE COMMENDED BY THE EMPEROR FOR WIPING OUT THE TRAITOR WHO ATTACKED THE AIR BASE.

I'VE BEEN DECLARED A TRAITOR!

FOLLOWING THE MYSTERIOUS ATTACK UPON THE AIR BASE, THE TRIGAN ARMOURED CORPS WERE PUT ON ALERT.

NONE OF THE SOLDIERS TOOK ANY NOTICE OF A GROUP OF BOYS WATCHING NEARBY.

WE'LL TAKE THESE WAR-MACHINES AND USE THEM TO DESTROY TRIGAN CITY!

PERIC WAS WORKING IN HIS LABORATORY THAT FATEFUL MORNING, WHEN A SOUND AT THE OPEN WINDOW MADE HIM TURN.

PERIC.

AAAAH...YOU.

THE GREAT SCIENTIST'S HAND GROPED FOR A BUTTON...

PERIC. SOMETHING TERRIBLE IS HAPPENING...

IMMEDIATELY, THE YOUNG AIR-FLEET PILOT WAS ENVELOPED IN TWIN-CLOUDS OF CHOKING RED GAS!

AAAAAAGH!

FOOL! DO YOU THINK I AM WITHOUT PROTECTION HERE?

JANNO RECOVERED CONSCIOUSNESS, TO FIND HIMSELF TOTALLY PARALYSED.

PERIC, YOU... YOU'VE GOT TO LISTEN TO ME.

I AM ALL ATTENTION. TO BEGIN WITH, YOU WILL EXPLAIN YOUR MOTIVES FOR ATTACKING THE AIR-FLEET BASE AND CAUSING SUCH HAVOC!

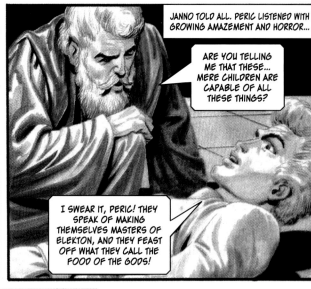

JANNO TOLD ALL. PERIC LISTENED WITH GROWING AMAZEMENT AND HORROR...

ARE YOU TELLING ME THAT THESE... MERE CHILDREN ARE CAPABLE OF ALL THESE THINGS?

I SWEAR IT, PERIC! THEY SPEAK OF MAKING THEMSELVES MASTERS OF ELEKTON, AND THEY FEAST OFF WHAT THEY CALL THE FOOD OF THE GODS!

PRESENTLY, THE FEELING CAME BACK INTO THE YOUNG MAN'S LIMBS.

WE MUST GO TO THE EMPEROR AT ONCE.

YES! I'VE SEEN WHAT THEY'RE CAPABLE OF, PERIC.

AT THAT VERY MOMENT, THE BOYS WERE CHATTING WITH SOLDIERS OF THE TRIGAN ARMOURED CORPS.

RIGHT, LADS. WE'VE SHOWN YOU HOW TO WORK THE CONTROLS, WHAT ELSE DO YOU WANT TO FIND OUT?

I THINK WE KNOW ALL WE NEED TO KNOW...

STRIKE!

AAAAAGHH!

START UP YOUR WAR-MACHINES. SURROUND THE CITY FROM ALL SIDES, THEN CLOSE IN, SHOOTING AS YOU GO!

DISASTER WAS ABOUT TO ENVELOP THE HEART OF THE TRIGAN EMPIRE.

YET ANOTHER PERIL THREATENED. A HERD OF ZARGOTS, SAVAGE KILLERS OF THE VORG PLAINS, CAME UPON SOME OF THE ALIEN PLANTS AND ATE THE FRUIT.

THE EFFECT OF EATING THE FOOD OF THE GODS WAS TO INCREASE THEIR NORMAL GREAT STRENGTH AND KILLING-INSTINCT A HUNDREDFOLD.

THE NEWS SPREAD LIKE A FOREST FIRE THROUGH THE SMALL VILLAGES AND TOWNSHIPS BORDERING THE PLAINS.

THE ZARGOTS ARE COMING!

THE MADDENED BEASTS TORE THROUGH THE STREETS.

THEY ARE NOW HEADING FOR... TRIGAN CITY!

PREPARE TO OPEN FIRE! NOT ONE STONE IS TO BE LEFT STANDING!

THEN THE LEADER SAW...

BY ALL THE STARS! ZARGOTS!

THIS HERD OF THE MOST SAVAGE PREDATORS ON ELEKTON HAD ALSO EATEN OF "THE FOOD OF THE GODS"

THEY FELL UPON THE WAR-MACHINES BEFORE THE BOYS HAD TIME TO BRING THEIR GUNS TO AIM...

...AND SCATTERED THEM LIKE TOYS.

JANNO AND PERIC HAD BROUGHT THE NEWS TO THE EMPEROR. THEY SAW THE DESTRUCTION FROM THE ROOF OF THE IMPERIAL PALACE.

THE BOYS SEEM TO HAVE ESCAPED – THEY'RE IN FULL FLIGHT.

THE ZARGOTS HAVE DESTROYED ALL THE WAR-MACHINES.

WE HAVE EXCHANGED ONE EVIL FOR ANOTHER! IT IS THE ZARGOTS WHO WILL POUND TRIGAN CITY TO RUBBLE.

INDEED, IT SEEMED THAT PERIC'S PREDICTION WOULD COME TRUE. BUT APPROACHING THE OUTSKIRTS OF THE CITY, THE HERD SIGHTED A PLANTATION OF FRUITS, THE DEADLY "FOODS OF THE GODS".

THE DEFEATED BOYS LAY AND WATCHED THE HERD BROWSING ON THE FRUIT.

THOSE BRUTES WON'T STOP TILL THEY'VE EATEN THE LOT.

I'M CRAVING FOR SOME OF THAT "FOOD OF THE GODS".

THERE'S NOTHING WE CAN DO. WE MAY BE SUPER-CREATURES, BUT WE CAN'T HANDLE SUPER-ZARGOTS.

IT WAS AT THAT TIME THAT THE BOTANIST, BERIS, ARRIVED AT THE IMPERIAL PALACE, TO SEE HIS FRIEND, PERIC.

PERIC, I HAVE ANALYSED THE STRUCTURE OF THE ALIEN PLANT AND HAVE ESTABLISHED THAT ITS AWFUL EFFECT UPON LIVING BEINGS IS ONLY TEMPORARY. FURTHERMORE, I HAVE DEVISED A CHEMICAL THAT WILL RAPIDLY KILL THE PLANT, IF SPRAYED UPON IT FROM THE AIR.

WE NEED SOME OF THAT CHEMICAL NOW, BERIS, TO SAVE TRIGAN CITY!

SOON AFTER, JANNO FLEW OVER THE ZARGOT HERD AND SPRAYED THE DEADLY PLANT. IT WITHERED TO THE TOUCH OF THE CHEMICAL. DISMAYED, THE ZARGOTS MOVED ON TO FIND FRESH PLANTATIONS, BUT JANNO WAS ALWAYS AHEAD OF THEM, KILLING, KILLING...

THE FOLLOWING DAY, A BEDRAGGLED MOB OF BOYS STRAGGLED SHAMEFACEDLY INTO TRIGAN CITY. THE EFFECTS OF "THE FOOD OF THE GODS" HAD LEFT THEM FOREVER.

I – I DON'T KNOW WHAT CAME OVER US. WE DIDN'T SEEM TO HAVE ANY CONTROL OVER OUR ACTIONS. ALL WE WANTED TO DO WAS DESTROY, DESTROY, DESTROY!

AS PERIC SAID LATER...

WE HAVE ALSO CONFIRMED THAT THE SEEDS OF THE PLANT CAME FROM THE FRAGMENT OF DESTROYED PLANET THAT WAS OBSERVED IN THE FOURTH LUNAR MONTH OF THIS YEAR. IT IS NOT HARD TO GUESS HOW THAT PLANET WAS DESTROYED – BY AN ATOMIC WAR!

THE SAME THING COULD HAVE HAPPENED ON ELEKTON!

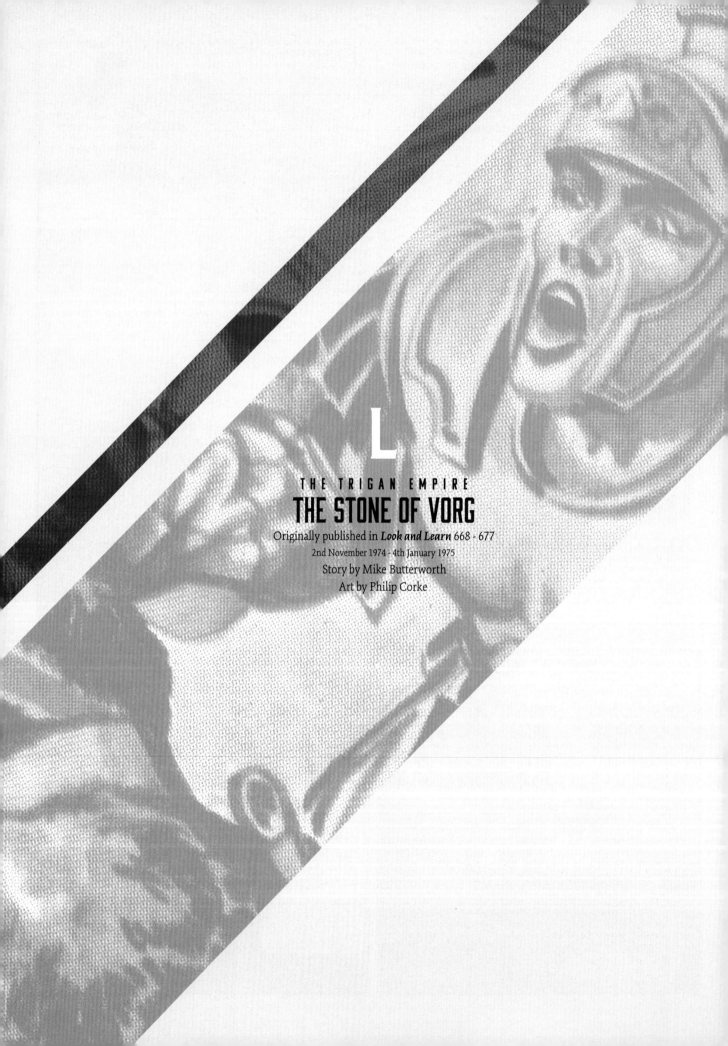

L

THE TRIGAN EMPIRE
THE STONE OF VORG

Originally published in *Look and Learn* 668 - 677

2nd November 1974 - 4th January 1975

Story by Mike Butterworth

Art by Philip Corke

ONE MEMORABLE DAY, A STRANGER CAME OUT OF THE WILDERNESS. ALTHOUGH HE WAS SIMPLY DRESSED, HE BORE HIMSELF LIKE A LEADER OF WARRIORS.

HE DISMOUNTED AT A KERBSIDE INN AND ATE HIS SIMPLE MEAL IN SILENCE.

LATER, CROSSING THE GREAT SQUARE OF THE CITY, THE STRANGER ESPIED A GREAT BOULDER PLANTED THERE.

HE HAILED A PASSER-BY.

TELL ME, FELLOW, WHAT IS THAT DOING HERE?

WHY, THAT IS THE STONE OF VORG! I WILL TELL YOU ITS STORY...

"MANY LUNAR YEARS AGO, BEFORE THE FOUNDATION OF THE EMPIRE, TARGO, THE FATHER OF THE EMPEROR TRIGO AND A GREAT CHIEF AMONG THE VORGS, WAS LOST WHILE HUNTING IN THE HILLS..."

I SHALL NEVER REACH CAMP NOW. IT WILL BE A CHILL NIGHT IN THE OPEN FOR ME.

"TARGO MADE A FIRE AND PREPARED SOME FOOD. PRESENTLY..."

WHO COMES? FRIEND OR FOE?

I COME IN PEACE.

MY SON, SPARE A MORSEL TO EAT FOR A POOR WANDERER, AND YOU WILL NOT REGRET IT.

BE SEATED, MASTER. HALF OF WHAT I HAVE IS GLADLY YOURS.

"THE MEAL OVER, THE SOOTHA MADE AN ASTOUNDING PREDICTION TO THE VORG CHIEF..."

YOU HAVE A SON AND HE WILL LEAD YOUR PEOPLE TO AN UNHEARD-OF GREATNESS. HE WILL BECOME THE PRINCIPAL RULER OF THE ENTIRE PLANET ELEKTON, UNTIL...

UNTIL WHEN, MASTER?

"THE SOOTHA POINTED."

UNTIL HE WHO IS ABLE TO SMITE THAT STONE ASUNDER WITH ONE BLOW OF HIS FIST, COMES AND TAKES YOUR SON'S IMPERIAL CROWN FROM HIM!

"IT WAS THE EMPEROR TRIGO HIMSELF WHO, MANY YEARS LATER, HAD THE STONE BROUGHT TO HIS OWN CAPITAL CITY AND SET UP IN THE GREAT SQUARE."

THAT STONE SHALL STAND HERE, AS A REMINDER TO ME THAT I MUST ALWAYS RULE YOU JUSTLY AND WELL. IF I FAIL IN MY TASK, MAY THE PROPHECY BE FULFILLED...MAY HE WHO CAN SMITE THE STONE ASUNDER COME AND TAKE MY IMPERIAL CROWN FROM ME!

THE STORY ENDED, THE STRANGER GAZED AT THE STONE OF VORG.

OF COURSE, IT WOULD BE IMPOSSIBLE TO BREAK THE STONE, EVEN WITH A WAR-CLUB, LET ALONE WITH THE BARE FIST.

I WONDER...

BEFORE THE ASTONISHED GAZE OF PASSERS-BY, THE STRANGER RAISED HIS FIST AND BROUGHT IT DOWN.

HAH!

...HUH!

HE'S DONE IT!

196

OVERCOME WITH AWE AND WONDER, THE ONLOOKERS IN THE GREAT SQUARE FELL ON THEIR KNEES.

THE PROPHECY HAS COME TRUE!

THE NEW EMPEROR OF ALL THE TRIGANS.

THE OBJECT OF THEIR VENERATION SMILED WRYLY.

EMPEROR OF THE TRIGANS! THAT WOULD BE QUITE SOMETHING.

TRIGO WAS AT BREAKFAST WHEN THE NEWS WAS BROUGHT TO HIM.

IMPERIAL MAJESTY! SOME FELLOW HAS SMASHED THE STONE OF VORG WITH HIS BARE FIST!

RUBBISH!

IT WAS SOME TIME BEFORE THE OFFICER COULD CONVINCE HIS EMPEROR THAT THE IMPOSSIBLE HAD, IN FACT, HAPPENED.

WHAT IS TO BE DONE, SIRE?

GET HOLD OF SOME MEMBERS OF THE IMPERIAL COUNCIL. ASK THEM TO QUESTION THIS STRANGER, FIND OUT WHO HE IS AND SO FORTH.

SO IT WAS THAT ZACHO AND SERRO, TWO MEMBERS OF THE COUNCIL, QUESTIONED THE STRANGER.

WHO ARE YOU FELLOW AND FROM WHERE DO YOU HAIL?

WHAT IS YOUR OCCUPATION?

CALL ME...Z!

THE CAPTAIN OF THE IMPERIAL GUARD COULD TOLERATE THE STRANGER'S INSOLENCE NO LONGER.

YOU HAVE USED SORCERY TO SMASH THE STONE, BUT YOUR SORCERY WILL NOT TAKE THE CROWN FROM MY EMPEROR'S HEAD.

LOOK YOUR LAST UPON THE SKY, ANIMAL.

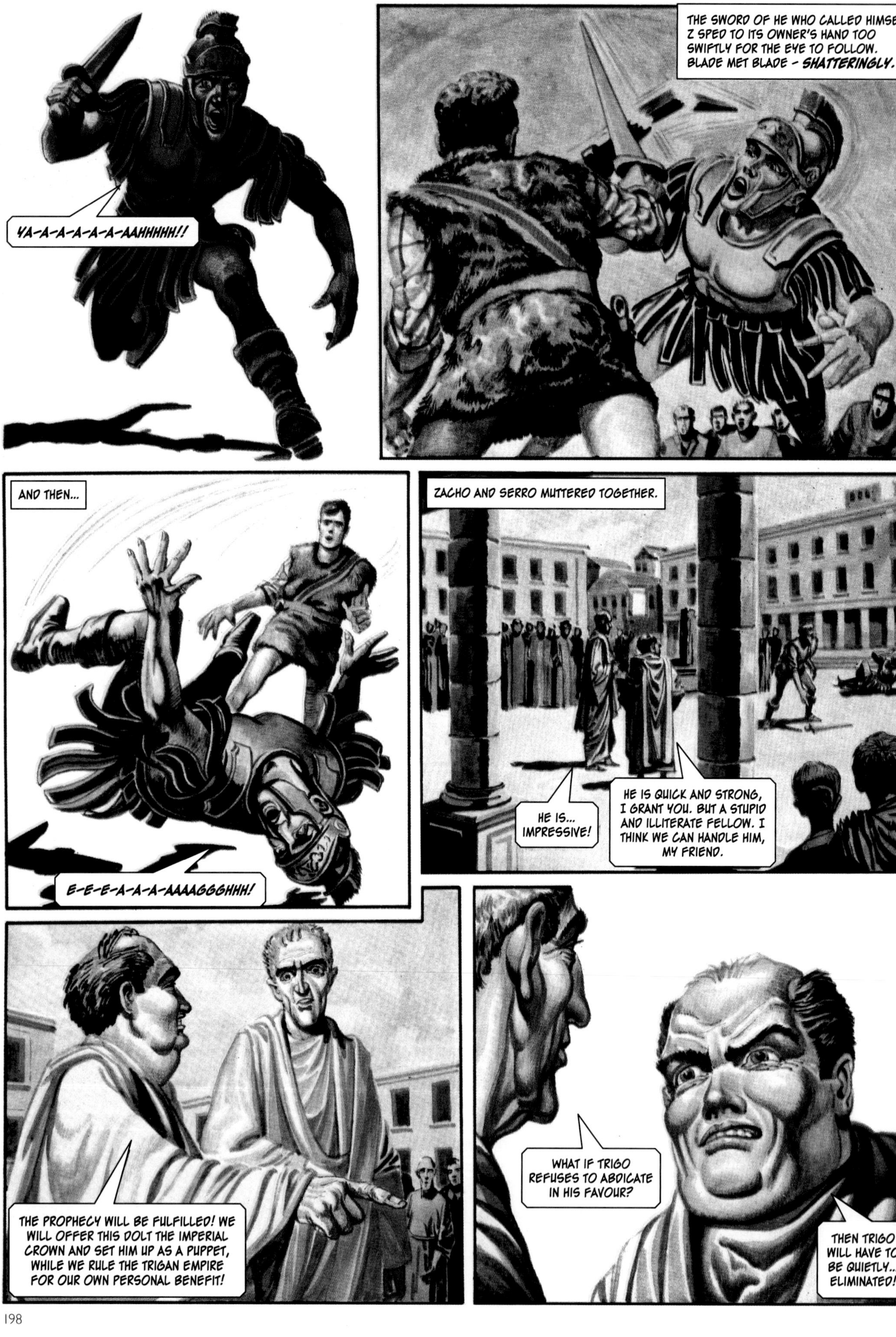
YA-A-A-A-A-A-AAHHHHH!!
THE SWORD OF HE WHO CALLED HIMSELF Z SPED TO ITS OWNER'S HAND TOO SWIFTLY FOR THE EYE TO FOLLOW. BLADE MET BLADE - SHATTERINGLY.
AND THEN...
E-E-E-A-A-A-AAAAGGGHHH!
ZACHO AND SERRO MUTTERED TOGETHER.
HE IS... IMPRESSIVE!
HE IS QUICK AND STRONG, I GRANT YOU. BUT A STUPID AND ILLITERATE FELLOW. I THINK WE CAN HANDLE HIM, MY FRIEND.
THE PROPHECY WILL BE FULFILLED! WE WILL OFFER THIS DOLT THE IMPERIAL CROWN AND SET HIM UP AS A PUPPET, WHILE WE RULE THE TRIGAN EMPIRE FOR OUR OWN PERSONAL BENEFIT!
WHAT IF TRIGO REFUSES TO ABDICATE IN HIS FAVOUR?
THEN TRIGO WILL HAVE TO BE QUIETLY... ELIMINATED!

TRIGO'S NEPHEW, JANNO, WAS ENJOYING A HOLIDAY AT A REMOTE PART OF THE GREAT OCEAN COAST.

THIS IS THE LIFE!

THEN HE RECEIVED A MESSAGE ON HIS PERSONAL CONTACT-SET.

THIS IS AN URGENT IMPERIAL SUMMONS. LORD JANNO WILL RETURN TO TRIGAN CITY AT ONCE AND REPORT TO THE PALACE.

ARRIVING IN HIS UNCLE'S THRONE ROOM, HE FOUND HIS FAMILY AND THE IMPERIAL COUNCIL ALREADY ASSEMBLED.

WHAT'S THE MATTER, FATHER?

SOME FELLOW HAS SMASHED THE STONE OF VORG WITH HIS BARE FIST AND THEREFORE CAN LAY CLAIM TO THE THRONE!

TRIGO CALLED FOR SILENCE. THEN HE SPOKE GRAVELY.

WHAT SHALL BE MY COURSE OF ACTION? IS IT MY DUTY TO REMAIN EMPEROR AND SERVE MY PEOPLE AS ONLY I KNOW BEST, OR MUST I RELINQUISH MY CROWN TO HE WHO CALLS HIMSELF Z?

GIVE ME YOUR VIEWS.

LONG LIVE THE EMPEROR TRIGO!

TO DAVELI WITH Z!

PERISH ALL PRETENDERS!

WE WANT NO STRANGER RULING US!

I THANK YOU FOR YOUR LOYAL SUPPORT. HOWEVER, I MUST GIVE THE MATTER CAREFUL THOUGHT. I SHALL DEPART INTO THE WILDERNESS FOR A WHILE AND, WHEN I RETURN, I WILL MAKE KNOWN MY DECISION.

THE TWO CONSPIRATORS, ZACHO AND SERRO, MUTTERED TO EACH OTHER.

WHAT NOW?

BEFORE WE TAKE THE NEXT STEP, WE MUST ASSURE OURSELVES THAT OUR THICK-HEADED FRIEND IS GOING TO CO-OPERATE.

THE STRANGER, Z, HAD BEEN GIVEN AN APARTMENT IN THE GUARDS' BARRACKS. ZACHO AND SERRO VISITED HIM THERE.

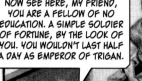

NOW SEE HERE, MY FRIEND, YOU ARE A FELLOW OF NO EDUCATION. A SIMPLE SOLDIER OF FORTUNE, BY THE LOOK OF YOU. YOU WOULDN'T LAST HALF A DAY AS EMPEROR OF TRIGAN.

WHAT MY COLLEAGUE IS TRYING TO SAY IS – YOU'RE GOING TO NEED OUR SUPPORT TO GET THE CROWN, AND YOU'RE GOING TO NEED OUR SUPPORT TO KEEP IT!

I UNDERSTAND. YOU HAVE ME CROWNED EMPEROR, AND YOU WILL BE REWARDED.

THAT NIGHT, IN A SEEDY QUARTER OF THE CITY, MONEY CHANGED HANDS.

THERE MUST BE NO MISTAKE.

WHEN ME AND MY FELLOWS ELIMINATE SOMEONE, HE STAYS ELIMINATED!

AT DAWN THE FOLLOWING DAY, TRIGO WAS FAR INTO THE ROLLING WILDERNESS OF VORG.

HOW SHALL I DECIDE...HOW?

THEY WERE UPON HIM BEFORE HE HAD TIME TO DEFEND HIMSELF.

YAAAAAA!

CUT HIM DOWN!

THE EMPEROR OF THE TRIGANS WAS STRUCK FROM HIS MOUNT.

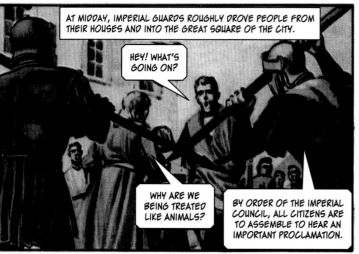

AT MIDDAY, IMPERIAL GUARDS ROUGHLY DROVE PEOPLE FROM THEIR HOUSES AND INTO THE GREAT SQUARE OF THE CITY.

HEY! WHAT'S GOING ON?

WHY ARE WE BEING TREATED LIKE ANIMALS?

BY ORDER OF THE IMPERIAL COUNCIL, ALL CITIZENS ARE TO ASSEMBLE TO HEAR AN IMPORTANT PROCLAMATION.

LATER, ONE OF THE CONSPIRATORS, ZACHO, SPOKE TO THE PEOPLE.

IT IS THE WILL OF THE IMPERIAL COUNCIL THAT, AS TRIGO HAS DECLARED THAT HE WOULD RELINQUISH HIS IMPERIAL CROWN TO HE WHO SMASHED THE STONE OF VORG, THE STRANGER CALLED Z BE CROWNED EMPEROR.

JANNO'S VOICE ROSE IN ANGRY PROTEST!

THAT'S NOT TRUE! MY UNCLE DID NOT SAY HE WOULD GIVE AWAY HIS CROWN UNCONDITIONALLY. WE MUST AWAIT HIS RETURN FROM THE WILDERNESS!

ZACHO HISSED TO THE GUARDS' COMMANDER...

HAVE HIM STRUCK DOWN... AND EARN YOURSELF PROMOTION.

INSTANTLY, MY LORD!

JANNO WAS SILENCED...AND HIS FATHER WITH HIM!

BY ALL THE STARS!

NOT SO FAST, LORD BRAG!

UUUUGH!

THERE WAS NO FURTHER PROTEST. BEFORE THE EYES OF THE ASSEMBLED MULTITUDE, THE STRANGER WHO HAD COME OUT OF THE WILDERNESS WAS CROWNED WITH THE IMPERIAL DIADEM OF THE TRIGAN EMPIRE.

BY VIRTUE OF THE AUTHORITY OF THE IMPERIAL COUNCIL, I PROCLAIM YOU LORD OF LIFE AND DEATH OVER THE PEOPLES OF THE EMPIRE!

IMMEDIATELY AFTER THE CEREMONY, ZACHO AND SERRO BROUGHT THEIR 'PUPPET EMPEROR' TO HIS STUDY.

WE EXPECT NO TROUBLE FROM THE REST OF THE COUNCIL, BUT THE IMPERIAL FAMILY MUST BE PUT UNDER RESTRAINT. HERE IS AN ORDER TO THAT EFFECT. IF YOUR MAJESTY WILL PLEASE SIGN...

Z SIGNED WITH A CROSS, A FACT THAT DID NOT ESCAPE THE TWO SNEERING CONSPIRATORS.

YOU CAN'T DO THIS TO US!

AS A RESULT OF THE IMPERIAL ORDER, JANNO AND BRAG WERE TAKEN TO THE DANK VAULTS BENEATH THE PALACE...

THROW THEM IN HERE.

FATHER AND SON WERE HURLED INTO A DARK CELL, THERE TO BROOD OVER THE FATE OF THE EMPIRE.

WHAT WILL HAPPEN TO UNCLE TRIGO WHEN HE RETURNS?

IF HE RETURNS. I'VE A FEELING THAT THEY'VE DONE FOR HIM ALREADY!

FAR OUT ACROSS THE WILDERNESS OF VORG, A BAND OF SAVAGE WARRIORS WERE JOURNEYING TO THEIR DESERT CITY. THEY ESPIED A STILL FORM IN THE DISTANCE.

SEE!

IT WAS THE DEPOSED EMPEROR OF THE TRIGANS, LEFT FOR DEAD BY THE RUFFIANS WHO HAD AMBUSHED HIM.

HE IS A TRIGAN. I CAN TELL BY HIS RAIMENT.

WHAT IS YOUR NAME, TRIGAN ANIMAL? SPEAK!

I...I....

WHAT HOPE REMAINED FOR THE TRIGAN EMPIRE? ITS FOUNDER AND TRUE LEADER HAD LOST ALL MEMORY OF HIS IDENTITY!

I DON'T KNOW MY NAME, OR WHO I AM!

THE RING OF BLADE ON BLADE RESOUNDED THROUGH THE GREAT COURTYARD OF THE IMPERIAL PALACE.

HA!

THE RASCALLY ZACHO AND SERRO WATCHED FROM A BALCONY ABOVE.

OUR FINE NEW EMPEROR KNOWS HOW TO DEFEND HIMSELF.

HE IS ALL BRAWN AND NO INTELLIGENCE. THE FELLOW CAN NEITHER READ NOR WRITE, AND HE WILL PUT HIS SIGNATURE TO ANYTHING.

THE UNEVEN CONTEST OF SWORD-PRACTICE CAME TO A SUDDEN AND DRAMATIC CLIMAX...

...AND A THRILLING FINISH!

HOLA!

AFTER SWORD-PRACTICE, THE NEW EMPEROR ATTENDED TO BUSINESS OF STATE.

TWO SMALL MATTERS REQUIRING YOUR SIGNATURE, IMPERIAL MAJESTY.

OH, YES...

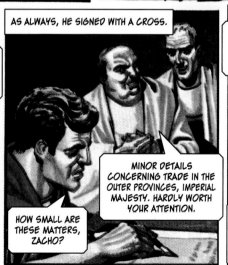

AS ALWAYS, HE SIGNED WITH A CROSS.

HOW SMALL ARE THESE MATTERS, ZACHO?

MINOR DETAILS CONCERNING TRADE IN THE OUTER PROVINCES, IMPERIAL MAJESTY. HARDLY WORTH YOUR ATTENTION.

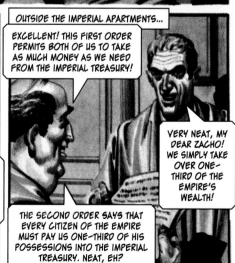

OUTSIDE THE IMPERIAL APARTMENTS...

EXCELLENT! THIS FIRST ORDER PERMITS BOTH OF US TO TAKE AS MUCH MONEY AS WE NEED FROM THE IMPERIAL TREASURY!

VERY NEAT, MY DEAR ZACHO! WE SIMPLY TAKE OVER ONE-THIRD OF THE EMPIRE'S WEALTH!

THE SECOND ORDER SAYS THAT EVERY CITIZEN OF THE EMPIRE MUST PAY US ONE-THIRD OF HIS POSSESSIONS INTO THE IMPERIAL TREASURY. NEAT, EH?

THE TAX ON ONE-THIRD OF A CITIZEN'S POSSESSIONS CAUSED RIOTS IN THE CITY.

DOWN WITH THE TYRANT!

BRING BACK TRIGO!

IN THE END, EVERYBODY PAID. SOME PAID PEACEFULLY, BUT WITH RELUCTANCE.

I AM THE MERCHANT ROCCA – AND I BRING THREE THOUSAND THULLARS.

ROCCA – THREE THOUSAND THULLARS.

NEXT!

OTHERS RESISTED THE RUINOUS TAX – TO THEIR COST!

SAYS HE HAS NO MONEY, EH? WHAT ABOUT...THIS?

YOU WILL PAY THE REQUIRED ONE-THIRD, PLUS AN EXTRA THIRD FOR CONCEALING YOUR FORTUNE AND MAKING A FALSE STATEMENT TO OFFICERS OF THE IMPERIAL CROWN!

MEANWHILE, FAR OUT ACROSS THE BARREN WILDERNESS OF VORG, A PARTY OF DESERT WARRIORS CAME IN SIGHT OF THEIR CITY. WITH THEM WAS A PRISONER.

THE PRISONER HAD LOST HIS MEMORY. UNKNOWN TO HIS CAPTORS, HE WAS THE RIGHTFUL EMPEROR OF THE TRIGANS.

WHO IS HE?

A TRIGAN ANIMAL! WE FOUND HIM LYING OUT IN THE DESERT. HE WILL MAKE A USEFUL SLAVE.

TAKE HIM AWAY, AND MAKE SURE THAT HE DOESN'T ESCAPE, BLIND HIM!

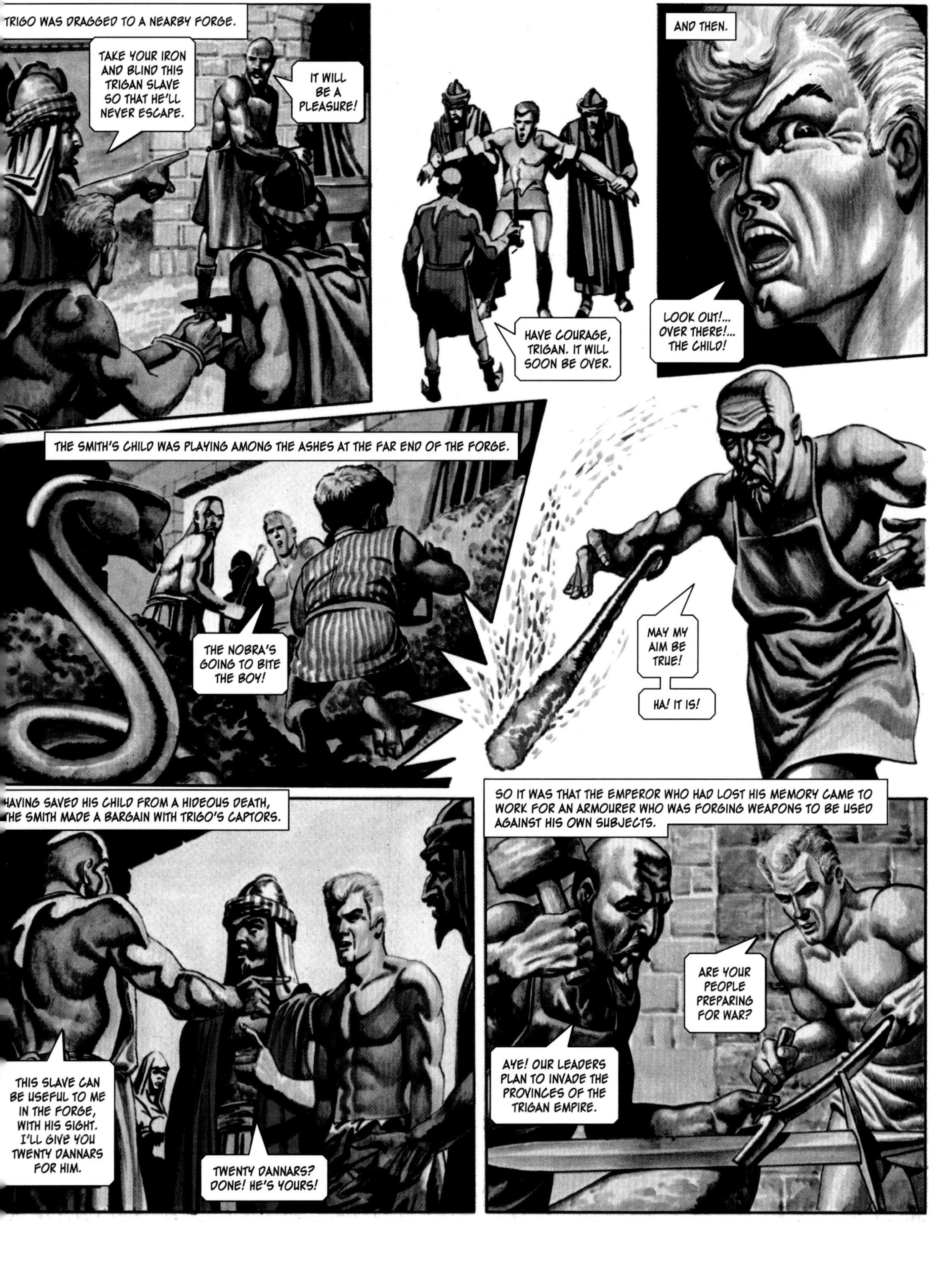
TRIGO WAS DRAGGED TO A NEARBY FORGE.
TAKE YOUR IRON AND BLIND THIS TRIGAN SLAVE SO THAT HE'LL NEVER ESCAPE.
IT WILL BE A PLEASURE!
HAVE COURAGE, TRIGAN. IT WILL SOON BE OVER.
AND THEN.
LOOK OUT!... OVER THERE!... THE CHILD!
THE SMITH'S CHILD WAS PLAYING AMONG THE ASHES AT THE FAR END OF THE FORGE.
THE NOBRA'S GOING TO BITE THE BOY!
MAY MY AIM BE TRUE!
HA! IT IS!
HAVING SAVED HIS CHILD FROM A HIDEOUS DEATH, THE SMITH MADE A BARGAIN WITH TRIGO'S CAPTORS.
THIS SLAVE CAN BE USEFUL TO ME IN THE FORGE, WITH HIS SIGHT. I'LL GIVE YOU TWENTY DANNARS FOR HIM.
TWENTY DANNARS? DONE! HE'S YOURS!
SO IT WAS THAT THE EMPEROR WHO HAD LOST HIS MEMORY CAME TO WORK FOR AN ARMOURER WHO WAS FORGING WEAPONS TO BE USED AGAINST HIS OWN SUBJECTS.
ARE YOUR PEOPLE PREPARING FOR WAR?
AYE! OUR LEADERS PLAN TO INVADE THE PROVINCES OF THE TRIGAN EMPIRE.

TRIGO SHRUGGED HIS SHOULDERS.

WELL, IT'S NO CONCERN OF MINE!

YOU FORGE A STRAIGHT BLADE, MASTER.

BACK IN TRIGAN CITY, THE NEW EMPEROR AMUSED HIMSELF BY WRESTLING WITH THE MEMBERS OF HIS PALACE GUARD.

HAH!

AAAAAAGH!

EEEEEGH!

...WHILE THE SCOUNDRELS ZACHO AND SERRO CONTINUED TO FEATHER THEIR NESTS.

I SHOULD LIKE MY NEPHEW TO BECOME A NOBLEMAN OF THE EMPIRE.

NOTHING SIMPLER, MY DEAR SERRO. MAKE OUT THE ORDER, AND OUR TAME EMPEROR WILL SIGN IT WITHOUT QUESTION.

THE NEXT DAY...

ANY MORE STATE BUSINESS?

JUST ONE MORE SMALL THING FOR YOU TO SIGN, IMPERIAL MAJESTY.

Z SCANNED THE DOCUMENT BRIEFLY, THEN...

MAKING YOUR WASTREL OF A NEPHEW A NOBLEMAN OF THE EMPIRE, AND GRANTING HIM A CASTLE AND A LIFE PENSION?

I THINK THIS NONSENSE HAS NOW GONE FAR ENOUGH.

THE EMPEROR CLAPPED HIS HANDS, AND A GUARD CAME RUNNING.

YOU...YOU CAN READ!

OF COURSE I CAN READ, YOU HALF-WITS.

PUT THESE TWO SCOUNDRELS IN CHAINS!

THE DOOR OF THE DANK CELL CREAKED OPEN, AND A HARSH VOICE SUMMONED TWO WRETCHED PRISONERS.

ON YOUR FEET, LORD BRAG AND LORD JANNO. YOUR TIME HAS COME!

FATHER AND SON CLASPED HANDS.

WE ARE BEING LED OUT TO EXECUTION! FAREWELL, JANNO.

FAREWELL, FATHER.

INSTEAD OF BEING LED TO THE EXECUTION BLOCK, THEY WERE TAKEN TO WHERE THE STRANGE USURPER SAT ALONE.

GOOD DAY TO YOU, MY LORDS. I SEE YOU ARE ALIVE AND WELL, IF A TRIFLE GRUBBY. YOU SHOULD HAVE PROVIDED WASHING FACILITIES WHEN YOU HAD THE CELLS CONSTRUCTED.

BRAG FOUND HIS VOICE.

I TAKE IT THAT WE ARE TO BE EXECUTED?

IT WAS TO SAVE YOUR LIVES THAT I LET ZACHO AND SERRO LOCK YOU UP. OTHERWISE THEY WOULD HAVE DESTROYED YOU, AS I FEAR, THEY HAVE ALREADY DESTROYED TRIGO.

SPEAKING OF ZACHO AND SERRO — THOSE TWO MISCREANTS HAVE ALREADY BEGUN TO SUFFER FOR THEIR CRIMES. COME AND SEE.

THE TWO RASCALLY EX-COUNCILLORS WERE CHAINED TO A WATER-WHEEL THAT IRRIGATED THE PALACE GARDENS.

WHERE DID WE GO WRONG ABOUT Z? WHERE?

IT'S ALL YOUR FAULT. YOU SAID HE COULDN'T READ OR WRITE.

WHO ARE YOU AND WHAT ARE YOU TRYING TO DO?

I AM Z...

AND I AM GOING TO SAVE THE TRIGAN EMPIRE!

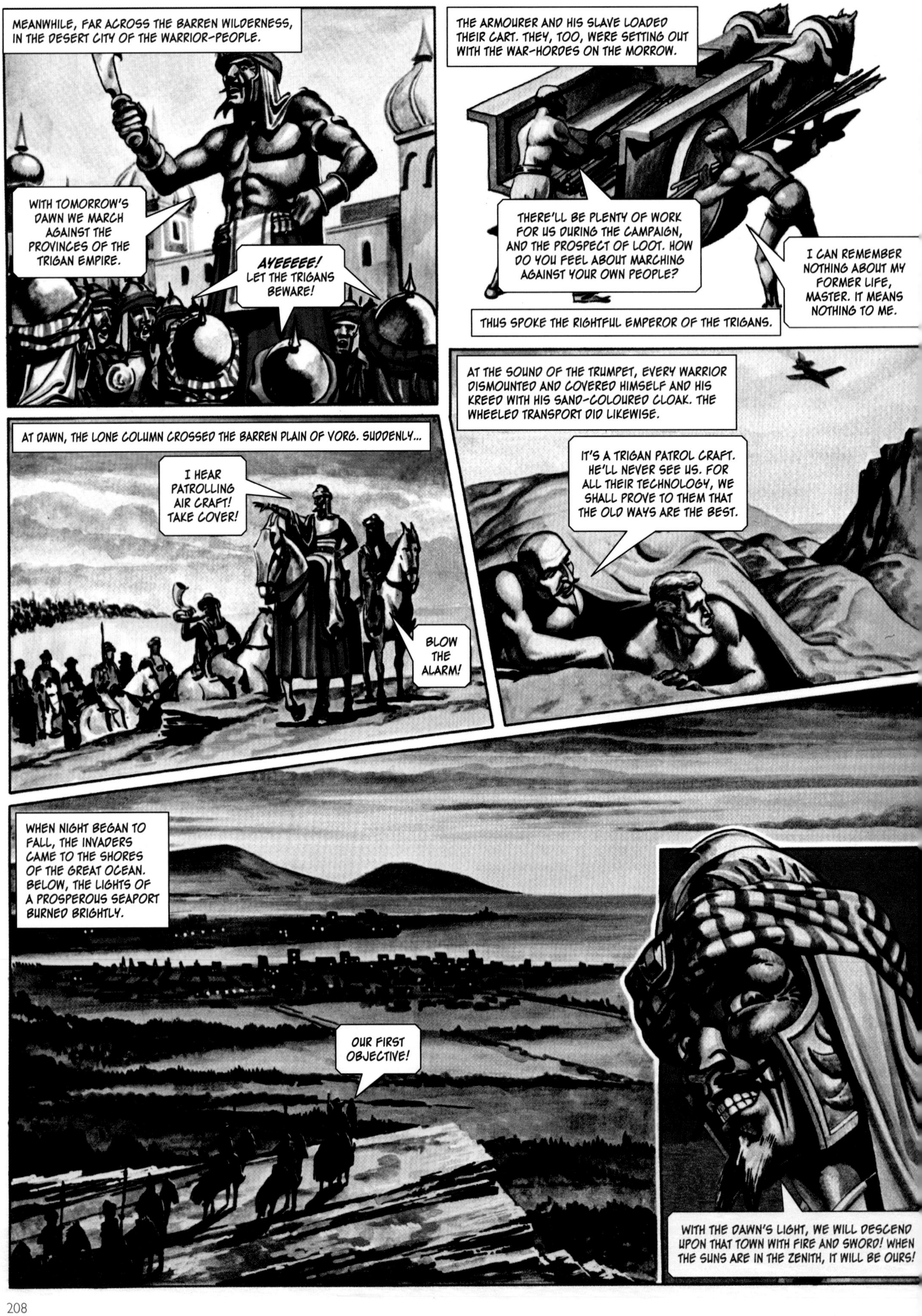

MEANWHILE, FAR ACROSS THE BARREN WILDERNESS, IN THE DESERT CITY OF THE WARRIOR-PEOPLE.
WITH TOMORROW'S DAWN WE MARCH AGAINST THE PROVINCES OF THE TRIGAN EMPIRE.
AYEEEEE! LET THE TRIGANS BEWARE!
THE ARMOURER AND HIS SLAVE LOADED THEIR CART. THEY, TOO, WERE SETTING OUT WITH THE WAR-HORDES ON THE MORROW.
THERE'LL BE PLENTY OF WORK FOR US DURING THE CAMPAIGN, AND THE PROSPECT OF LOOT. HOW DO YOU FEEL ABOUT MARCHING AGAINST YOUR OWN PEOPLE?
I CAN REMEMBER NOTHING ABOUT MY FORMER LIFE, MASTER. IT MEANS NOTHING TO ME.
THUS SPOKE THE RIGHTFUL EMPEROR OF THE TRIGANS.
AT DAWN, THE LONE COLUMN CROSSED THE BARREN PLAIN OF VORG. SUDDENLY...
I HEAR PATROLLING AIR CRAFT! TAKE COVER!
BLOW THE ALARM!
AT THE SOUND OF THE TRUMPET, EVERY WARRIOR DISMOUNTED AND COVERED HIMSELF AND HIS KREED WITH HIS SAND-COLOURED CLOAK. THE WHEELED TRANSPORT DID LIKEWISE.
IT'S A TRIGAN PATROL CRAFT. HE'LL NEVER SEE US. FOR ALL THEIR TECHNOLOGY, WE SHALL PROVE TO THEM THAT THE OLD WAYS ARE THE BEST.
WHEN NIGHT BEGAN TO FALL, THE INVADERS CAME TO THE SHORES OF THE GREAT OCEAN. BELOW, THE LIGHTS OF A PROSPEROUS SEAPORT BURNED BRIGHTLY.
OUR FIRST OBJECTIVE!
WITH THE DAWN'S LIGHT, WE WILL DESCEND UPON THAT TOWN WITH FIRE AND SWORD! WHEN THE SUNS ARE IN THE ZENITH, IT WILL BE OURS!

AT DAWN, THE SLEEPY QUIET OF THE TRIGAN SEAPORT TOWN OF RILLI WAS SPLIT BY THE WAR-SHRIEKS OF THE DESERT MARAUDERS.

THE SMALL GARRISON GALLANTLY TURNED OUT – BUT WAS IMMEDIATELY OVERRUN AND CUT DOWN.

AYEEEEEEEEEEEEH! HI! HI! HI!

BY NOON, RILLI WAS A BLAZING MASS, AND THE WAR-HORDE WAS ON ITS WAY BACK TO THE DESERT, LOADED DOWN WITH LOOT.

THE ARMOURER AND HIS SLAVE – WHO WAS NONE OTHER THAN THE EMPEROR TRIGO, WHO HAD LOST HIS MEMORY – WERE CARRYING LOOT IN PLENTY.

MEANWHILE, BACK IN TRIGAN CITY, BRAG AND JANNO WERE LISTENING TO THE AMAZING NEW EMPEROR ADDRESSING THE COUNCIL.

THE COUNCIL LISTENED WITH RESPECT AND AWE TO THE STRANGER WHO HAD RIDDEN IN FROM THE WILDERNESS AND TAKEN THE IMPERIAL CROWN FOR HIMSELF.

DID YOU SEE THE WAY OUR WARRIORS SLICED THROUGH YOUR TRIGAN GUARDS, EH?

THEY ARE NOT MY TRIGAN GUARDS, MASTER. MY FORMER LIFE IS MEANINGLESS TO ME!

I HAVE FOUND MUCH THAT IS WRONG WITH THE TRIGAN EMPIRE, FIRSTLY, I HAVE FOUND GREAT INEQUALITY BETWEEN THE VERY RICH AND THE VERY POOR, WHICH WAS WHY I PERMITTED ZACHO AND SERRO TO IMPOSE THE ONE-THIRD TAX ON ALL CITIZENS...

THOSE SCOUNDRELS PLANNED TO PUT THE MONEY TO THEIR OWN USE. I SHALL SEE THAT IT IS EMPLOYED TO FEED AND HOUSE THE POOR PEOPLE OF OUR EMPIRE. TRIGANS MUST LEARN TO STAND TOGETHER AND HELP EACH OTHER.

AT THAT MOMENT, THERE CAME AN INTERRUPTION...

WHAT IS IT, MESSENGER?

SIRE! I HAVE JUST RIDDEN FROM RILLI. A HORDE OF DESERT WARRIORS ATTACKED AT DAWN. THE CITY IS IN FLAMES AND THE DEMONS ARE DEPARTING BACK INTO THE WILDERNESS WITH THEIR LOOT.

THERE WAS AN IMMEDIATE UPROAR IN THE COUNCIL CHAMBER.

LET US SEND THE AIR FLEET TO BLAST THEM.

NO!

THOSE BARBARIANS MUST BE TAUGHT A SHARP LESSON.

A SQUADRON OF ARMOURED FIGHTING-VEHICLES WILL DO THE TRICK.

YOU WILL NEVER CATCH THE DESERT HORDE THAT WAY. THEY MOCK YOUR FIGHTING MACHINES. ONLY THE OLD METHODS WILL SERVE. WE MUST RIDE AND SEEK THEM OUT. WE MUST FIGHT THEM, BLADE TO BLADE AND SINEW TO SINEW.

WILL YOU RIDE AT MY SIDE, BRAG? AND YOU, JANNO?

I WILL!

AND I!

I KNEW I COULD RELY ON YOU!

CATCH, BRAG.

WITHIN A SHORT SPACE OF TIME EVERY ABLE BODIED WARRIOR IN THE CITY WAS MOUNTED AND READY. THEY THUNDERED OUT OF THE GATES WITH THE AMAZING EMPEROR AT THEIR HEAD.

DEATH TO THE INVADERS!

FATHER, THIS IS JUST LIKE OLD TIMES.

LIKE RIDING TO BATTLE BEHIND TRIGO! YES. THE SAME THOUGHT HAD JUST OCCURRED TO ME.

ALL THAT DAY AND THE FOLLOWING NIGHT, Z LED HIS WARRIORS AT BREAKNECK PACE THROUGH THE WILDERNESS.

YOU MUST SLOW THE PACE! OUR WARRIORS ARE FALLING OUT. HALF THE FORCE IS GONE!

THE BEST WILL KEEP UP MY PACE! THEY ARE THE ONES I WANT TO FIGHT ALONGSIDE ME IN THE COMING BATTLE!

AT DAWN ON THE NEXT DAY, Z HALTED ON A HILLCREST AND LOOKED DOWN AT THE HORDE ENCAMPED IN A VALLEY BELOW.

WE HAVE OVERTAKEN THEM!

AND NOW WE WILL DESTROY THEM!

THE DESERT WARRIORS, CONVINCED THAT THEY WERE SAFE FROM PURSUIT, WERE FEASTING UPON THE RICH FOOD AND DRINK THAT THEY HAD LOOTED.

IT WAS TRIGO — THE SLAVE-EMPEROR WITH THE LOST MEMORY — WHO RAISED THE ALARM!

WE ARE BEING ATTACKED!

THE TRIGANS RODE THROUGH THE ENCAMPMENT WITH FIRE AND SWORD.

TRIGO'S MASTER TOSSED HIM A WEAPON.

FIGHT FOR YOUR LIFE, SLAVE! THE ACCURSED TRIGANS WILL NOT BE GIVING ANY QUARTER THIS DAY!

BRAG SPURRED FORWARD AS HE SAW A TALL FIGURE SWINGING A LONG BLADE. THE FIGURE TURNED TO FACE HIM...AND HE WAS LOOKING INTO THE COUNTENANCE OF HIS OWN BROTHER.

BY ALL THE STARS!... TRIGO!

THERE WAS NO ANSWERING CRY OF RECOGNITION. INSTEAD BRAG'S WORLD DISSOLVED IN A SEA OF PAIN, AS HIS SWORD WAS BEATEN DOWN AND HE FELL FROM HIS CAREERING KREED WITH STUNNING FORCE.

AAAAAGH!

TRIGO VAULTED ASTRIDE THE RIDER LESS MOUNT...

I'VE NO PART OF THIS QUARREL! – I'M GETTING OUT OF HERE!

HE WAS NEARLY CLEAR OF THE SCENE OF BATTLE, WHEN A TRIGAN GUARDSMEN TOOK AIM AND FIRED AT THE FIGURE ON THE GALLOPING KREED.

SOON AFTER, THE LAST OF THE DESERT HORDE WERE OVERPOWERED, AND THE FIGHTING CEASED. Z LOOKED ABOUT HIM.

WHAT OF THE PRISONERS, IMPERIAL MAJESTY?

THEY ARE TO BE SPARED. SEND THEM BACK HOME ON FOOT, WITHOUT THEIR KREEDS. THEY WILL NEVER RAID TRIGAN TERRITORY AGAIN!

MEANWHILE, JANNO WAS TENDING HIS FATHER. BRAG TRIED TO RISE, AND HE CALLED OUT FRANTICALLY.

TRIGO! TRIGO WAS HERE! WHAT HAPPENED TO HIM?

CALM YOURSELF, FATHER...

HE'S WANDERING IN HIS MIND!

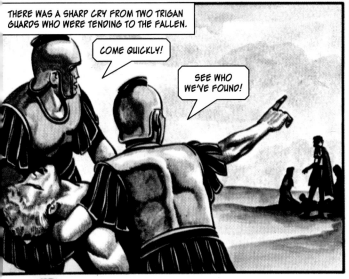

THERE WAS A SHARP CRY FROM TWO TRIGAN GUARDS WHO WERE TENDING TO THE FALLEN.

COME QUICKLY!

SEE WHO WE'VE FOUND!

JANNO GAZED INTO THE FAMILIAR FACE OF HIS UNCLE.

IT'S THE EMPEROR! MY FATHER WAS RIGHT! HE DID SEE HIM IN THE BATTLE.

HIS IMPERIAL MAJESTY IS GRAVELY HURT.

ALL EYES WERE TURNED TO Z, WHO GAZED EXPRESSIONLESSLY DOWN UPON THE MAN WHOSE CROWN HE HAD USURPED.

WHAT'S HE GOING TO DO? ORDER UNCLE TRIGO TO BE SLAIN?

BEAR THE FORMER EMPEROR BACK TO THE CITY. SEE THAT HE IS GIVEN EVERY ATTENTION, AND ASK PERIC TO KEEP ME INFORMED OF HIS PROGRESS.

NEWS OF THE SURVIVAL OF TRIGO PRECEDED THEIR RETURN TO THE CAPITAL. AS THE PROCESSION BEARING THE WOUNDED EX-EMPEROR ENTERED THE GATES OF TRIGAN CITY, A MULTITUDE WAS GATHERED TO PAY SILENT TRIBUTE.

THEY LAID HIM IN AN UPPER CHAMBER OF THE IMPERIAL PALACE THAT HAD ONCE BEEN HIS.

HE IS BEYOND THE SKILL OF MY HEALING ARTS. WE CAN ONLY WAIT AND HOPE THAT NATURE WILL SPARE HIM.

I WILL GUARD HIM, DAY AND NIGHT.

THAT NIGHT, THE POPULATION OF THE CITY WAS SWOLLEN BY COUNTLESS OTHERS WHO CAME IN FROM THE SURROUNDING COUNTRYSIDE AND THE FAR-FLUNG PROVINCES. THE GREAT SQUARE BELOW THE IMPERIAL PALACE WAS A SEA OF WINKING LIGHTS, EACH CARRIED BY A SILENT ONLOOKER.

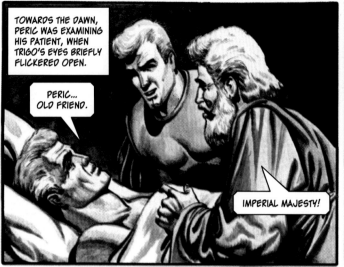

TOWARDS THE DAWN, PERIC WAS EXAMINING HIS PATIENT, WHEN TRIGO'S EYES BRIEFLY FLICKERED OPEN.

PERIC... OLD FRIEND.

IMPERIAL MAJESTY!

I MUST GO STRAIGHT AND TELL THE EMPEROR. HE WILL LIVE, AND HIS MEMORY HAS RETURNED.

IN THE DARKNESS JUST BEFORE THE DAWN OF ELEKTON'S TWIN SUNS, JANNO SAW A FIGURE FLIT ACROSS THE CHAMBER AND APPROACH THE UNCONSCIOUS FORM.

HEY!

JANNO SWUNG HIS BLADE, BUT THE BLOW NEVER LANDED. NEXT INSTANT, THE YOUNG TRIGAN WAS VIOLENTLY OVERTURNED.

AAAAAAAGHH!

HE LOOKED UP INTO THE FACE OF...Z!

DID YOU THINK I HAD COME TO SLAY YOUR EMPEROR?

NOT SO. I HAD MERELY COME TO LOOK UPON HIS FACE, BY WAY OF FAREWELL, BEFORE I DEPART.

Z GAZED OUT ACROSS THE WATCHING MULTITUDE BELOW. HIS VOICE WAS WISTFUL.

I COULD HAVE BEEN A GOOD EMPEROR. I HAD EVEN BEGUN TO WIN THEIR RESPECT...

...BUT NOT THEIR AFFECTION. ONLY TRIGO HAS THAT. HE IS THEIR TRUE EMPEROR. I WISH HIM A LONG LIFE!

IN THE DAWN LIGHT, THE STRANGER WHO HAD COME OUT OF THE WILDERNESS AND BRIEFLY REIGNED AS THE EMPEROR OF THE TRIGANS, RODE BACK THE WAY HE HAD COME.

THE TRIGAN EMPIRE
THE WEATHER CONTROLLER

Originally published in *Look and Learn* 682 - 689

8th February 1975 - 29th March 1975

Story by Mike Butterworth

Art by Philip Corke

ON THE THIRD HOUR OF THE TWENTY-FIFTH DAY OF THE YEAR OF HOTH, PEOPLE IN THE STREETS OF TRIGAN CITY BEGAN SUDDENLY TO ACT IN A MOST REMARKABLE MANNER.

AAAAH! THE COLD! THE ICY COLD!

WHAT'S HAPPENING TO US?

WITHIN INSTANTS, ICE WAS FORMING EVERYWHERE.

GET UNDER COVER, BEFORE WE ALL FREEZE TO DEATH!

HELP ME WITH THIS OLD MAN BEFORE HE PERISHES.

DOWN IN THE HARBOUR, THE SUDDEN AND FANTASTIC FALL IN TEMPERATURE FROZE THE SEA. SHIPS WERE CRUSHED IN THE GRIP OF THE MOUNTAINOUS ICE FORMATIONS.

THE TRIGAN BAY BRIDGE, WEIGHED DOWN BY THE SUDDEN ADDITION OF THE ICE MASS, SAGGED AND BROKE...

...WITH DISASTROUS RESULTS!

AT NOONDAY, THE TEMPERATURES ROCKETED BACK TO NORMAL AND THE STREETS OF THE CITY RAN DEEPLY WITH MELTED ICE.

IT'S UNBELIEVABLE! FANTASTIC!

THE EMPEROR TRIGO SUMMONED AN IMPERIAL COUNCIL MEETING TO DISCUSS THE STRANGE DISASTER. PERIC, ELEKTON'S TOP SCIENTIST, GAVE HIS OPINION.

IT IS MY THEORY THAT THE PHENOMENON OF THE FALLING TEMPERATURE HAD NO NATURAL CAUSE.

ARE YOU SUGGESTING, PERIC, THAT IT WAS CAUSED DELIBERATELY?

I AM, MAJESTY! I BELIEVE THAT A PERSON OR PERSONS UNKNOWN HAVE DISCOVERED A MEANS TO CONTROL THE MAGNETIC FIELD OF THIS PLANET, AND CONSEQUENTLY CONTROL THE WEATHER CLIMATE.

I DO NOT HAVE TO REMIND YOU THAT SUCH TOTAL COMMAND OVER LIFE ON ELEKTON MAKES THIS PERSON OR PERSONS VIRTUAL DICTATORS.

I AM CONVINCED, HOWEVER, THAT THE SOURCE OF THIS MAGNETIC POWER CAN BE DETECTED FROM THE AIR. SO I HAVE DEVISED A PIECE OF EQUIPMENT WHICH CAN BE CARRIED IN AN ORDINARY AIR CRAFT.

THE GREAT SILENCE WAS INTERRUPTED BY JANNO, THE EMPEROR'S NEPHEW.

I'LL DO IT! I'LL FLY THE DETECTOR CRAFT!

I HALF GUESSED THAT MY YOUNG FRIEND WOULD VOLUNTEER!

TWO DAYS LATER, JANNO TOOK OFF IN HIS SPECIALLY-EQUIPPED AIR CRAFT. HIS TASK, TO CIRCUMNAVIGATE THE PLANET AT ZERO HEIGHT, SEARCHING FOR THE SOURCE OF THE SINISTER POWER.

THAT SAME DAY, TOTALLY WITHOUT WARNING...IT HAPPENED!

AAAAH! THE HEAT, THE HEAT!

I MUST HAVE WATER!

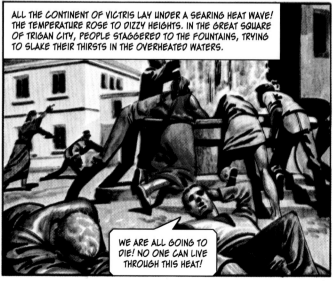

ALL THE CONTINENT OF VICTRIS LAY UNDER A SEARING HEAT WAVE! THE TEMPERATURE ROSE TO DIZZY HEIGHTS. IN THE GREAT SQUARE OF TRIGAN CITY, PEOPLE STAGGERED TO THE FOUNTAINS, TRYING TO SLAKE THEIR THIRSTS IN THE OVERHEATED WATERS.

WE ARE ALL GOING TO DIE! NO ONE CAN LIVE THROUGH THIS HEAT!

THE SEARING HEAT BUCKLES THE ROADWAYS, CAUSING MULTIPLE TRAFFIC DISASTERS.

SPONTANEOUS COMBUSTION FROM THE FANTASTIC TEMPERATURE CAUSED WIDESPREAD FIRES. A WHOLE AREA OF THE CAPITAL CITY WAS SOON A SEA OF FLAMES.

THE FLAMES ARE SPREADING! EVACUATE THE ENTIRE CITY!

NIGHT FELL, BRINGING SCREAMS OF INDESCRIBABLE CHAOS AS PANIC-STRICKEN PEOPLE FLED THE CONFLAGRATION.

JANNO SAW THE FLAMES BELOW HIM, FROM THE COCKPIT OF HIS SPEEDY FIGHTING CRAFT.

HALF THE CITY IS WIPED OUT ALREADY!

NEVERTHELESS, HE STAYED WITH HIS TASK, REPORTING BACK CONSTANTLY TO HIS CONTROL CENTRE.

I AM CHANGING COURSE FOR MY TENTH CIRCUMNAVIGATION, WHICH WILL TAKE ME OVER THE GREAT BARRIER MOUNTAINS AT APPROXIMATELY MIDNIGHT, TRIGAN CITY TIME.

JANNO WAS FILLED WITH A SENSE OF AWE AND WONDER AS THE MASSIVE, SNOW-CLAD RANGE APPEARED AHEAD: A MOUNTAIN FASTNESS THAT FEW HAD EVER PENETRATED ON FOOT.

I SHALL HAVE TO CLIMB HIGHER TO GET OVER THEM.

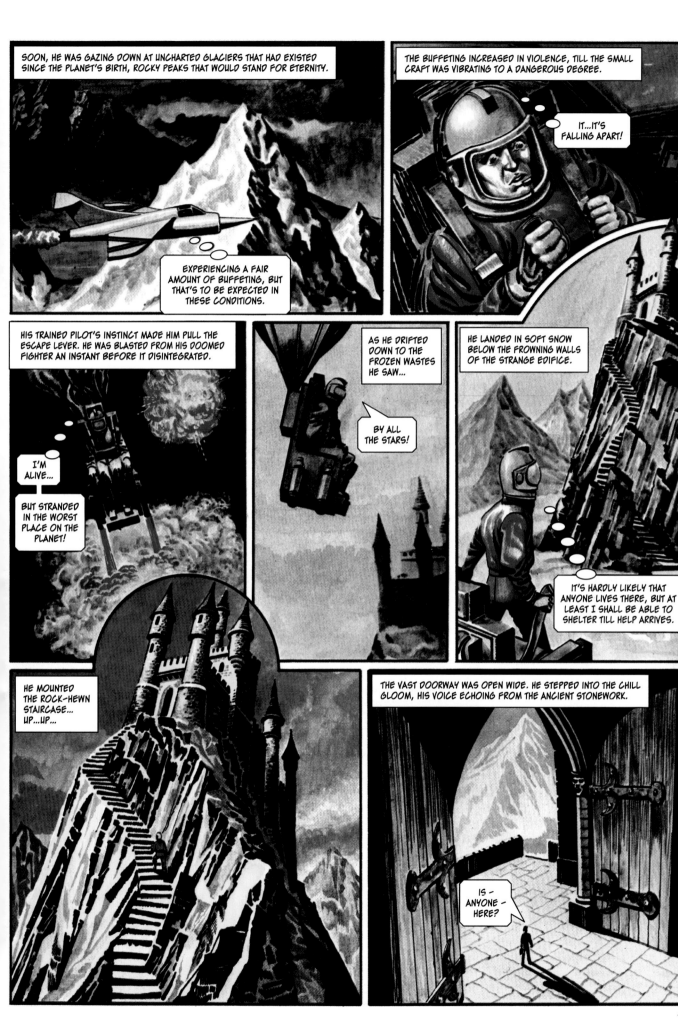

SOON, HE WAS GAZING DOWN AT UNCHARTED GLACIERS THAT HAD EXISTED SINCE THE PLANET'S BIRTH, ROCKY PEAKS THAT WOULD STAND FOR ETERNITY.

EXPERIENCING A FAIR AMOUNT OF BUFFETING, BUT THAT'S TO BE EXPECTED IN THESE CONDITIONS.

THE BUFFETING INCREASED IN VIOLENCE, TILL THE SMALL CRAFT WAS VIBRATING TO A DANGEROUS DEGREE.

IT...IT'S FALLING APART!

HIS TRAINED PILOT'S INSTINCT MADE HIM PULL THE ESCAPE LEVER. HE WAS BLASTED FROM HIS DOOMED FIGHTER AN INSTANT BEFORE IT DISINTEGRATED.

I'M ALIVE...

BUT STRANDED IN THE WORST PLACE ON THE PLANET!

AS HE DRIFTED DOWN TO THE FROZEN WASTES HE SAW...

BY ALL THE STARS!

HE LANDED IN SOFT SNOW BELOW THE FROWNING WALLS OF THE STRANGE EDIFICE.

IT'S HARDLY LIKELY THAT ANYONE LIVES THERE, BUT AT LEAST I SHALL BE ABLE TO SHELTER TILL HELP ARRIVES.

HE MOUNTED THE ROCK-HEWN STAIRCASE... UP...UP...

THE VAST DOORWAY WAS OPEN WIDE. HE STEPPED INTO THE CHILL GLOOM, HIS VOICE ECHOING FROM THE ANCIENT STONEWORK.

IS - ANYONE - HERE?

A HARSH, GRATING VOICE MADE JANNO TURN.

WELCOME, TRIGAN! I HAVE BEEN EXPECTING ONE SUCH AS YOU.

MY INSTRUMENTS DETECTED THAT YOUR CRAFT WAS SPECIALLY EQUIPPED, SO I HAD TO ENCOMPASS ITS DESTRUCTION.

SO YOU ARE RESPONSIBLE FOR THIS FIENDISH BUSINESS!

NOT SO FAST!

CALM YOURSELF AND I WILL SHOW YOU SOMETHING THAT WILL FILL YOU WITH AWE AND WONDER.

AAAAAH!

HELPLESS, JANNO WAS DRAGGED OUT ON TO THE TERRACE.

WATCH CAREFULLY...

THERE CAME A RUMBLING OF HEAVY MACHINERY. THE FLOOR OF THE VALLEY MOVED ASIDE AND A VAST DISC OF BRIGHT METAL ROSE SKYWARDS.

WHAT... WHAT IS IT?

IT IS THE HEAT CONTROLLER! BY MEANS OF ITS POWER, I AM ABLE TO DICTATE THE TERMS OF LIFE OR DEATH TO ALL LIVING THINGS ON THIS PLANET!

YOU HAVE SEEN ITS EFFECT IN CERTAIN MILD DEMONSTRATIONS RECENTLY. WHAT YOU HAVE NOT SEEN IS THE HEAT CONTROLLER AT FULL POWER.

THE OLD MAN POINTED ACROSS THE AGELESS GLACIER.

REGARD THAT MOUNTAIN! IT HAS CARRIED SNOW AND ICE ON ITS CREST SINCE ELEKTON WAS FORMED. NOW OBSERVE...

JANNO'S AGED CAPTOR TOUCHED A CONTROL ON HIS CHAIR. INSTANTLY, A BAND OF PURPLE LIGHT STABBED FROM THE HEAT CONTROLLER.

THEY SAW IT ALL QUITE CLEARLY... SNOW AND ICE TURNED TO SUPER-HEATED STEAM...A CATACLYSMIC AVALANCHE...AND THE PEAKS CHANGED TO **MOLTEN ROCK!**

AT A SIGNAL FROM SLATTA, TWO BURLY GUARDS CAME FORTH.

SOON THE WHOLE MOUNTAIN HAD BEEN REDUCED TO A HEAP OF SMOKING ASH.

WHO ARE YOU, AND WHAT ARE YOU TRYING TO DO?

MY NAME IS SLATTA. AND, AS THE INVENTOR AND BUILDER OF THE HEAT CONTROLLER, I CLAIM THAT IT IS I – AND NOT PERIC – WHO DESERVES THE TITLE OF ELEKTON'S TOP SCIENTIST.

YOU HAVE SEEN WHAT I DID TO THE MOUNTAIN. THIS I CAN ALSO DO TO INDIVIDUAL CITIES. UNLESS THE NATIONS OF ELEKTON BOW TO MY DICTATORSHIP, THEY WILL ALL BE DESTROYED!

THIS TRIGAN CAN BE OF SOME USE TO ME. TAKE HIM AWAY. BREAK HIS SPIRIT AND HIS WILL, AND LOCK HIM UP!

AWAY WITH HIM! BREAK HIM IN BODY AND SPIRIT!

THE YOUNG TRIGAN ZIPPED INTO ACTION.

GUUUUUUUUGH!

HOLA!

NOT SO FAST, TRIGAN.

YAAAAAA-A-A-AHH!

HE PLUMMETED DOWN – DOWN – DOWN!

AAAAAA-AAA-AAAAHH!

HE LANDED IN SOFT SNOW, ROLLING OVER AND OVER.

IT WAS A MIRACLE! AND IF I CAN CONTINUE TO MAKE MIRACLES HAPPEN, I MIGHT BE ABLE TO TAKE THE NEWS BACK TO TRIGAN CITY.

SLATTA'S VOICE ROSE IN THE CHILL AIR.

AFTER HIM, YOU FOOLS! IF HE REACHES CIVILISATION, WE SHALL HAVE EVERY AIR-FLEET ON ELEKTON BOMBING THE HEAT CONTROLLER.

PRESENTLY, A PARTY OF GUARDS BURST OUT OF THE CASTLE DOOR, TAKING WITH THEM A PAIR OF SAVAGE GORDS, THE HUNTING HOUNDS OF ELEKTON.

LET SLIP THE GORDS.

JANNO HEARD THE BAYING OF THE HOUNDS, AND HIS HEART SANK.

THEY'LL TEAR ME TO PIECES!

AHEAD LAY A PERILOUS-LOOKING SNOW BRIDGE.

HALF WAY ACROSS, THE NEAREST GORD WAS ALL BUT UPON HIM.

THE BRUTE'S GAINING WITH EVERY YARD!

AND THEN, HE SAW...*IT!*

BY ALL THE STARS!

THE MASSIVE CREATURE LURCHED AT JANNO, WHO DUCKED UNDER THE SLASHING TALONS.

THE MONSTER MET THE GORDS IN THE SLENDEREST PART OF THE SNOW BRIDGE.

UNDER ITS MASSIVE WEIGHT, THE BRIDGE COLLAPSED.

WA-A-A-A-AAAAAHHH:

WHEN THE GUARDS ARRIVED ON THE SCENE, THEY DREW THEIR OWN CONCLUSIONS.

THE SINISTER FIGURE IN THE WHEELED CHAIR LISTENED WITH SATISFACTION TO THE NEWS.

GOOD, GOOD! IT WOULD HAVE BEEN FATAL FOR THE TRIGAN TO HAVE REPORTED OUR WHEREABOUTS!

I MUST GET OUT OF SIGHT. SLATTA'S GUARDS CAN'T BE FAR BEHIND!

THE GORDS MUST HAVE CAUGHT UP WITH THE TRIGAN HERE.

AND THEY ALL FELL TOGETHER! WE'D BETTER REPORT THIS TO THE MASTER.

HOWEVER, HIS ARRIVAL HERE PROVIDES THE WARNING THAT I MUST MOVE QUICKLY.

THIS VERY DAY, I WILL COMMENCE TO TAKE OVER THE PLANET.

STARTING WITH... THE STATE OF CATO!

CATO: A WARLIKE STATE, HOSTILE TO THE TRIGAN EMPIRE. RULED OVER BY A DICTATORIAL COUNCIL. THAT VERY DAY, THE CATON COUNCIL WAS THROWN INTO TURMOIL.

MY LORDS, THIS MESSAGE HAS JUST COME IN FROM AN UNKNOWN SOURCE. IT SAYS "YOUR PROVINCIAL CITY OF NAGGAR WILL BE ENTIRELY DESTROYED AT DAWN TOMORROW. AFTER THAT, YOU WILL NOT HESITATE TO OBEY MY ORDERS."

WHA-A-A-AT?

IS THIS THE WORK OF A MADMAN?

MAD, PERHAPS; BUT THIS THREAT MUST REFER TO THE FANTASTIC TEMPERATURE CHANGES.

WHAT'S TO BE DONE?

NAGGAR MUST BE EVACUATED IMMEDIATELY!

SO IT WAS THAT ONE OF THE LARGEST CITIES OF THE STATE WAS EMPTIED OF ITS PEOPLE. THE EVACUATION TOOK MANY HOURS.

WHY ARE YOU DRIVING US FROM OUR HOMES LIKE THIS?

IF YOU STAY, YOU WILL DIE! AND NO ONE DIES WITHOUT PERMISSION OF THE COUNCIL!

IN THE DAWN LIGHT, *THE HEAT CAME!* THE WATER OF THE HARBOUR *BOILED!* THE TREES TOOK *FIRE!* THE VERY STONES MELTED!

HALF WAY ACROSS THE PLANET, TREKKING THROUGH THE TRACKLESS WASTE OF THE GREAT BARRIER MOUNTAINS, JANNO SAW THE LURID GLOW OF THE SKY.

SLATTA IS AT HIS FIENDISH WORK AGAIN!

MALEVOLENT EYES GLARED OUT AT THE YOUNG TRIGAN.

ALL AT ONCE A KILLING-SPEAR BURIED ITS POINT INTO THE ICE CLOSE TO JANNO'S HEAD.

THEN HE WAS SURROUNDED.

YOU DARED TO VENTURE INTO THE HUNTING GROUND OF THE VORZ. FOR THIS YOU WILL PAY!

JANNO KNEW THE VORZ TO BE ONE OF THE MANY TRIBES OF WARRIOR-HUNTERS WHO CARRIED ON A NOMADIC EXISTENCE AMONG THE VALLEYS AND GLACIERS OF THE GREAT BARRIER MOUNTAINS. THEY TOOK HIM TO THEIR CAMP NEARBY.

AN ANCIENT LEADER-PRIEST PRONOUNCED A MERCILESS SENTENCE UPON THE CAPTIVE.

THE INTRUDER SHALL BE SACRIFICED TO THE GOD WHO DWELLS BENEATH THE ICE, SO THAT THE VORZ MAY HAVE MUCH LUCK AT THE HUNT!

HE WAS BOUND TO A SACRIFICIAL STAKE. ONE OF THE VORZ SMASHED A HOLE IN THE ICE OF THE FROZEN LAKE.

THE TRIBE DEPARTED SOME DISTANCE AWAY AND JANNO WAS LEFT ALONE.

WHAT WILL EMERGE FROM THAT HOLE?

MEANWHILE, THE LEADERS OF CATON STATE WERE GAZING UPON A SCREENING OF THEIR PROVINCIAL CITY OF NAGGAR, NOW A PILE OF DESTRUCTION.

APPALLING!

MY MUST AGREE TO ANYTHING TO PREVENT ITS REPETITION!

A MESSENGER ARRIVED.

MY LORDS, THE UNKNOWN ONE HAS SENT THIS ORDER... "YOU WILL INSTANTLY SURRENDER YOUR POWERS AND LEAVE THE COUNCIL CHAMBER. ONE MOMENT'S HESITATION WILL BRING THE IMMEDIATE DESTRUCTION OF CATON CITY."

IN THE RUSH TO LEAVE THE COUNCIL CHAMBER, SEVERAL OF THE OLDER MEMBERS WERE TRAMPLED UNDERFOOT.

LET'S GET OUT OF HERE!

HELP ME, FRIENDS.

FAR AWAY, IN HIS STRONGHOLD IN THE GREAT BARRIER MOUNTAINS, SLATTA RECEIVED THE NEWS.

CATO IS WITHOUT A GOVERNMENT. WITH ONE STROKE, I HAVE TAKEN OVER AN ENTIRE NATION AND ITS PEOPLE.

NEXT... THE TRIGAN EMPIRE!

IT WAS AT ABOUT THAT SAME TIME THAT JANNO SAW A DISTURBANCE IN THE PATCH OF BROKEN ICE.

SOMETHING'S... COMING!

THAT WHICH MET HIS EYES SENT A SHOCK-WAVE OF PANIC THROUGH HIS FRAME.

BY ALL THE STARS! NO!

THE SO-CALLED "ICE-GOD" WAS A LARGE SPECIMEN OF THE CARNIVOROUS SEA-BEAST CALLED THE UGGA.

JANNO CLOSED HIS EYES, AND GAVE HIMSELF UP FOR LOST.

AND THEN, A SHOWER OF ARROWS AND STONES.

AS THE SEA-BEAST PLUNGED BACK TO THE DEEPS FROM WHENCE IT CAME, A PARTY OF YELLING WARRIORS CHARGED DOWN UPON THE ENCAMPMENT TO PUT THE VORZ TO FLIGHT.

A BONE KNIFE SLASHED THROUGH HIS BONDS, AND JANNO FOUND HIMSELF LOOKING INTO A GRINNING FACE.

LATER, OVER A CAMPFIRE MEAL, THE LEADER OF THE RAIDERS TOLD JANNO ABOUT HIMSELF AND HIS PEOPLE.

FROM THE LOOK OF YOU, YOU ARE FROM THE OUTER LANDS. HOWEVER, ANYONE WHOM THE ACCURSED VORZ WOULD WISH TO SACRIFICE IS A FRIEND OF MINE!

WE ARE THE ZAGGS, INTELLIGENT PEOPLE, NOT MINDLESS NOMADS LIKE THE VORZ. TILL RECENTLY, WE HAD OUR OWN VALLEY, WITH AN ANCIENT STRONGHOLD THAT WAS BUILT BY OUR FOREFATHERS. BUT THAT WAS TAKEN FROM US.

WHO TOOK IT FROM YOU?

HE WHO LIVES IN THE MOVING CHAIR. HE WHO HAS BUILT THE GREAT MACHINE IN THE MIDDLE OF OUR VALLEY.

SLATTA!

YOU HAVE IT IN YOUR POWER TO REGAIN YOUR VALLEY AND YOUR STRONGHOLD, AND ALSO TO DO A GREAT SERVICE TO THE ENTIRE POPULATION OF THE PLANET.

LISTEN TO ME...

MEANWHILE, IN FAR OFF TRIGAN CITY, THE EMPEROR TRIGO WAS WITH HIS IMPERIAL COUNCIL.

MY LORDS! TODAY COMES NEWS THAT THE CATON STATE HAS CAPITULATED TO THIS UNKNOWN POWER. NOW THAT SAME POWER DEMANDS THE SURRENDER OF THE TRIGAN EMPIRE OR THIS CAPITAL CITY WILL SUFFER THE SAME FATE AS NAGGAR.

JANNO HAS NOT BEEN HEARD OF, SO WE MUST ASSUME THAT HE IS LOST. THERE IS, THEN, NO HOPE OF LOCATING THE WHEREABOUTS OF THE MAGNETIC POWER.

BUT IT IS NOT MY INTENTION TO SUBMIT! OPEN THE CITY GATES AND LET ANY LEAVE WHO WISH.

I, FOR ONE, AM STAYING HERE. BETTER TO PERISH A TRIGAN, THAN TO LIVE AS A SLAVE!

LATER THAT DAY, IN THE FAR-OFF VALLEY, THE DEADLY HEAT-CONTROLLER STABBED A BAND OF PURPLE LIGHT SKYWARDS.

MOST OF THE CITIZENS OF TRIGAN CITY HAD FOLLOWED THEIR EMPEROR'S EXAMPLE AND REMAINED. WHEN THE TEMPERATURE BEGAN TO RISE, THEIR SUFFERING COMMENCED.

AAAAH! THE VERY WATER IN THE FOUNTAIN IS STEAMING!

ON THE RAMPARTS OF HIS STRONGHOLD, SLATTA DIRECTED THE BEAM OF THE HEAT-CONTROLLER.

THE TEMPERATURE IS RISING IN TRIGAN CITY. THIS WILL TEACH THAT PROUD EMPEROR TO DEFY ME.

ABOVE THE VALLEY, TWO BRAWNY ZAGG TRIBESMEN STRAINED TO DISLODGE A BOULDER...

THE MASSIVE LUMP TOPPLED DOWN THE SLOPE.

NOTHING WILL STOP IT NOW!... NOTHING!

SLATTA'S HENCHMEN SAW THE PERIL...

MASTER! – AN AVALANCHE! – DESCENDING UPON THE HEAT CONTROLLER!

IT'S FINISHED SLATTA. NOTHING COULD WITHSTAND THE FORCE OF THE AVALANCHE MY FRIENDS HAVE CREATED!

YOU!

SLATTA TOUCHED A CONTROL.

TRIGAN ANIMAL! I WILL CRUSH THE LIFE FROM YOU!

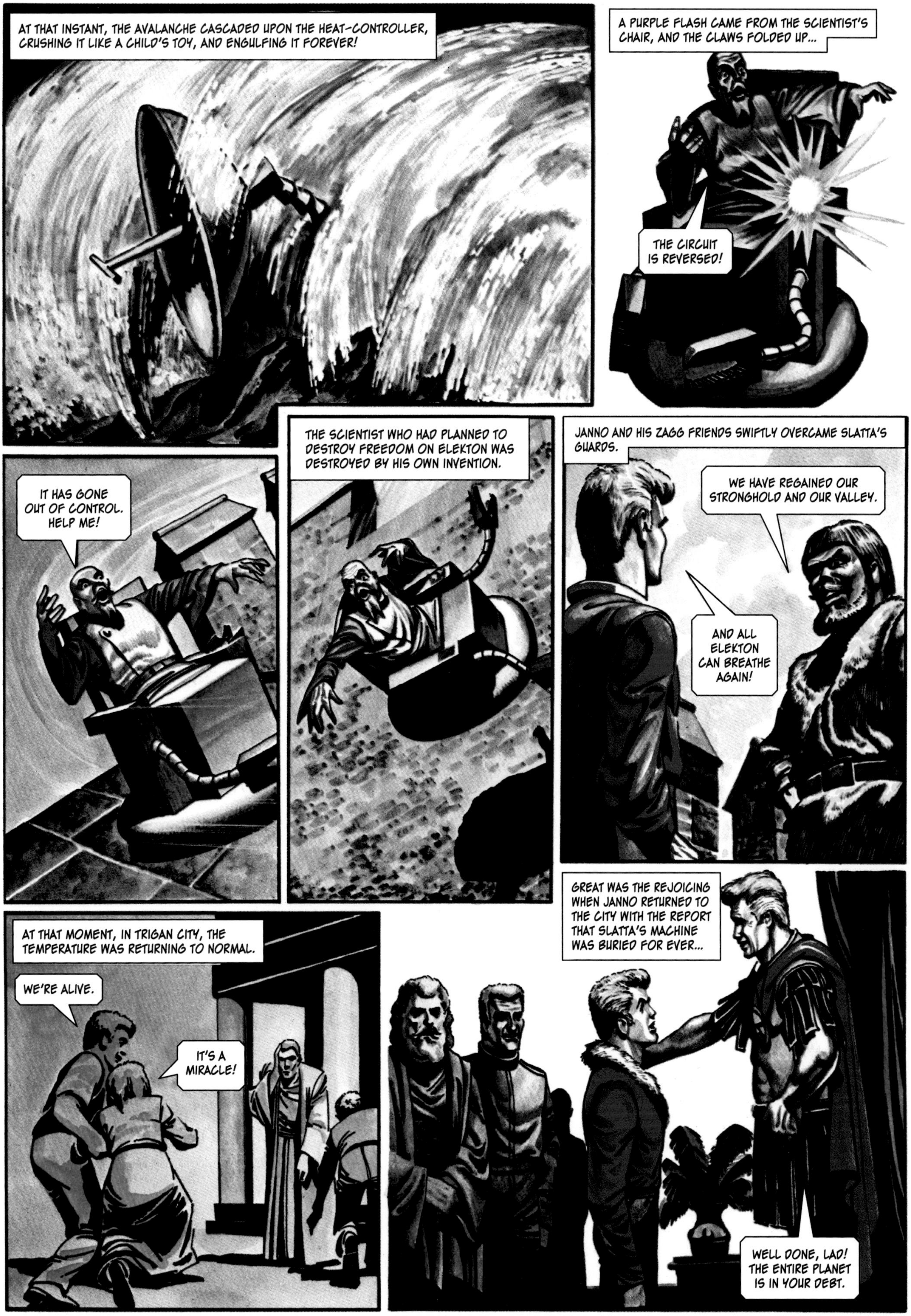
AT THAT INSTANT, THE AVALANCHE CASCADED UPON THE HEAT-CONTROLLER, CRUSHING IT LIKE A CHILD'S TOY, AND ENGULFING IT FOREVER!
A PURPLE FLASH CAME FROM THE SCIENTIST'S CHAIR, AND THE CLAWS FOLDED UP...
THE CIRCUIT IS REVERSED!
IT HAS GONE OUT OF CONTROL. HELP ME!
THE SCIENTIST WHO HAD PLANNED TO DESTROY FREEDOM ON ELEKTON WAS DESTROYED BY HIS OWN INVENTION.
JANNO AND HIS ZAGG FRIENDS SWIFTLY OVERCAME SLATTA'S GUARDS.
WE HAVE REGAINED OUR STRONGHOLD AND OUR VALLEY.
AND ALL ELEKTON CAN BREATHE AGAIN!
AT THAT MOMENT, IN TRIGAN CITY, THE TEMPERATURE WAS RETURNING TO NORMAL.
WE'RE ALIVE.
IT'S A MIRACLE!
GREAT WAS THE REJOICING WHEN JANNO RETURNED TO THE CITY WITH THE REPORT THAT SLATTA'S MACHINE WAS BURIED FOR EVER...
WELL DONE, LAD! THE ENTIRE PLANET IS IN YOUR DEBT.

BONUS STORY

THE WISE MAN OF VORG

Originally published in *Ranger Book* 1967

Story by Mike Butterworth

IN THE EARLY DAYS OF THE TRIGAN EMPIRE THE PEOPLE OF TRIGAN STRIVED TO LIVE IN THEIR FABULOUS CITY IN PEACE AND TRANQUILLITY...

FROM ALL OVER THE PLANET, ELEKTON MERCHANTS BROUGHT THEIR WARES TO THE THRIVING CITY... BUT IT WAS OFTEN IN THE FACE OF DIRE PERIL...

THE LOKANS ARE COMING!

[T]HE LOKANS WERE AN EVIL AND WARLIKE [N]ATION RULED BY THE TYRANT KING ZORTH.

YOUR GOODS ARE FORFEITED TO THE STATE OF LOKA!

THE LOKANS!

BESIDE ROBBING THE CARAVANS THEIR PLANES ALSO ATTACKED INNOCENT PASSENGER CRAFT BOUND FOR TRIGAN...

TIME AND TIME AGAIN THE TRIGAN PLANES [W]ERE SENT TO THEIR DESTRUCTION.

NEWS OF THE CONTINUED, UNPROVOKED ATTACKS BY THE LOKANS EVENTUALLY DROVE THE GALLANT TRIGO TO FURY. HE ADDRESSED THE ELDERS OF HIS COUNCIL...

I SAY WE HAVE SUFFERED ENOUGH! NOW MY THOUGHTS ARE TURNING TO...WAR!

233

BUT THE OLDER MEN SHOOK THEIR HEADS...

LORD TRIGO, WE HAVE NEITHER THE POWER NOR THE WEALTH TO CARRY ON A WAR WITH LOKA!

THEN WHAT IS *YOUR* ADVICE?

THE OLD MAN'S ANSWER FILLED TRIGO WITH A NEW FURY...

I AM SURE IF WE WERE TO PAY KING ZORTH A LARGE AMOUNT OF MONEY EVERY YEAR...

PAY HIM? SO THAT HE MAY GRACIOUSLY CONDESCEND TO LEAVE OFF MURDERING AND ROBBING OUR INNOCENT PEOPLE? *NEVER!*

TRIGO'S DECISION WAS MADE...

I SHALL JOURNEY TO THE GREAT MOUNTAIN... AND CONSULT THE WISE MAN OF VORG!

THE FOLLOWING DAY TRIGO JOURNEYED FAR ACROSS THE WILDERNESS OF VORG, TO THE GREAT MOUNTAIN...

THE WISE MAN HAS AIDED OUR PEOPLE IN THE PAST... NOW PERHAPS HE WILL DO SO AGAIN!

HIGH ON THE MOUNTAIN SLOPE HE FOUND A VAST CAVERN – AND AT THE MOUTH OF THE CAVERN HE STRUCK A MASSIVE GONG...

IT IS I, TRIGO! I SUMMON THE WISE MAN OF VORG!

BEFORE LONG A GENTLE VOICE ANSWERED HIM...

ENTER TRIGO. YOUR VISIT WAS EXPECTED. SPEAK!

OVERCOME WITH AWE BY THE ANCIENT FIGURE, TRIGO SPOKE HALTINGLY OF THE PROBLEM THAT CONFRONTED THE TRIGAN EMPIRE.

SO – DO WE SWALLOW THE INSULTS AND OUTRAGES OF THESE FIENDISH LOKANS... OR DO WE TAKE ARMS AGAINST THEM?

I SEE THE ANSWER IN YOUR EYES, TRIGO.

I SEE THE WAR-HORDES RIDING OUT FROM TRIGAN. I HEAR THE DRUMS OF WAR BEATING AND I SEE THE GREAT REJOICINGS OF VICTORY IN THE STREETS OF TRIGAN...

TRIGO'S EYES BLAZED WITH A FIERCE DELIGHT...

YOU HAVE ANSWERED ME, WISE MAN!

NO TRIGO - YOU HAVE ANSWERED YOURSELF.

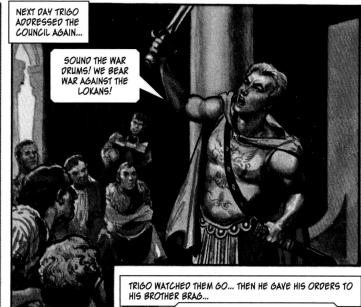

NEXT DAY TRIGO ADDRESSED THE COUNCIL AGAIN...

SOUND THE WAR DRUMS! WE BEAR WAR AGAINST THE LOKANS!

TRIGO WATCHED THEM GO... THEN HE GAVE HIS ORDERS TO HIS BROTHER BRAG...

BRAG - YOU WILL COMMAND THE GROUND FORCES - YOU WILL RIDE FOR LOKA AT ONCE AND JOIN BATTLE!

YES TRIGO!

WITHIN THE HOUR THE SMALL TRIGAN AIR FLEET TOOK OFF...

SET COURSE FOR LOKA!

BUT THEN CAME DISASTER! THE ILL-FATED AIR FLEET WAS SMASHED TO PIECES BY RELENTLESS GROUND FIRE, BEFORE IT WAS EVEN IN SIGHT OF LOKA...

THE TRIGAN CAVALRY WAS A SPLENDID SIGHT AS IT SET OFF FOR BATTLE...

FORWARD!

...AND THE SPLENDOUR OF TRIGAN'S CAVALRY WAS MOWN DOWN BEFORE THE WARRIORS WERE CLOSE ENOUGH TO STRIKE WITH THEIR SWORDS AND LANCES...

IT WAS BRAG HIMSELF WHO BROUGHT NEWS OF THE DISASTER TO TRIGO...

BRAG — WHAT HAS HAPPENED?

YOU HAVE DESTROYED US ALL WITH YOUR FOLLY...I AM THE ONLY SURVIVOR OF THE TRIGAN CAVALRY!

TRIGO COULD NOT MEET THE FURY AND CONTEMPT IN THE EYES OF HIS BROTHER...

I WILL TAKE MY OWN SWORD AND DIE IN BATTLE!

THEN PREPARE TO DIE SWIFTLY BROTHER, FOR THE LOKANS ARE NEARLY AT THE GATES!

NEXT MORNING THE HIGHLY MECHANISED FORCES OF LOKA ASSAULTED THE CITY...

SWORD IN HAND TRIGO WAS STRUCK DOWN BY A MASS OF FALLING MASONRY IN THE CITY SQUARE...

UUUUGH!

HE LAY WHERE HE FELL, UNRECOGNISED IN THE GENERAL CHAOS... AND THERE, AFTER DARK, HIS FAITHFUL ZOLT SLAVE FOUND HIM, AND CARRIED HIM TO SAFETY...

WE WILL TAKE HIM TO A PLACE OF HIDING...

WITH THE ZOLT WENT SALVIA, DAUGHTER OF ONE OF TRIGO'S SCIENTISTS... AS THEY STOLE THROUGH THE SMOKING RUINS OF THE CITY THEY HEARD HOARSE CRIES OF TRIUMPH...

THE WISE MAN SPOKE THE TRUTH... THERE IS REJOICING FOR VICTORY IN TRIGAN THIS NIGHT... BUT IT IS THE LOKANS WHO REJOICE!

IN THE GRIM MONTHS THAT FOLLOWED TRIGO WAS NURSED SLOWLY BACK TO HEALTH IN THE MOUNTAINS BY THE SKILL OF SALVIA...

HE WILL LIVE!

THE FIRST DAY THAT TRIGO WAS STRONG ENOUGH TO STAND HE WENT TO GAZE DOWN AT HIS UNHAPPY CITY IN THE PLAINS BELOW...

WHAT ARE THEY BUILDING OVER THERE? BETWEEN THE MOUNTAINS?

IN THE WEEKS SINCE THEIR VICTORY THE LOKANS HAD BUILT A MASSIVE DAM... WITH TRIGAN SLAVE LABOUR...

GENTLY SALVIA GAVE HIM THE TERRIBLE NEWS...

THE LOKANS ARE PLANNING TO FLOOD THE PLAINS, AND TRIGAN WITH IT, TO PROVIDE FOR THEIR COUNTRY. IN A FEW WEEKS OUR CITY WILL BE NO MORE.

TRIGO FLING HIMSELF TO THE GROUND IN BITTER DESPAIR...

AND IT IS I WHO BROUGHT THEM TO THIS... WHAT CAN I DO?

I SHALL GO TO THE WISE MAN OF VORG... AND THIS TIME...

ONCE AGAIN HE STOOD BEFORE THE WISE MAN...

SO YOU HAVE RETURNED, TRIGO.

YOU SPOKE THE TRUTH TO ME BEFORE, OLD MAN, BUT I DID NOT PERCEIVE YOUR WISDOM. MY FOLLY LED TO THE DEFEAT OF MY PEOPLE. BUT NOW I HAVE LEARNED MY LESSON, AND MUST TRY TO MAKE AMENDS.

THE ANCIENT EYES WERE HOODED, AND THE VOICE CAME THROUGH SOFTLY AT LENGTH...

SINGLE HANDED YOU MUST SAVE YOUR PEOPLE, TRIGO. THEN THE WATERS WILL CLOSE OVER YOUR ENEMIES.

TRIGO LEFT THE GREAT MOUNTAIN SORELY TROUBLED...

I DO NOT UNDERSTAND HIS WORDS... HOW MANY I CONQUER LOKA SINGLEHANDED... OR CAUSE MY ENEMIES TO BE DESTROYED BY THE WATERS?

A WEEK LATER, AS THE WATERS OF THE RIVER ROSE HIGH AGAINST THE MASSIVE DAM TRIGO GAZED DOWN... AND THE MEMORY OF THE OLD MAN'S WORDS CAME TO HIM...

THE WATERS! YES!

THAT NIGHT THE CARELESS LOKAN SENTRIES DID NOT SEE THE DARK FIGURE THAT CREPT STEALTHILY INTO THEIR CAMP...

FROM THE CLOSELY GUARDED AMMUNITION STORE HE STOLE A LARGE-CALIBRE DISINTEGRATOR BOMB...

A SMALL ENOUGH THING... BUT IT WILL SERVE!

BY THE RIVER'S EDGE A SMALL FLEET OF SPEEDY AQUACRAFT LAY AT ANCHOR...

FELLING THE SENTRY WITH ONE BLOW, TRIGO LEAPT ABOARD ONE OF THE AQUACRAFT...

A TOUCH OF THE CONTROLS AND THE SPEEDY CRAFT WAS RACING ACROSS THE DARK WATERS...

TO THE DAM!

SENTRIES ON THE MASSIVE DAM SAW THE APPROACHING CRAFT, AND RAISED THE ALARM.

UNAUTHORISED CRAFT APPROACHING DAM AT SPEED – *OPEN FIRE!*

DISINTEGRATOR SHELLS BURST ALL ROUND THE ZIG-ZAGGING CRAFT, AS TRIGO MADE HIS PREPARATIONS...

AT THE LAST MOMENT TRIGO FLUNG HIMSELF FROM THE CAREERING CRAFT...

THE AQUACRAFT STRUCK THE WALL OF THE DAM, AND WITH A GREAT BLINDING FLASH THE MASSIVE WALL WAS TORN ASUNDER...

CAUGHT IN A SEETHING MAELSTROM OF RUSHING WATER, TRIGO FOUGHT FOR A HAND-HOLD ON THE ROCKY SHORE...

THE PENT-UP WATERS TORE THROUGH THE SHATTERED DAM AND POURED OUT THROUGH THE MOUNTAINS, SWEEPING EVERYTHING BEFORE THEM...

...FINALLY ENGULFING THE CITY OF LOKA...

NEXT DAY THE ONCE TRIUMPHANT LOKANS ABANDONED THEIR CONQUESTS AND RETURNED TO THEIR OWN DEVASTATED HOMELAND...

THEN TRIGO RETURNED TO HIS OWN CITY WHERE THE PEOPLE COULD STILL HARDLY BELIEVE THAT THE NIGHTMARE WAS INDEED OVER...

IT IS TRIGO!

OR HIS GHOST!

HUMBLY, TRIGO ADDRESSED HIS COUNCIL IN THE RUINED COUNCIL CHAMBER OF TRIGAN...

I WAS HOT-HEADED AND HASTY, UNWILLING TO LISTEN TO THE ADVICE OF MY ELDERS. IN FUTURE YOUR ADVICE SHALL BE PRECIOUS TO ME, I SWEAR IT!

AND THEN IN RINGING TONES HE CRIED...

AND NOW – LET US REBUILD OUR GLORIOUS CITY! LET US REBUILD AGAIN!